THE ENVIRONMENT
AND MENTAL HEALTH
A Guide for Clinicians

✧ ✧ ✧

THE ENVIRONMENT AND MENTAL HEALTH

A Guide for Clinicians

Edited by

Ante Lundberg

Washington, DC Commission on Mental Health Services

Routledge
Taylor & Francis Group
New York   London

First published by Lawrence Erlbaum Associates, Inc.
10 Industrial Avenue, Mahwah
New Jersey 07430

Published 2009 by Routledge
711 Third Avenue, New York, NY 10017
2 Park Square, Milton Park, Abingdon, Oxfordshire OX14 4RN

First issued in paperback 2014

Routledge is an imprint of the Taylor and Francis Group, an informa business

Cover design by Kathryn Houghtaling Lacey

Library of Congress Cataloging-in-Publication Data

The environment and mental health : a guide for
clinicians / editor, Ante Lundberg.
     p. cm.
   Includes bibliographical references and indexes.
   ISBN 0-8058-2907-5 (alk. paper).
   1. Mental illness—Environmental aspects. 2. Mental
health—Environmental aspects. 3. Environmentally induced diseases. I. Lundberg, Ante.
   [DNLM: 1. Mental Disorders—etiology. 2. Environmental Exposure—adverse effects. 3. Environmental Illness. WM 140 E61 1998]
RC455.4.E58E528 1998
616.89'071—dc21
DNLM/DLC
for Library of Congress   97-43761
                                      CIP

ISBN 13: 978-0-8058-2907-5 (hbk)
ISBN 13: 978-1-138-01248-6 (pbk)

The greatest delight which the fields and woods minister
is the suggestion of an occult relation between man and the vegetable.
—R. W. Emerson, *Nature* (1836)

Nature, to be commanded, must be obeyed.
—Francis Bacon, *Novum Organum* (1620)

Contents

Foreword

Howard Frumkin
Emory University

Those of us who practice environmental and occupational medicine are grateful for the simple cases—the battery worker with fatigue, headaches, abdominal pain, and an elevated lead level; the assembly worker with pain and numbness in her hand and delayed median nerve conduction; the patient who develops typical contact dermatitis after working with epoxies. But few of our cases are straightforward. We often recognize complex and challenging psychological issues, and we often lack the training or wisdom to handle them well.

Environmental and occupational medicine intersects mental health in at least five ways. First, some chemicals have direct toxic effects. Mercury causes irritability and paranoia, a syndrome known as *erethism*. Manganese causes psychosis, dubbed *locura manganica* by Chilean miners. Carbon disulfide causes depression so striking that, according to legend, early British viscose rayon factories had to install bars on upper floor windows to prevent suicidal jumps by workers. And these are only the obvious syndromes that occur at high-dose exposures; milder neurotoxicity is seen with a range of toxins, including solvents, metals, and pesticides, at currently permissible levels.

Second, patients with occupational or environmental illnesses or injuries, like any other sick patients, may suffer from stress or develop reactive depression. If the illness is longlasting, poorly understood, or disabling; if the patient has a sense of injustice, invalidation, or abandonment; or if the diagnosis is contested or litigated, the depression may be aggravated. The care of these patients must include attention to mental health issues.

Third, environmental and occupational physicians confront a variety of poorly defined and in some cases overlapping syndromes, including multiple chemical sensitivity, closed building syndrome, Gulf War syndrome, and chronic fatigue syndrome. Patients present with diffuse symptoms, often including constitutional and psychiatric symptoms, that they associate with environmental exposures. Often they are firmly convinced of the environmental origin of their ailment by the time they visit the physician. In at least some cases, there is psychiatric co-morbidity. In most cases psychiatric evaluation is helpful.

Fourth, a deeply rooted link with nature may lie at our core, a part of who we are as a species, contributing to our spirituality and our sense of wholeness. E. O. Wilson called this affinity biophilia, and in recent years ecopsychology has proposed a therapeutic paradigm based on it. As clinicians, we may find this a useful perspective, recognizing the value of such "therapies" as time outdoors or with a pet. As advocates, we may also find this a useful perspective, recognizing that the public health importance of environmental protection extends to mental health.

Finally, in a field that sometimes offers more questions than answers, that lacks some of the easy certainties of surgery or pediatrics, and in which some of our patients are needy, demanding, and difficult, there is another lesson we can learn from our psychiatric colleagues. We need to take a close look at our own behavior. The defensive reactions of some physicians to patients with multiple chemical sensitivity go beyond scientific skepticism, suggesting that our own backgrounds and emotions color our therapeutic perspective.

For all these reasons, environmental and occupational health professionals need to collaborate with mental health professionals. Dr Lundberg is to be congratulated for assembling this splendid collection of essays on the environment and mental health. I hope it will be widely read by professionals in both fields, stimulating greater awareness of the areas of overlap and fruitful interdisciplinary exchanges. Ultimately, this can only advance the goals that are important to us all: better care of individual patients, and more effective advocacy for a clean, healthy environment.

Acknowledgments

This book has benefited from the suggestions and criticism of many people. It developed from a symposium on the topic that I chaired at the 1994 annual meeting of the American Psychiatric Association, with presentations by Aristide Esser, Aaron Katcher, Robert Lifton, Herbert Needleman, Richard Restak, and Bernard Weiss.

Producing a book turned out to be laborious but highly rewarding; the patience, flexibility, and professionalism of the authors made it an instructive and enjoyable experience. I am particularly grateful for the editorial help and advice of Randall White and the interest and encouragement of Howard Frumkin.

Among others who commented on parts of the manuscript or contributed material, I wish to thank Dan Oren, NIMH; Rosie Sokas, George Washington University; Phyllis Windle, formerly of the congressional Office of Technology Assessment; David Wallinga, NRDC; Pamela Tucker, ATSDR; and Kate Oliver, NIH, who prepared the appendix.

On countless occasions I could rely on the advice of members of my family. My wife read and worked on the manuscript in all its versions; the final result owes much to her skills and experience as a writer and editor. I am deeply grateful for her work, her interest, and her never failing support.

Any remaining editorial shortcomings are my responsibility.

—*Ante Lundberg*

Chapter 1

Introduction

Ante Lundberg
Washington, DC Commission on Mental Health Services

By the term *environment* mental health professionals usually mean an individual's family and immediate social circle. Psychotherapy tends to focus on intrapsychic events and on interaction with the closest family and social group. In recent decades, the focus has shifted to biological determinants of individual experience and behavior, to the genetics of serious mental illness, and to pharmacotherapy for psychiatric disorders.

Genetics and family environment combine to mold a person (Eisenberg, 1995), but growing evidence shows that the nonsocial environment—biological and physical—is important as well, not only for health and psychological functioning, but also for psychiatric morbidity (Lundberg, 1996; Schottenfeld, 1992). Toxins and traumatic experiences such as natural disasters cause illness and vulnerability. Epidemiological data show a sharp rise in depression among adolescents and young adults (Kessler et al., 1994). On the other hand, interacting with the living world, even contemplating pictures of nature, can have therapeutic effects (Katcher & Wilkins, 1993; Ulrich, 1993).

Anecdotal evidence indicates that clinicians see more and more patients who have been exposed to environmental poisons or environmental stress, who worry about environmental threats, or who are preoccupied with the fate of the environment. Often such concerns are irrational and can be seen as representing cognitive dysfunction or neurotic defense such as displacement or rationalization. But in some cases the fears are well founded.

Psychiatric teaching and research has paid only sporadic attention to these often elusive but powerful influences. Searles (1960) explored the topic from a psychoanalytic perspective in *The Nonhuman Environment in Normal Development and in Schizophrenia*:

> It is my conviction that there is within the human individual a sense, whether at a conscious or unconscious level, of relatedness to his nonhuman environment, that this relatedness is one of the transcendentally important facts of human living, that—as with other very important circumstances in human existence—it is a source of ambivalent feelings to him, and that, if he tries to ignore its importance to himself, he does so at peril to his psychological well-being. (p. 6)

An annotated bibliography, *Environmental Pollution and Mental Health*, was published by Williams, Leyman, Karp, and Wilson (1973). The editors pointed out that the "complex processes through which degraded aspects of the physical environment affect man's mental health are poorly understood. Aside from the literature on lead, there is little that can be said with confidence about the effects of pollution and a deteriorated physical environment on mental health" (pp. 2–3).

In 1979, a task force of the American Psychiatric Association produced a bibliography, *Relating Environment to Mental Health and Illness: The Ecopsychiatric Data Base* (Shurley, 1979). It was organized around the concepts of General Systems Theory and contained a comprehensive listing of the relevant literature up to that year. Its emphasis was largely theoretical and conceptual. Freeman's *Environment and Mental Health* was published in 1984 (a new edition is planned). It assembled experts from many fields including medicine, social sciences, architecture, zoology, and law who reviewed available information about the psychosocial effects of the man-made environment.

There is still not much empirical research devoted to environment and mental health in the behavioral and clinical sciences. Seasonal affective disorder has been studied since the 1980s (Oren & Rosenthal, 1992) and seasonal pattern has been added as a specifier to mood disorders in the *Diagnostic and Statistical Manual of Mental Disorders* (4th ed. [*DSM–IV*]; American Psychiatric Association, 1994). The *DSM–IV* also allows referring to environmental problems under Axis IV of the multi-axial assessment. Psychologists have shown more interest in the effects of the environment than psychiatrists. A two-volume *Handbook of Environmental Psychology* was published by Stokols and Altman (1987). Of particular interest is the work of Kaplan and Kaplan (1989) on the experience of nature, discussed in chapter 11. A review of many of these topics for the general reader can be found in *The Power of Place* (Gallagher, 1993).

Sociology, geography, and philosophy have contributed to the study of the interaction between man and his environment; a large body of essays and popular writing show the degree of public interest and concern. A movement among nonmedical therapists, ecopsychology, addresses grief for environmental destruction and our perceived alienation from the natural world. Its philosophical-spiritual premise assumes that human sanity requires an ongoing relationship, even identification with the wider world; its practitioners advocate an ecological definition of self (Conn, 1995). Their arguments are compelling, even if they are experiential and poetic rather than scientific.

There are scientific, economic, and clinical reasons to treat mental illness separately from mental health (Torrey, 1995). Biological etiology has been proven for some major psychoses, insurance coverage is more readily available, and treatment fits the "medical model." But the distinction is not clear-cut; much psychological suffering and disability is not due to major mental illness but to psychological or physical stress and trauma (Mazure, 1995). Furthermore, health, not only disease, is the proper concern of physicians.

The interaction between environment and mental health and illness has many dimensions. Interaction with animals and nature has been shown to be beneficial, whereas environmental illness (EI) can be caused by toxins and other hazards in combination with unavoidable psychological stressors and individual vulnerability. An EI patient must be evaluated in physiological as well as psychological terms. Clinicians working with these patients must understand how stress affects physiology as well as mood and behavior, and be familiar with the behavioral manifestations of neurotoxins. EI patients have to contend with a particular set of secondary stressors: Their symptoms are often vague and nonspecific, defy diagnosis and invite a skeptical response, and the presumed cause is usually invisible and elusive. They worry that exposure to toxins or radiation may have delayed effects, perhaps affecting their future children. The same questions worry those who are not ill but fear that they were exposed. Inadequate and untrustworthy information from officials adds to feelings of helplessness and alienation. Exposed individuals can feel stigmatized. When groups and communities get involved, the debate (e.g., over the placement of a dangerous waste facility or who will get compensated) often becomes emotional and politicized. Controversy and lack of scientific data in many areas further increase the patient's uncertainty. The clinician also needs to know how social context, perception of risk, and coping style affect experience.

The stressors described here apply in varying degree to the whole range of conditions discussed in this book, but particularly to the sick veterans of Operation Desert Storm in the Persian Gulf War, who are still trying to find out what ails them.

Some of the chapters in this book are controversial; in most areas there is a shortage of scientific data. This book is designed to introduce the new field of environmental psychiatry, to illustrate its importance for clinical practice, and to serve as a practical guide.

REFERENCES

American Psychiatric Association. (1994). *Diagnostic and statistical manual of mental disorders* (4th ed.). Washington, DC: Author.

Conn, S. (1995). When the earth hurts, who responds? In T. Roszak, M. E. Goves, & A. D. Kanner (Eds.), *Ecopsychology: Restoring the earth, healing the mind* (pp. 156–171). San Francisco: Sierra Club Books.

Eisenberg, L. (1995). The social construction of the human brain. *American Journal of Psychiatry, 152*, 1563–1575.

Freeman, H. (Ed.). (1984). *Mental health and the environment.* New York: Churchill Livingstone.

Gallagher, W. (1993). *The power of place: How our surroundings shape our thoughts, emotions and actions.* New York: Poseidon Press.

Kaplan, R., & Kaplan, S. (1989). *The experience of nature: A psychological perspective.* Cambridge, England & New York: Cambridge University Press.

Katcher, A., & Wilkins, G. (1993). Dialogue with animals: Its nature and culture. In S. R. Kellert & E. O. Wilson (Eds.), *Biophilia hypothesis* (pp. 173–197). Washington, DC: Island Press.

Kessler, R. C., McGonagle, K. A., Nelson, C. B., Hughes, M., Swartz, M., & Blazer, D. G. (1994). Sex and depression in the national comorbidity survey II: Cohort effects. *Journal of Affective Disorders, 30*, 15–26.

Lundberg, A. (1996). Psychiatric aspects of air pollution. *Otolaryngology Head and Neck Surgery, 114*, 227–231.

Mazure, C. M. (Ed.). (1995). *Does stress cause psychiatric illness?* Washington, DC: American Psychiatric Press, Inc.

Oren, D. A., & Rosenthal, N. E. (1992). Seasonal affective disorders. In E. S. Paykel (Ed.), *Handbook of affective disorders* (pp. 551–556). New York: Guilford Press.

Schottenfeld, R. S. (1992). Psychologic sequelae of chemical and hazardous materials exposures. In J. B. Sullivan & G. R. Krieger (Eds.), *Hazardous materials toxicology* (pp. 463–470). Baltimore: Williams & Wilkins.

Searles, H. (1960). *The nonhuman environment in normal development and in schizophrenia.* New York: International Universities Press.

Shurley, J. T. (1979). *Relating environment to mental health and illness: The ecopsychiatric data base* (Rep. No. 16). Washington, DC: American Psychiatric Association Task Force.

Stokols, D., & Altman, I. (Eds.). (1987). *Handbook of environmental psychology.* New York: Wiley.

Torrey, E. F. (1995, October). *The marriage of mental illness and mental health: Isn't it time for a divorce?* Lecture presented at the American Psychiatric Association's Institute on Psychiatric Services, Boston, MA.

Ulrich, R. S. (1993). Biophilia, biophobia, and natural landscapes. In S. R. Kellert & E. O. Wilson (Eds.), *The biophilia hypothesis* (pp. 73–137). Washington, DC: Island Press.

Williams, J. S., Leyman, E., Karp, S. A., & Wilson, P. T. (1973). *Environmental pollution and mental health.* Washington, DC: Information Resources Press.

Chapter 2

Environmental Change and Human Health

Ante Lundberg
Washington, DC Commission on Mental Health Services

Changes in the world around us test our ability to adapt and may threaten health and well-being. In industrialized societies most people lead lives very different from their grandparents, who were often directly dependent on the natural world. The electronic revolution continues to change how we live and work. Elsewhere, political and economic conditions force vast numbers of people to leave their homes. We are all exposed to the consequences of pollution, climate change, and loss of stratospheric ozone: real but insidious new threats from toxic substances, infections, and ultraviolet (UV) radiation.

In the community, environmental threats such as a hazardous waste site, a polluting factory, or a nuclear power plant can be seen and confronted, even if the danger they represent is invisible and technically complicated. Acid rain due to industrial activity in a remote area is a more abstract notion, even though its consequences, for example, dying trees and fish, are starkly visible. Global issues such as climate change, ozone depletion, and loss of biodiversity have potentially catastrophic consequences, yet to most people they seem distant and theoretical, obscured by a debate that is technical and driven by ideology, special interests, and emotion. But pressures on the environment will continue to build: Population and consumption are growing, and we can expect greater environmental health problems.

Mental health is inseparable from physical health. Both depend to a large extent on socioeconomic and environmental conditions. A report on world mental health (Desjarlais, Eisenberg, Good, & Kleinman, 1995) points out that the remarkable improvement in health care and life expectancy in some developing countries has been accompanied by "an increase in depression, schizophrenia, dementia, and other forms of chronic mental illness, primarily because more people live into the age of risk. Along with economic growth and various social transformations have come a marked increase in rates of alcoholism and suicide" (p. 4). At the same time, every year about 15 million people die of hunger, and malnutrition affects the lives of almost 24% of the global population. Lack of adequate nutrition is accompanied by disease, congenital anomalies, and attention and cognitive deficits. Illness in the family creates additional stress, depression, and impaired health (Kaplan, 1994; Ursin, 1994).

The effects of pollution and other environmental threats on human health are reviewed in a report by the Physicians for Social Responsibility (PSR), *Critical Condition: Human Health and the Environment* (Chivian, McCally, Hu, & Haines, 1993). Its underlying themes are:

- The physical environment, our habitat, is the most important determinant of human health.
- Protection of the environment and preservation of ecosystems are, in public health terms, the most fundamental steps in preventing human illness.
- Physicians should be the health officials most knowledgeable about the environmental factors that cause disease, and should be prominent spokespersons in communicating with the public about environmental hazards.

This book deals with clinical aspects of the interaction between environment and mental health. For information about other areas of environmental medicine the reader is referred to other sources. The remainder of this chapter deals with some of the environmental forces that undermine, or strengthen, mental health.

CHEMICAL POLLUTION

Every year between 2,000 and 3,000 new chemicals are registered by the U.S. Environmental Protection Agency (USEPA) and added to the 75,000 unique chemicals and millions of mixtures already in use. Most are not carefully studied for health effects, and only a handful have been thoroughly evaluated for neurotoxic effects (National Research Council, 1992). They may present health hazards in the workplace or as pollutants in air, water, or food.

The principal outdoor air pollutants are sulfur dioxide, carbon monoxide, lead and other metals, particulates, nitrogen dioxide, ozone, and acid aerosols. The last two are secondary pollutants, formed through photochemical oxidation by sunlight. The 1970 Clean Air Act and subsequent amendments have led to a significant reduction of airborne pollution. USEPA reports that over a recent 5-year period, the number of Americans living in areas that violate federal clean air standards has dropped from 140 million to 62 million (USEPA, 1995). A disproportionate number of non-White and poor people live in such nonattainment areas (Sexton et al., 1993).

Studies from the United States and Europe show that people in industrialized nations spend more than 90% of their time indoors (USEPA, 1989). Indoor pollution consists primarily of carbon monoxide, suspended particles, and volatile organic compounds, mainly from cigarette smoke and heating and cooking fuels. Environmental tobacco smoke (ETS) is the most important carcinogenic environmental toxin. It is thought to be responsible for approximately 3,000 lung cancer deaths per year among nonsmokers in the United States (USEPA, 1992). Research has shown that ETS cannot be removed by ventilation or by air filters (Repace & Lowrey, 1985).

Despite improvement, contamination of drinking water and food is still a problem in many areas of the United States. In addition to pathogens like cryptosporidium, the following are of particular concern: pesticides, nitrates, volatile organic compounds, lead, arsenic, mercury, cadmium, copper and other heavy metals, polychlorinated biphenyls (PCBs), and radionuclides such as strontium 90 and cesium 137.

- Lead exposure in the United States has decreased dramatically since leaded gasoline was phased out, but an estimated 1.7 million children between 1 and 5 years old have blood lead levels equal to, or greater than, 10 micrograms per 100 ml, the maximum level considered safe for normal neurological development. Main sources for lead exposure in the United States are old paint and old water pipes; in other parts of the world leaded gasoline is still used. Exposure to lead mainly occurs through inhalation and through ingestion of lead in food, paint, water, soil, or dust.

- Methylmercury (MeHg) is considered one of the most dangerous chemicals in the world's environment. Human exposure to MeHg primarily occurs through the consumption of contaminated food such as fish, although catastrophic exposures due to industrial pollution have occurred. The fetus is particularly sensitive to MeHg exposure and adverse effects on infant development have been associated with levels of exposure that result in few, if any, signs of maternal clinical illness or toxicity (Gilbert & Grant-Webster, 1995).

• A report on herbicides in drinking water by the Environmental Working Group states: "14.1 million people routinely drink water contaminated with five major agricultural herbicides (atrazine, cyanazine, simazine, alachlor, and metolachlor) . . . 11.7 million of these people live in the heart of the corn belt and in Louisiana, including every major midwestern city south of Chicago. Within this population an estimated 65,000 infants drink these herbicides from birth via infant formula reconstituted with herbicide-contaminated tap water. An additional 2.4 million people are exposed to these herbicides via drinking water in the Chesapeake Bay watershed" (Wiles, Cohen, Campbell, & Elderkin, 1994, p. 1).

Plants and animals tend to concentrate certain toxins. PCBs and other chlorinated hydrocarbons, together with lead and mercury, are among the toxic pollutants that accumulate in biological systems in the Great Lakes and other bodies of water. PCBs enter the water from the air in minute amounts. They are taken up by plankton, then by fish feeding on plankton, then by birds and mammals higher on the food chain. It is estimated that concentrations of PCBs can be 15 to 25 million times higher in birds' eggs than in the water (Colborn, Dumanoski, & Myers, 1996).

The long list of chemical pollutants that an individual encounters in today's world can contribute to cancer (PSR, 1997) and a wide range of other medical and behavioral problems. PCBs, DDT, DDE, kepone, heptachlor and breakdown products of detergents have estrogenic effects, dioxin and many other chemicals have multiple endocrinological effects. They may partly explain the reproductive changes observed in wildlife and the decline in human sperm count reported in several studies (Colborn et al., 1996). The central nervous system is particularly vulnerable to heavy metals, carbon monoxide, pesticides, and other organic compounds (chapter 3). Delayed neurological development and reduced stress tolerance have been found in children of mothers whose diet contained Great Lakes fish (Golub & Jacobsen, 1995). The developmental consequences of prenatal toxic exposure were described in a volume edited by Needleman and Bellinger (1994). Another recent book, *Toxic Deception: How the Chemical Industry Manipulates Science, Bends the Law, and Endangers Your Health* (Fagin & Lavelle, 1996), describes the influence of powerful commercial interests on research and public information about environmental toxins.

CLIMATE CHANGE, HEAT, RADIATION

The earth's climate has been getting warmer over the past century: 1995 was the warmest year since records were first kept in 1856. Most scientists now attribute the continuing increase in temperature to human activities and believe that climate changes brought about by the heat-trapping effect of CO_2 and other greenhouse gases are accelerating. The exact rate of warming cannot be predicted, but its consequences are likely to be complex and drastic (McMichael, Haines, Sloof, & Kovats, 1996).

More extremes of hot, cold, and violent weather are predicted by some models. Heat waves will cause more deaths among the old and infirm, but human health will mostly be affected through food shortages (Parry & Rosenzweig, 1994), spread of infections and social disruption connected with mass migration from low lying areas as sea the level rises, and spread of malaria, dengue fever, and other communicable diseases due to increased range and activity of insect vectors (Loevinsohn, 1994).

Very hot weather is accompanied by increased mortality, particularly from cardiovascular, cerebrovascular, and respiratory diseases. During three heat waves in Los Angeles, the peak mortality at all ages was several times the expected rate, especially among the elderly (Haines, 1993). Data from New York and St. Louis indicate that most of the excess deaths were not just displaced, that is, those who died would not necessarily have died soon afterward if the heat wave had not occurred. Studies from other U.S. cities strongly suggest that weather has a greater impact on acute mortality than air pollution (Kalkstein, 1997). During the summer of 1995, nearly 600 deaths in Cook County, Illinois (which includes Chicago) were attributed at least in part to extreme heat. A disproportionately high number of the fatalities were old, poor, and African American.

Several studies, both in the laboratory and in the community, have found a positive correlation between ambient temperature and violent or aggressive behavior (Cotton, 1986; Rotton & Frey, 1984). The outcome of schizophrenia, broadly defined, was found to be positively related to mean environmental temperature by Gupta and Murray (1992), who reanalyzed data from two World Health Organization (WHO) studies comparing schizophrenia in several different countries. They also found that the risk of developing schizophrenia was positively related to the mean daily range of temperature. The authors cautioned, however, that other variables also contribute.

Exposure to low level radiation from radon, nuclear sites, and medical radiology contributes to lung cancer and leukemia, but has no known direct effect on psychological health (USEPA, 1995). The increased levels of UV-B radiation observed in recent years as a consequence of the thinning of the stratospheric ozone layer have added to rates of skin cancer and cataracts, and in addition, UV-B has been found to interfere with the cellular immune system (JeeVan & Kripke, 1993). Exposure to strong sunlight induces a state of immunosuppression, probably through the mediation of epidermal cytokines.

Immune deficiency is believed by many to play a central role in the etiology of the Chronic Fatigue Syndrome (CFS; Farrar, Locke, & Kantrowitz, 1995). This obscure but often debilitating illness is not covered in this volume, although it is sometimes included in the term *environmental illness* (EI). The reader is referred to the many scientific studies and popular books dealing specifically with CFS. It is interesting to note that several types of environmental exposure affect the immune system, including pesticides (Repetto & Baliga, 1996), stress (Maier, Watkins, & Fleshner, 1994), and UV-B.

MIGRATION

Climate change and severe pollution lead to starvation, social disruption, and dislocation of large numbers of people, and contribute to war (Haines, 1993; Kane, 1995). The number of armed conflicts in the world has increased, and almost all are internal (Kane, 1995). Widespread poverty and social and political conflicts add to the pressures to migrate.

The world's refugee population remained at around 2.5 million throughout the 1950s and 1960s; since the mid-1970s it has risen sharply (Kane, 1995). Nearly 4 million new refugees fled their homes in 1994. In addition to the 23 million official refugees (who leave their country to escape persecution or violence and who cannot return), there is an equal number of internally displaced people, and a much greater number who seek to improve their lives by moving from rural areas to cities (Kane, 1995). Almost one half of the global population now lives in cities. Research into the mental health aspects of noise and crowding is summarized in chapter 10.

Most refugees live in third world countries; the United Nations High Commissioner for Refugees (UNHCR) reports that only about 17% have come to live in North America, western Europe, and Australia. Almost 80% of refugees are women and children (UNHCR, 1993). A recent United Nations report on mental health problems in low-income countries discusses the plight of the displaced (Desjarlais, Eisenberg, Good, & Kleinman, 1995). Fear, uncertainty, and despair are widespread. Several studies have found increased rates of suicide, domestic violence, alcohol abuse, apathy, hopelessness, and depression among people in refugee camps.

Millions of people are relocated in the course of public works projects, such as major hydroelectric dams. The United Nations report states:

> The common consequences of dislocation include impoverishment, malnutrition, increased morbidity, dependency, and the breakdown of community norms and mutual support systems. Resettlement projects mean not only loss of home and the identity that comes from a sense of place; they can obliterate generations of practical cultural knowledge and effort. To this is added insecurity, nutritional deficiencies, sanitation risks, poor water supply, insufficient and infertile land, alcohol abuse, increased risk of illness, and barriers to health services. (pp. 19–20)

The United States accepts 900,000 immigrants a year and at least the same number enter the country illegally. Most of the latter group soon leave; the estimated number of undocumented immigrants in the country is between 3.5 and 4 million (U.S. Bureau of the Census, 1995). Refugees resettled in Western countries face problems most often having to do with acculturation and social ties. Children typically acculturate faster than adults, and as a consequence intergenerational conflicts increase rather than decrease over time. Among resettled Cambodian refugees, anger over separation from their homeland was one of the strongest and most widespread feelings even for those who did not leave family behind. In general, refugees stand a better chance of being psychologically healthy if they maintain strong social and community ties and a sense of cultural identity. Refugee populations may be highly vulnerable to behavior problems such as alcoholism, drug abuse, and delinquency. A study of Cambodian refugees in Oregon found a pattern of disruption of early attachment among delinquent individuals who often lack role models for culturally appropriate social behavior (Desjarlais et al., 1995). Religious affiliation and political commitment seem to offer protection.

STRESS

It is widely accepted that stressful experiences can cause psychological vulnerability and impairment. Research in psychiatry has mainly focused on the consequences of acute, life threatening, and horrifying events. *The Diagnostic and Statistical Manual of Mental Disorders* (4th ed. [*DSM–IV*]; American Psychiatric Association, 1994) defines two stress-related diagnoses: acute stress disorder and posttraumatic stress disorder (PTSD). Cases of PTSD provide convincing clinical examples of the connection between specific experience and psychiatric morbidity. The symptoms overlap with those of several other disorders, including mood, panic, obsessive compulsive, psychotic, dissociative, and organic mental disorders. Research during the past decade has also demonstrated that the behavioral manifestations are accompanied by lasting physiological changes (Lombardi et al., 1994). Psychological stress is thought to undermine host resistance to infection through neuroendocrine-mediated changes in immune competence (Leonard & Song, 1996). Stressful life events also play a role in the development of dissociative, mood, panic, and other mental disorders (Mazure, 1995).

Natural and man-made disasters satisfy the diagnostic criteria for traumatic stress as do many chronically menacing situations. Living near a hazardous waste site or a nuclear plant, or on the shore of a lake where the fish has become inedible, constitutes a vague but constant threat to health and quality of life. Elevated incidence of anxiety disorder, posttraumatic stress disorder, and depression have been documented after disasters such as the Exxon Valdez oil spill. Several studies have found signs of long-term effects, including impaired concentration, insomnia, and elevated urinary catecholamine excretion, among people living near toxic waste sites and nuclear facilities. The health consequences of such technological threats are discussed in chapter 5.

Understanding how people perceive and cope with environmental risk and trauma is necessary to help those who have been exposed. The degree of stress depends on the individual's cognitive appraisal of danger and injury, which often differs from that of the experts (Schottenfeld, 1992), and on his sense of loss of control (Gibbs & Belford, 1993). Both are influenced by the quality of information available, by community response to the threat, by distrust of government and industry officials, and by anticipated financial and health effects. Other factors that render risk more or less acceptable include whether it is voluntary or not, under individual or government control, natural or man-made, familiar or alien, visible or not. Ethical considerations and perception of fairness also determine response to environmental threats (Dohrenwend et al., 1981; Eyles, Baxter, Johnson, & Taylor, 1993; Wandersman & Hallman, 1993).

Social support and active behavioral and cognitive interventions are protective and lead to more positive psychiatric outcomes (Snow & Kline, 1995). Studies show that problem-focused coping moderates the effect of stressors and improves adjustment. Emotion-focused coping, on the other hand, is consistently shown to be associated with poor mental health outcomes. Avoidance coping (e.g., choosing to ignore the situation) leads to poor adjustment and is statistically related to greater psychological impairment and increased use of alcohol and tobacco. Research on risk perception and coping is reviewed in chapter 8.

WAR

The experience of warfare has always involved physical danger, fatigue, and extreme psychological stress. Today's troops are also likely to encounter toxic chemicals, biological agents, and radiation. When a veteran is ill, the somatic and psychological consequences of multiple insults sustained in combat make diagnosis difficult. Inadequate and classified records as well as social and political conflicts add to the difficulty. All these factors are part of the experience of those who served in the Persian Gulf War (PGW).

Tens of thousands of returning PGW veterans reported a wide range of distressing symptoms that they attributed to their wartime assignments. Symptoms included arthralgia, weakness, fatigue, headache, memory loss and other mental impairment, skin rashes, and so on. No established etiology could account for what became known as the *Persian Gulf War Syndrome*, but large numbers of veterans were sick and they and their families worried. They were soon asking questions that could not be answered for lack of reliable information, particularly regarding exposure to toxic and other hazardous agents in the field. Their experience of uncertainty, fear, frustration, and mistrust illustrates dramatically what many sufferers of environmental illness have to contend with.

The U.S. Department of Veterans' Affairs (VA) created a Persian Gulf health registry in 1992, to include all U.S. troops that had served in the Persian Gulf. A large number of investigations of the Persian Gulf War Syndrome followed; the U.S. House and Senate both convened committees and held hearings; and the National Institute on Health (NIH) conducted a workshop (NIH, 1994). In 1994, the U.S. Department of Defense instituted a clinical evaluation program (CCEP) to evaluate and treat the health problems of PGW veterans, and at the same time asked the Institute of Medicine (IOM) of the National Academy of Sciences to evaluate this program. In addition, President Bill Clinton appointed a special advisory committee on veterans' illnesses, and the U.S. General Accounting Office (GAO) conducted a review of the medical care of PGW veterans and research into their illnesses.

The IOM reports (1995, 1996) were critical of the confusion, duplication and poor planning of many government efforts, the paucity of reliable data, and, ultimately, the lack of diagnostic criteria or treatment recommendations for veterans of the PGW. Of the first 10,020 patients seen in the CCEP program, 37% were diagnosed with a psychiatric condition, most commonly depression or PTSD. Many of the psychiatric conditions identified have both physical and psychiatric symptoms. The IOM emphasized that psychosocial stressors can produce physical and psychological effects that are as real and potentially devastating as physical, chemical, or biological stressors.

Similarly, the Presidential Advisory Committee (1996) reported that it could find no evidence that exposure to chemical or biological weapons had caused their ailments, and that aftereffects of wartime stress is likely to be an important contributing factor to the broad range of illnesses they report. The committee also said that more research into the long-term effects of low level exposure to toxins was urgently needed.

In July 1997, the U.S. GAO published its review of the government's care of PGW veterans and medical research into their illnesses. The report stressed that psychiatric illness is a real illness, but also pointed out that various toxins can produce both psychological symptoms and neurological changes. It discussed the strong criticism leveled at previous reports by scientists and veterans' groups.

The GAO pointed out that the extent of the exposure to chemical agents has not been fully resolved. Chemical agents were present at Khamisiyah, Iraq, and elsewhere on the battlefield. During the war, 16 of 21 Iraqi sites identified by Gulf War planners as nuclear, biological, and chemical (NBC) facilities were destroyed. Additional NBC sites have been identified since the end of the war; one of these was located close to the Kuwait-Iraq border, where coalition ground forces were based. In June 1996, the U.S. Department of Defense (DoD) acknowledged that some veterans may have been exposed to the nerve agent sarin following the postwar demolition of Iraqi ammunition facilities.

It further states that the United States had no effective method for detecting biological weapons during the war. The Iraqis were known to have stockpiles of aflatoxin, a group of carcinogens whose toxicology is not well understood. Infection with indigenous *Leishmania tropica* has been suggested as a cause of some of the veterans' problems. The GAO pointed out that it should not be ruled out because the prevalence is unknown; it can remain asymptomatic for a very long time and emerge when the patient's immune system fails.

Troops were also exposed to other potentially hazardous substances. These include compounds used to decontaminate equipment, fuel used as a sand suppressant in and around encampments, fuel oil used to burn human waste, fuel in shower water, leaded vehicle exhaust used to dry sleeping bags, depleted uranium, parasites, pesticides, drugs to protect against chemical warfare agents (such as pyridostigmine bromide), and smoke from oil-well fires.

The GAO report suggested that the prevalence of PTSD and other serious psychiatric illnesses among PGW veterans was overestimated in studies that did not exclude neurological conditions, or that used overly broad and heterogenous groups of diagnoses (e.g., psychological conditions ranging from tension headache to major depression). Although there have been many studies of the role of stress in the veterans' illnesses, many toxicological questions remain unanswered.

Most of these concern the chronic effects of exposure to very low levels of hazardous substances. The report summarizes research results suggesting that low-level exposure to chemical warfare agents as well as organophosphate pesticides can cause delayed, chronic neurotoxic effects, which could explain some of the PGW veterans' ill-defined symptoms. Agents like pyridostigmine bromide and DEET, may alter the metabolism of organophosphates in ways that activate their delayed, chronic effects on the brain. Exposure to combinations of such agents has been shown in animal studies to be far more likely to cause morbidity and mortality than any of the chemicals acting alone. Pyridostigmine bromide was given to troops as protection against the immediate, potentially lethal effect of nerve gas.

Research in this area is complicated by the fact that the DoD did not maintain complete records of pyridostigmine bromide use during the war. Continued revelations by the DoD, the Central Intelligence Agency, and the United Nations indicate that large numbers of troops may have been exposed to low levels of poison gas and other noxious agents. The ongoing discovery and slow release of exposure data has created more suspicion and doubt, adding to the distress and worry of the sick veterans. A contentious, emotional, and increasingly politicized debate continues in the media.

Despite the effort spent on research of illnesses reported by PGW veterans, there are as yet no criteria for a comprehensive diagnosis. The etiology of various complaints remains a mystery. There is no definitive answer to who was contaminated and what the long-term consequences may be for the individual soldiers. In the meantime, thousands of veterans suffer from muscle and joint pain, stomach ailments, rashes, sleeplessness, loss of memory, and a variety of other psychiatric and psychosocial problems. Symptoms from fatigue to depression and joint pain may in part have been caused by toxic environmental exposure, in some cases resulting in objective neurological changes. Chapter 6 discusses the PGW veterans' illnesses problem from a medical perspective and describes experiences from the U.S. Army's Specialized Care Center. Chapter 7 reports on research into the psychological aftermath of service in the war.

The ailments of PGW veterans pose disturbing questions. Politics have clouded the issues, but many of the difficulties in establishing diagnoses seem inherent in the basic dilemma of environmental illness: Is it psychological or is it somatic? Unfortunately no such convenient division is possible. The answer will certainly turn out to be a number of different diagnoses combining both toxic, infectious, and psychologically based etiology.

LIGHT

Seasonal and diurnal changes in light and heat affect biological rhythms and health. Seasonality of depressive disorders has been noted in isolated reports ever since Hippocrates about 400 B.C. (Oren & Rosenthal, 1992). Contemporary investigators have found a strong statistical association among the seasons, affective disorders, and suicide. Depression and other mental disorders peak in late spring and early summer (Näyhä, Väisänan, & Hassi, 1994).

In a series of studies beginning in 1982, a group of investigators at NIMH described seasonal affective disorder (SAD), a syndrome characterized by atypical depressive symptoms, including hypersomnia and fatigue, increased appetite, carbohydrate craving, and weight gain that recurs every winter or in some cases every summer (Rosenthal et al., 1984). Exposure to bright light was therapeutic for winter depression. Numerous reports (reviewed in Oren & Rosenthal, 1992) have since confirmed the existence of this syndrome in several other countries. Some studies indicate that the prevalence of winter SAD and of subclinical versions of the syndrome increase with increasing latitude. A survey in the Washington, DC area found approximately 4% of the population to have winter SAD, and many more to have milder seasonal symptoms. This high incidence seems to conflict with epidemiological data showing that most depression occurs in the early summer. Most suicides occur in late spring and early summer both in the northern and the southern hemisphere (McCleary, Chew, Hellsten, & Flynnbransford, 1991). Biometeorological and sociological factors are believed to interact to produce these patterns. In a study of suicide in Japan between 1900 and 1982, Abe (1987) found that the seasonal pattern had become less pronounced over the years; Tietjen and Kripke (1994) found no seasonal variation in suicides in Los Angeles and Sacramento between 1968 and 1977. Data from Italy showed that seasonality was greater in rural than in urban settings (Miccioli, Williams, Zimmerman-Tansella, & Tansella, 1991).

Although Tietjen and Kripke (1994) found no seasonal variation, there was some evidence of fewer suicides following days of above average sunshine and increased suicides after 10 days of below average sunshine. Monitoring light exposure among randomly chosen volunteers, Kripke's team also found an association between low illumination and atypical depressive symptoms (Espiritu et al., 1994).

Exposure to bright light has been recommended as a treatment for depression since antiquity, but formally studied only the past 20 years. Rosenthal and colleagues reported on the first controlled clinical trial of light therapy in SAD. Numerous studies have since confirmed the efficacy of light treatment in this condition (Rosenthal, Sack, Skwerer, Jacobsen, & Wehr, 1988). Light treatment of nonseasonal depression has also been studied with promising results, but more thorough studies are needed to determine its usefulness (Kripke, Mullaney, Klauber, Risch, & Gillin, 1992).

The timing of light exposure is somewhat controversial; several studies indicate that morning doses are most effective, but several others indicate no therapeutic difference between morning and evening effects. Light seems to synchronize disturbed biological rhythms. Most investigators believe this occurs via the suprachiasmatic nuclei that control the circadian variation in melatonin production in the pineal gland. It is unclear what role melatonin itself plays in SAD. This hormone has been the object of much research in recent years and of sudden public enthusiasm for its ability to induce sleep in most people and alleviate jet lag. A range of other beneficial effects is also claimed. Preparations of melatonin have long been available in health food stores and can now be found in all pharmacies, but the requisite clinical studies of its safety and efficiency have not been done.

BIOLOGICAL DIVERSITY

The world's biological diversity is increasingly threatened by human activities. Species loss has accelerated. Preservation of biodiversity is important for practical as well as esthetic reasons, where the term *esthetic* does not only connote pleasure but includes our awareness of complexity derived from billions of years of evolution that is our heritage.

Many environmental changes made by humans are reversible but the extinction of species and the wholesale loss of ecosystems are not. Thus, the loss of biological diversity is different from other environmental problems, and possibly more threatening to all aspects of human well-being. Delegates to the American Medical Association (AMA) annual conference in 1995 passed a resolution declaring that "human health is inseparable from the health of the natural world," and urging "physicians and health care professionals to become more aware of the importance of the protection of biological diversity and its relationship to human health" (AMA, 1995).

Biological diversity has always fluctuated and mass extinctions have occurred, perhaps because of abrupt geological or climate changes. But in general, species have been added more rapidly than they have disappeared. Now that process has been reversed: Biological diversity is being lost at an alarming rate, and this impoverishment is clearly attributable to human activity. The most optimistic view of the consequences of reduced biological diversity is that resources that otherwise might improve the quality of human life will not be available. At worst, reductions could mean a serious disruption of the ecological processes on which civilization depends (U.S. Congress, Office of Technology Assessment, 1987).

By 1989, tropical rainforests covered less than one half of their prehistoric area (Myers, 1991). The populations of mid-Atlantic migratory songbirds, U.S. freshwater fish and mollusks, and the fungi of western Europe are declining; the Mediterranean-style vegetation of California and central Chile, Australian coral reefs and heaths are shrinking. Significant reduction in total global species diversity is likely if the present rate of environmental destruction continues (Wilson, 1992).

Biological diversity has many tangible benefits. It has fueled improvements in food production and other agriculture-based industries. No major U.S. crop is entirely native: Each originated with genetic material from elsewhere and those sources are used continuously to increase productivity and add other desirable features. For example, the genetic material that provided the basis for the Green Revolution in rice came from Japan, Korea, Mexico, and the United States (Pinstrup-Andersen, Lundberg, & Garrett, 1995).

For physicians, the most powerful argument for the preservation of biodiversity is that the natural world provides raw material for new medicines. The AMA resolution acknowledged that 79 of the 100 most widely prescribed drugs "are derived either primarily or secondarily from the natural world and its biological diversity." For example, Reserpine, the first drug used to treat psychosis, is derived from a plant (*Rauwolfia serpentina*). Medicinal plants and microbials from developing countries already contribute at least $30 billion to the global pharmaceutical industry and an estimated 200 companies and research organizations are screening plant and animal compounds for medicinal properties (Rural Advancement Foundation International, 1994).

The potential for further discoveries is enormous. Of more than 250,000 known flowering species, fewer than one half of 1% have been surveyed for possible medicinal value (Cox, 1995). Researchers at the National Cancer Institute (NCI) have collected between 9,000 and 10,000 species, and are now examining 3 anti-HIV agents derived from plants (Mays, 1995). In addition, the behavior of certain animals can provide information for disease prevention or treatment. For example, understanding how bears can hibernate without losing bone mass may help to prevent bone loss in elderly and bedridden patients (Chivian, 1995).

In many cases, the value of species and forests can be measured in dollars, but usually the benefits of diversity are not so readily calculated. For many people, even the attempt to assign economic estimates misses the point. They believe that creatures and ecosystems have value independent of their use to humans. Today's large-scale losses of biological diversity are likely to have a severe impact on human well-being beyond the loss of potential drugs.

From a letter to the *Audubon Naturalist News*:

My friend George went home from the hospital last week. In his five years he has been in and out of the hospital more times than anyone can remember. He is also one of the toughest kids I have met in my 15 years of practicing pediatrics.

George was three when he developed severe hepatitis. One of the key laboratory tests that was done used the polymerase chain reaction (PCR), a technique to amplify genetic information requiring an enzyme called Taq polymerase. Taq polymerase was isolated from bacteria living in the thermal hot springs in Yellowstone National Park.

It soon became apparent that George suffered from acute leukemia. One of the drugs central to his chemotherapy was vincristine, a complex molecule isolated from rosy periwinkle found in the Madagascar rain forest.

Ultimately George needed a bone marrow transplant, and once again PCR was used to determine the best donor. He was put on cyclosporin, a drug isolated from fungi that live in wet dark areas like marshes and rain forests. Without this drug bone marrow and organ transplants would be virtually impossible. George may not be the first image that comes to mind when one thinks about the quality of our environment and the importance of protecting rain forests and endangered species. Yet it is because of programs designed to protect irreplaceable resources that he is alive today. (Eskenazi, 1995, p. 6; from a letter to the *Audubon Naturalist News*)

THE EXPERIENCE OF NATURE

When people move from their old neighborhoods either by necessity or by choice, they usually lose the support of a familiar community, familiar customs, and direct interaction with people they know.

In moving from country to city people may gain in comfort and escape hardships, but they also lose contact with animals, plants, and rural landscapes. At the start of World War I, 50% of the U.S. population worked on farms; in the 1990s only 2% do, mostly on large mechanized enterprises. People in the developed world are no longer intimately connected with the predictable rhythms of nature, no longer responsible for animals and crops. Perhaps personality development has been affected by these changes. Definitive scientific data are not available, but our need for contact with living nature has been the object of much speculation and research (chapter 13). We are rapidly moving into the electronic era: Many people already spend a part of both their working and leisure time on computer networks, that is, in fluid virtual communities that do not exist in physical space. The psychosocial consequences of this accelerating change are unforeseeable, but may remove us even further from the natural world.

Love of nature and longing for a "simple country life" have inspired art and literature since antiquity, but most writers celebrate nature tamed in gardens, vineyards, and farms. Deep forests, vast open spaces, and the oceans were mainly viewed with fear. Veneration of nature unspoiled by man, the notion of Eden as wilderness rather than a garden, was a product of the romantic movement of the late 18th and early 19th centuries and interpreted by Emerson, Thoreau, and their contemporaries. Contrast, however, Thoreau's (1856) maxim "In wildness is the preservation of the world" with a more obscure and reflective passage:

It is in vain to dream of a wildness distant from ourselves. There is none such. It is a bog in our brains and bowels, the primitive vigor of Nature in us, that inspires that dream. I shall never find in the wilds of Labrador any greater wildness than in some recess of Concord, i.e. than I import into it.

The great pleasure most people get from natural landscapes, the intense sadness we can feel when watching a forest fire or dying dogwood trees, the strong feelings we can have about animals, all seem to point to a fundamental affinity with the living environment. Wilson (1984) named this human attribute *biophilia*, and researchers from several disciplines have established that experience of nature can indeed have restorative powers (chapters 12 and 13).

Psychotherapists with an ecological viewpoint maintain that emotional responses to the environment are healthy and worth examining as primary mental phenomena. Ecopsychologists challenge notions of individual separateness, of self and other, of mind and matter (Hillman, 1995; Lifton, 1993). They aim to expand awareness beyond the individual and to develop a sense of connectedness with the world. Among their targets are existential isolation, denial, and grief related to destruction of the environment. Their insights and their purpose merit our attention.

The evidence is inescapable that human activity now modifies the environment everywhere, often irreversibly, sometimes drastically, and that nature itself is hostage to our actions (McKibben, 1989). We used to assume that nature was large enough to be forgiving, too large even to notice our insults, and almost eternal. In the span of only two generations we have discovered that we have the power to destroy nature, with nuclear weapons or with waste—and that we may in fact do so, unless we learn to cooperate and take responsibility for our actions. We can still hope that this collective coming-of-age will inform how we see ourselves individually, that we can develop a species consciousness (Lifton, 1993). The survival of the human species may ultimately depend on it.

REFERENCES

Abe, K. (1987). Secular trends of suicide seasonality: Association with per capita GNP and sunshine. In *Seasonal effects on reproduction, infection and psychoses: Progress in biometeorology* (Vol. 5, pp. 205–212). The Hague: SPB Academic Publishing.

American Medical Association, House of Delegates (AMA). (1995). *Human health and the protection of biodiversity* (Resolution 403). Resolution presented at the American Medical Association annual meetings, Washington, DC.

American Psychiatric Association. (1994). *Diagnostic and statistical manual of mental disorders* (4th ed.). Washington, DC: Author.

Chivian, E. (1995, April). *Species extinction: The loss of biodiversity and its implications for human health*. Paper presented at the conference on Biodiversity and Human Health, Smithsonian Institution, Washington, DC.

Chivian, E., McCally, M., Hu, H., & Haines, A. (Eds.). (1993). *Critical condition: Human health & the environment*. Cambridge, MA: MIT Press.

Colborn, T., Dumanoski, D., & Myers, J. P. (1996). *Our stolen future*. New York: Dutton.

Cotton, J. L. (1986). Ambient temperature and violent crime. *Journal of Applied Social Psychology, 16,* 786–801.

Cox, P. A. (1995, April). *Conservation: Indigenous peoples and medicinal plants.* Paper presented at the conference on Biodiversity and Human Health, Smithsonian Institution, Washington, DC.

Desjarlais, R., Eisenberg, L., Good, B., & Kleinman, A. (Eds.). (1995). *World mental health: Problems and priorities in low income countries.* New York: Oxford University Press.

Dohrenwend, B. P., Martin, J. L., Goldsteen, K., Goldsteen, R. L., Bartlett, G. S., Warheit, G. J., & Dohrenwend, B. S. (1981). Stress in the community: A report to the President's Commission on the Accident at Three Mile Island. *Annals of the New York Academy of Sciences, 365,* 159–174.

Eskenazi, A. (1995). A letter for George. *Audubon Naturalist News, 21,* 9.

Espiritu, R. C., Kripke, D. F., Ancoli-Israel, S., Mowen, M. A., Mason, W. J., Fell, R. L., Klauber, M. R., & Kaplan, O. J. (1994). Low illumination experienced by San Diego adults: Association with atypical depressive symptoms. *Biological Psychiatry, 35,* 403–407.

Eyles, J., Baxter, J., Johnson, N., & Taylor, S. M. (1993). Worrying about waste: Living close to solid waste disposal facilities in southern Ontario. *Social Science and Medicine, 37,* 805–812.

Fagin, D., Lavelle, M., & The Center for Public Integrity. (1996). *Toxic deception: How the chemical industry manipulates science.* Secaucus, NJ: Birch Lane Press, Carol Publishing Group.

Farrar, D. J., Locke, S. E., & Kantrowitz, F. G. (1995). Chronic fatigue syndrome. 1: Etiology and pathogenesis. *Behavioral Medicine, 21,* 5–16.

General Accounting Office. (1997). *Gulf War illnesses: Improved monitoring of clinical progress and reexamination of research emphasis are needed* (Letter Report No. GAO/NSIAD-97-163). Washington, DC: Author.

Gibbs, M., & Belford, S. (1993). Toxic threat, coping style and symptoms of emotional distress. *Toxicollegian, 2,* 1–4.

Gilbert, S. G., & Grant-Webster, K. S. (1995). Neurobehavioral effects of developmental methylmercury exposure. *Environmental Health Perspectives, 103* (Suppl. 6), 135–142.

Golub, M. S., & Jacobson, S. W. (1995). Workshop on perinatal exposure to dioxin-like compounds. IV. Neurobehavioral effects. *Environmental Health Perspectives, 103* (Suppl. 2), 151–155.

Gupta, S., & Murray, R. M. (1992). The relationship of environmental temperature to the incidence and outcome of schizophrenia. *British Journal of Psychiatry, 160,* 788–792.

Haines, A. (1993). The possible effects of climate change on health. In E. Chivian, M. McCally, H. Hu, & A. Haines (Eds.), *Critical condition: Human health & the environment* (pp. 151–170). Cambridge, MA: MIT Press.

Hillman, J. (1995). A psyche the size of the earth. In T. Roszak, M. E. Gomes, & A. D. Kanner (Eds.), *Ecopsychology.* San Francisco: Sierra Club Books.

Institute of Medicine. (1995). *Health consequences of service during the Persian Gulf War: Initial findings and recommendations for immediate action.* Washington, DC: National Academy Press.

Institute of Medicine. (1996). *Evaluation of the U.S. Department of Defense Persian Gulf comprehensive clinical evaluation program.* Washington, DC: National Academy Press.

JeeVan, A., & Kripke, M. L. (1994). Ozone depletion and the immune system. *Lancet, 342,* 1159–1160.

Kalkstein, L. S., & Greene, J. S. (1997). An evaluation of climate/mortality relationships in large U.S. cities and the possible impacts of a climate change. *Environmental Health Perspective, 105,* 84–93.

Kane, H. (1995). Leaving home. In L. Starke (Ed.), *State of the world 1995* (pp. 132–149). New York: W. W. Norton & Co.

Kaplan, H. I. (1994). *Kaplan and Sadock's synopsis of psychiatry.* Baltimore: Williams & Wilkins.

Kripke, D. F., Mullaney, D. J., Klauber, M. R., Risch, S. C., & Gillin, J. C. (1992). Controlled trial of bright light for nonseasonal major depressive disorders. *Biological Psychiatry, 31,* 119–134.

Leonard, B. E., & Song, C. (1996). Stress and the immune system in the etiology of anxiety and depression. *Pharmacology, Biochemistry and Behavior, 54,* 299–303.

Lifton, R. (1993). *The protean self: Human resilience in an age of fragmentation.* New York: Basic Books.

Loevinsohn, M. E. (1994). Climatic warming and increased malaria incidence in Rwanda. *Lancet, 343,* 714–718.

Lombardi, G., Covelli, V., Gignante, M., Rossi, R., Tommaselli, A. P., Selleri, A., Valentino, R., & Savastano, S. (1994). Neuroendocrine axis and behavioral stress. *Annals of the New York Academy of Sciences, 741,* 216–222.

Maier, S. F., Watkins, L. R., & Fleshner, M. (1994). Psychoneuroimmunology. The interface between behavior, brain, and immunity. *American Psychologist, 49,* 1004–1017.

Mays, T. (1995, April). *A paradigm for the equitable sharing of benefits resulting from biodiversity research and development.* Paper presented at the conference on Biodiversity and Human Health, Smithsonian Institution, Washington, DC.

Mazure, C. M. (Ed.). (1995). *Does stress cause psychiatric illness?* Washington, DC: American Psychiatric Press.

McCleary, R., Chew, K. S. Y., Hellsten, J. J., & Flynnbransford, M. (1991). Age-specific and sex-specific cycles in United States suicides, 1973 to 1985. *American Journal of Public Health, 81,* 1494–1497.

McKibben, B. (1989). *The end of nature.* New York: Random House.

McMichael, A. J., Haines, A., Sloof, R., & Kovats, S. (Eds). (1996). *Climate change and human health: An assessment prepared by a task group on behalf of the World Health Organization, the World Meteorological Organization and the United Nations Environmental Programme* (Rep. No. WHO/EHG/96.7). Geneva: WHO.

Miccioli, R., Williams, P., Zimmerman-Tansella, C., & Tansella, M. (1991). Geographical and urban–rural variation in the seasonality of suicide: Some further evidence. *Journal of Affective Disorders, 21,* 39–43.

Myers, N. (1991). Tropical deforestation: The latest situation. *BioScience, 41,* 282.

National Institute of Health. (1994). Technology assessment workshop panel: The Persian Gulf experience and health. *Journal of the American Medical Association, 272,* 391–396.

National Research Council. (1992). *Environmental neurotoxicology.* Report of the Committee on Neurotoxicology and Models for Assessing Risk. Washington, DC: National Academy Press.

Näyhä, S., Väisänen, E., & Hassi, J. (1994). Season and mental illness in an arctic area of northern Finland. *Acta Psychiatrica Scandinavica* (Suppl. 377), 46–49.

Needleman, H. L., & Bellinger, D. (Eds.). (1994). *Prenatal exposure to toxicants: Developmental consequences.* Baltimore: Johns Hopkins Press.

Oren, D. A., & Rosenthal, N. E. (1992). Seasonal affective disorders. In E. S. Paykel (Ed.), *Handbook of affective disorders* (pp. 551–556). New York: Guilford Press.

Parry, M. L., & Rosenzweig, C. (1994). Food supply and risk of hunger. *Lancet, 342,* 1345–1347.

Pinstrup-Andersen, P., Lundberg, M. K. A., & Garrett, J. L. (1995). *Foreign assistance in agriculture: A win–win proposition. Food policy report.* Washington, DC: International Food Policy Research Institute.

Physicians for Social Responsibility. (1997). *Cancer and the environment: What the primary care physician should know.* Washington, DC: Author.

Presidential Advisory Committee. (1997). *Gulf War veterans' illnesses: Final report.* Washington, DC: U.S. Government Printing Office (No. 040-000-00683-4).

Repace, J. L., & Lowrey, A. H. (1985). An indoor air quality standard for ambient tobacco smoke based on carcinogenic risk. *New York State Journal of Medicine, 85,* 381–383.

Repetto, R., & Baliga, S. S. (1996). *Pesticides and the immune system: The public health risks.* Baltimore: World Resources Institute.

Rosenthal, N. E., Sack, D. A., Gillin, J. C., Lewy, A. J., Goodwin, F. K., Davenport, Y., Mueller, P. S., Newsome, D. A., & Wehr, T. A. (1984). Seasonal affective disorder: A description of the syndrome and preliminary findings with light therapy. *Archives of General Psychiatry, 41,* 72–80.

Rosenthal, N. E., Sack, D. A., Skwerer, A. G., Jacobsen, F. M., & Wehr, T. A. (1988). Phototherapy for seasonal affective disorder. *Journal of Biological Rhythms, 3,* 101–120.

Rotton, J., & Frey, J. (1984). Psychological costs of air pollution: Atmospheric conditions, seasonal trends, and psychiatric emergencies. *Population and Environment, 7,* 3–16.

Rural Advancement Foundation International. (1994, November/December). Bioprospecting/biopiracy and indigenous peoples, *RAFI Communiqué.* Ottawa, Canada: RAFI.

Schottenfeld, R. S. (1992). Psychologic sequelae of chemical and hazardous materials exposures. In J. B. Sullivan & G. R. Krieger (Eds.), *Hazardous materials toxicology* (pp. 463–470). Baltimore: Williams & Wilkins.

Sexton, K., Gong, H., Jr., Bailar, J. C. III, Ford, J. G., Gold, D. R., Lambert, W. E., & Utell, M. J. (1993). Air pollution health risks: Do class and race matter? *Toxicology and Industrial Health, 9,* 843–878.

Snow, D. L., & Kline, M. L. (1995). Preventive interventions in the workplace to reduce negative psychiatric consequences of work and family stress. In C. M. Mazure (Ed.), *Does stress cause psychiatric illness?* (pp. 221–270). Washington, DC: American Psychiatric Press.

Thoreau, H. D. (1962). Journal, August 30, 1856. In J. W. Krutch (Ed.), *Walden and other writings.* New York: Bantam.

Tietjen, G. H., & Kripke, D. F. (1994). Suicides in California (1968–1977): Absence of seasonality in Los Angeles and Sacramento counties. *Psychiatry Research, 53,* 161–172.

UNHCR. (1993). *The state of the world's refugees 1993: The challenge of protection.* New York: Penguin.

Ursin, H. (1994). Stress, distress, and immunity. *Annals of the New York Academy of Sciences, 741,* 204–211.

U.S. Bureau of the Census. (1995). *Statistical abstract of the United States* (115th ed., pp. 12–13). Washington, DC: Author.

U.S. Congress, Office of Technology Assessment. (1987). *Technologies to maintain biological diversity* (Publication No. OTA-F-330). Washington, DC: U.S. Government Printing Office.

United States Environmental Protection Agency, Office of Air and Radiation. (1989). *Report to congress on indoor air quality, volume II: Assessment and control of indoor air pollution* (EPA Publication No. 400-1-89-001C, pp. i, 4–14). Washington, DC: Author.

United States Environmental Protection Agency, Office of Air and Radiation. (1992). *Respiratory and health effects of passive smoking: Lung cancer and other disorders* (EPA Publication No. 600-6-90-006F). Washington, DC: Author.

United States Environmental Protection Agency, Office of Air and Radiation. (1995). *Air quality trends 1994* (EPA Publication No. 454/F-95-003). Washington, DC: Author.

Wandersman, A. H., & Hallman, W. K. (1993). Are people acting irrationally? *American Psychologist, 48,* 681–686.

Wiles, R., Cohen, B., Campbell, C., & Elderkin, S. (1994). *Herbicides in drinking water.* Washington, DC: Environmental Working Group.

Wilson, E. O. (1984). *Biophilia.* Cambridge, MA: Harvard University Press.

Wilson, E. O. (1992). *The diversity of life.* Cambridge, MA: Belknap Press.

Chapter 3

Behavioral Manifestations
of Neurotoxicity

Bernard Weiss
University of Rochester

Behavioral toxicology embraces the adverse behavioral effects of chemicals, particularly those to which we are exposed in the environment (Weiss & Cory-Slechta, 1994). Behavioral toxicology surfaced as a discipline around 1970, at a time when toxicology remained rooted in death or pathology as endpoints. Its importance quickly grew evident as functional disorders ascribed to environmental pollutants attracted the attention of both the public and regulatory authorities. Behavior gained further stature as one of the criteria specified by Congress in the Toxic Substances Control Act (TSCA) of 1976.

Psychiatry still seems reluctant to concede the role of toxicology in explaining some behavioral disorders. Neurotoxicity is barely mentioned in psychiatric textbooks, except in the guise of gross poisoning, such as overdoses of medication. But flagrant toxicity is not the core subject matter of contemporary neurobehavioral toxicology. Its principal theme, rather, is the detection and characterization of subtle dysfunction, and its tools consist of test methods adapted from neuropsychology and experimental psychology. One aim of this chapter is to familiarize psychiatrists with a body of work that is directly pertinent to their clinical activities; an allied purpose is to encourage their participation in further developing the discipline.

HISTORY

The origins of behavioral toxicology lie in a diversity of sources (see Table 3.1). Behavioral pharmacology burgeoned with the introduction in the 1950s of chemotherapy for psychiatric disorders. Workplace exposure cri-

TABLE 3.1
Historical Origins of Behavioral Toxicology

- Behavioral pharmacology
- Workplace exposure criteria
- Public awareness and concerns
- Toxic torts
- U.S.S.R. emphasis on the central nervous system

teria set standards for many chemicals on the basis of behavioral deficits such as an increase in accidents. Public awareness and concerns over subtle effects such as learning disabilities helped to mobilize actions by governments. Toxic torts, which now earn generous fees for attorneys and expert witnesses, brought behavioral toxicology into the courtroom. The former U.S.S.R.'s emphasis on the nervous system as the prime site for toxicity, which bears the imprint of Pavlov, generated both curiosity and skepticism on the part of Western experts. Soviet experts claimed that their more rigorous exposure standards, often many times lower than ours, could be traced to their reliance on behavior and brain function, rather than tissue damage, as markers of toxicity (Glass, 1975).

SILENT DAMAGE

The central nervous system is particularly vulnerable to toxicants. No other organ system contains so many specialized components that must mutually coordinate their operations if the organism is to function adequately, and no other organ system is as diverse. Furthermore, although neurons may develop increasingly complex branching with time (e.g., Coleman & Flood, 1987), some areas of the brain, such as the substantia nigra, lose neurons with age. One aspect of this process, not widely appreciated, is that brain damage early in life, particularly during fetal and neonatal development, may not emerge until, late in life, the brain's reserve capacity is sufficiently compromised. Such covert damage, which remains in a latent stage until challenged by aging or additional stressors, has been termed *silent damage* (Weiss & Reuhl, 1994).

WORKPLACE EXPOSURE

Neurotoxic chemicals pervade the workplace. Of 588 chemicals for which ambient exposure standards are published by the American Conference of Governmental Industrial Hygienists (ACGIH), the values for 167 are based on neurobehavioral endpoints (Anger & Johnson, 1985). Of particular interest to psychiatrists, investigations of many workplace chemicals indicate that psychological disturbances are among the principal health consequences of chronic exposure. Because symptoms are easy to attribute to other factors psychiatrists must be alert to the patient's total environment. Patients who see themselves as victims of multiple chemical sensitivity, sick building syndrome, and similar afflictions complain that physicians are unresponsive to the health hazards posed by environmental chemicals (National Research Council, 1992). Psychiatrists are seeing increasing numbers of such patients.

The workplace is the site of much behavioral toxicology research. Its findings indicate that even at exposure levels insufficient to induce clinically detectable signs of toxicity, psychological testing can unearth functional deficits. The potential of behavioral testing was cogently asserted by Gamberale (1985):

> The growing interest in the measurement of performance is most probably due to the sensitivity shown by these methods in unveiling changes in the human organism that otherwise would not be detected. . . . These changes are some of the earliest indicators of the occurrence of health effects. . . . (p. 72)

METALS

Metals constitute the largest group in the periodic table, and many of them are essential for life. But even the essential metals, at elevated doses, can prove toxic. Clinical reports, epidemiological studies, and laboratory findings demonstrate the span of disorders associated with metal exposure (see Table 3.2). Some of these elements have been the target of intensive research, whereas the connection of others with neurobehavioral complaints is more tenuous.

The signs and symptoms of metal neurotoxicity range from vague, subjective complaints such as depression and fatigue to clear neurological

TABLE 3.2
Metals Associated With Behavioral Toxicity

• Aluminum	• Mercury
• Arsenic	• Nickel
• Bismuth	• Selenium
• Boron	• Tellurium
• Cadmium	• Thallium
• Lead	• Tin
• Manganese	• Vanadium

TABLE 3.3
Symptoms Ascribed to Metal Toxicity

• Anosmia	• Incoordination
• Appetite loss	• Irritability
• Depression	• Paresthesias
• Disorientation	• Polyneuritis
• Dizziness	• Somnolence
• Fatigue	• Tremor
• Headache	• Visual disturbances
• Insomnia	• Weakness

indications such as tremor and polyneuritis (see Table 3.3). All, however, can be quantified with the appropriate psychological and behavioral test procedures. As noted earlier, subtle degrees of impairment often escape conventional clinical examinations.

Manganese

Manganese is an essential metal, but, at high exposure levels, produces a constellation of neurotoxic signs (see Table 3.4). Manganese miners have provided the classic cases; they inhale the ore dust, and the manganese, once dissolved in blood, makes its passage from the lung to the brain. The lung, in fact, serves as a reservoir, continuing to transfer inhaled manganese to the brain via the blood (Newland, Cox, Hamada, Oberdorster, & Weiss, 1987). The anatomical foundations of manganese neurotoxicity are evident from magnetic resonance imaging (MRI), which locates the highest concentrations of manganese in basal ganglia structures (Nelson, Golnick, Korn, & Angle, 1993; Newland, Ceckler, Kordower, & Weiss, 1989).

Even more interesting are the behavioral features, especially the hysterical laughing and weeping. In South American mining communities, the syndrome is called *locura manganica,* or manganese madness. But even in factories, where workers are exposed to much lower levels and do not exhibit overt neurological signs, psychological tests can expose behavioral deficits. (see Table 3.5, based on Mergler et al., 1994). Roels, Ghyselen,

TABLE 3.4
Signs and Symptoms of Manganese Neurotoxicity

• Abnormal gait	• Weakness
• Retropulsion	• Difficulty walking
• Diminished leg power	• Somnolence
• Impaired coordination	• Clumsiness
• Abnormal laughter	• Bradykinesia
• Expressionless face	• Lack of balance
• Dysarthria	• Muscle pains

TABLE 3.5
Prominent Differences in Reported Symptoms Between
Manganese-Exposed Workers and Referents (Mergler et al., 1994)

- Fatigue
  —No inclination to do anything
  —tired after sleeping, somnolent
  —tiredness in legs
- Mood
  —sudden changes
  —agitated, nervous, aggressive feelings
- Memory
  —absentminded, difficulty concentrating
  —memory loss noted by others
- Motor
  —difficulty articulating words (dysarthria)
  —cramps, ataxia

Buchet, Ceulemans, and Lauwerys (1992) reported similar findings. Although recent literature reports a correlation between levels of manganese in hair samples and a proclivity to engage in violent behavior (Gottschalk, Rebello, Buchsbaum, Tucker, & Hodges, 1991), the relationship of hair to blood and brain levels is currently unknown.

Mercury

Mercury is a neurotoxic metal recognized as a poison since antiquity. Elemental mercury vapor readily penetrates into and lodges in brain tissue. It is such a potent neurotoxicant that miners in the famed mercury mines of Almadén, in Spain, are allowed to work only a few hours each week. Mercury's toxic potency is partly a property of its volatility. It evaporates so readily that even a small amount in an enclosed space can be inhaled in high enough concentrations to induce toxic signs.

The cardinal neurological sign of mercury vapor intoxication is tremor. One victim, despite a marked tremor (Wood, Weiss, & Weiss, 1973), had to diagnose her own affliction; physicians in the community in which she lived treated her with tranquilizers. Tremor evaluation in workers exposed to low ambient levels of mercury vapor cannot be accomplished with only a simple neurological examination. Its evaluation requires complex instrumentation. Quantitative analyses of tremor, in fact, can serve as biomarkers of excessive exposure in the absence of any clinical indications of impairment.

The classical psychological component of mercury neurotoxicity is a syndrome known as Erethism. The word comes from the Greek root for "irritation" or "red." Its more advanced manifestations were graphically described in a survey of women exposed to mercury vapor in a factory (Benning, 1958):

I had dizzy spells, and I began to be so weak and tired that it was hard to even get my supper. I got so grouchy and nervous I would cry at nothing. . . . I would awaken suddenly and have a fluttery feeling like I was scared or floating in space. . . . I kept feeling worse and getting trembly and nervous . . . and I seemed to forget things so easily. . . . (p. 335)

Psychological testing of workers can detect neurobehavioral toxicity even in workers exposed to far lower mercury concentrations than those evoking the classical signs (Andersen, Ellingsen, Morland, & Kjuus, 1993; Echeverria et al., 1995). Moreover, in workers long since retired from jobs that exposed them to elemental mercury, neurobehavioral deficits seem to linger even decades later (Albers et al., 1988; Kishi et al., 1993). Table 3.6 summarizes the results of many studies designed to explore the neurobehavioral toxicity of workplace exposure. Elemental mercury toxicity has lately assumed a new dimension. Some critics of current dental practices assert that silver fillings, which contain a large percentage of mercury, release mercury vapor, especially during chewing, and that the inhaled vapor engenders a broad spectrum of medical and psychological illness.

Amalgam dental restorations have been assailed since their introduction in the middle of the last century, but many patients now seek their removal because they are convinced, despite no cogent evidence (e.g., Ahlqwist, Bengtsson, Furunes, Hollender, & Lapidus, 1988) that they are source of illness. Their urinary mercury levels typically fall considerably below the maxima set for workplace exposure. Furthermore, the process of removal itself raises urinary levels of mercury (Molin et al., 1990).

Infants and young children seem especially vulnerable to mercury, and display a syndrome, characterized by irritability and erythema, known as Pink Disease (Weiss & Clarkson, 1982). Although the developing brain may be exquisitely susceptible to organic mercury (Cox, Clarkson, Marsh, & Amin-Zaki, 1989), the hazards of gestational exposure to mercury vapor are equivocal. Mercury evaporating from amalgam reconstructions appar-

TABLE 3.6
Typical Neuropsychological Indices of
Workplace Exposure to Elemental Mercury

- Cognitive
  —Lower intelligence test scores
  —Impaired memory test performance
- Motor
  —Abnormal tremor characteristics
  —Slowed response speed
  —Impaired movement coordination
- Affect
  —Personality changes

ently traverses the placenta as readily as it passes into the brain (Drasch, Schupp, Hofl, Reinke, & Radier, 1994).

Lead

Lead is the most notorious of the toxic metals, and the subject of a massive literature. Like mercury, its history extends into antiquity. It is now seen as primarily a developmental neurotoxicant, and the blood levels currently considered tolerable for the developing brain have fallen, during the past 20 years, from 40 µg/dl to 10 µg/dl. But even that level cannot be construed as free from risk. The bulk of current work relies on IQ scores as the defining index of excessive exposure, but the seminal paper that initiated the present standard (Needleman et al., 1979) showed its most compelling results on behavior rating scales completed by teachers in the early primary grades. Ratings of behaviors such as "impulsive" and "distracted" revealed striking dose-response functions based on lead levels in deciduous teeth.

Although children are now the targets of most current studies, adults are also susceptible to lead neurotoxicity, as recognized since at least the time of Galen. Workers whose exposure levels are too low to provoke the more classical signs such as wrist-drop may still exhibit signs that bring them to psychiatric attention. The following passage describes a group of workers exposed in the course of removing lead-based paint from ship hulls (Rieke, 1969):

> Severe, classically described symptoms are infrequent. More commonly symptoms are vague; these metal burners are a little achy, dyspeptic, mentally sluggish and moderately fatigued . . . symptoms are attributed to other causes and the condition remains undiagnosed and untreated . . . these workers do not feel fit . . . they drink too much . . . are often tested for wrong ailments . . . they make errors which lead to . . . accidental injuries. (p. 521)

At still lower exposure levels, at which even these nonspecific indices are not apparent, neurobehavioral testing finds evidence of impairment. Table 3.7 is a summary of the published literature on workplace exposure.

TABLE 3.7
Typical Neuropsychological Indices of
Workplace Exposure to Inorganic Lead

- Cognitive
  —Lower intelligence test scores
  —Impaired memory test performance
  —Impaired vigilance
  —Reduced scores on learning tests
- Motor
  —Interference with coordination
  —Slowed response speed

The entries are based on controlled studies comparing exposed and control groups or on correlations between blood levels and performance.

PESTICIDES

Pesticides are notorious neurotoxicants. Most insecticides were designed to act on the nervous systems of insects, so it is not surprising that they also act on the nervous systems of humans (Ecobichon & Joy, 1993). The organophosphorous (OP) compounds are structurally and functionally similar to nerve gases such as those deployed by Iraq and that were used in the 1995 terrorist attacks in the Tokyo subway. They act by inhibiting acetylcholinesterase. Acute effects range from symptoms such as dizziness, visual disturbances, nausea and vomiting, and weakness to serious responses such as difficulty in breathing and severe diarrhea.

Episodes of OP poisoning occur in the United States with surprising frequency. The first, the Ginger Jake epidemic in 1930, even made its poignant way into the blues repertoire (Morgan, 1982). Victims show progressive distal weakness, sensory loss, ataxia, altered pain, vibration, and position sense, muscle weakness, and psychiatric signs such as depression, psychotic reactions, anxiety, and hallucinations.

But the signs of OP exposure can be a good deal more subtle than clear neurological damage (Weiss, 1988a). In one study, OP-exposed farm workers showed significant differences from control workers on several items (see Table 3.8) from a standardized scale of anxiety (Levin, Rodnitzky, & Mick, 1976). None of the exposed workers displayed any clinical indications of toxicity.

Several studies now indicate that acute poisoning may leave a subtle residue of dysfunction. Savage et al. (1988) studied patients who had suffered a poisoning episode a year earlier and who apparently had recovered

TABLE 3.8
Anxiety Scale Items Differentiating Control
and OP-Exposed Farm Workers

	Control.%	Exposed %	p-value
Work under tension	21	50	0.005
Fitful sleep	0	21	0.050
Restlessness	21	54	0.040
More nervous	4	33	0.025
Chronically anxious	8	33	0.072
Easily upset	8	39	0.036
Nervous when waiting	46	83	0.020
Tends to blush	25	54	0.080

TABLE 3.9
Chronic Neurological Sequelae of Acute Organophosphate
Pesticide Poisoning (from Savage et al., 1988)

	100 Cases	100 Controls	p-value
WAIS Verbal IQ	105.40	111.86	0.001
WAIS Performance	108.41	110.13	0.242
WAIS Full Scale	107.50	111.77	0.001
Impairment Rating	1.07	0.91	0.001
Halstead Index	0.30	0.23	0.020
Pegboard	148.34	137.96	0.002
Card Sorting	17.07	12.91	0.001

completely. But psychological testing comparing poisoned workers and controls one year later (see Table 3.9) disclosed that recovery was not complete. Earlier investigations also suggested enduring alterations in brain electrical activity (Duffy & Burchfiel, 1980).

Kepone™ (chlordecone) is a distant relative of DDT and belongs to the class of organochlorine insecticides. A manufacturing plant in Virginia exposed workers to high levels (Cannon et al., 1978). Some of them visited physicians with health complaints, which alerted health authorities. The earliest sign of excessive exposure turned out to be nervousness. How many plant physicians would suspect chemical exposure rather than family or employment problems as the source of the complaint? How many psychiatrists would even consider such a possibility?

SOLVENTS

Workers are exposed to volatile organic solvents in many industrial settings (paint manufacture, degreasing, printing, etc.) These compounds, such as toluene, also appear in many household products. They easily penetrate into the brain and, at high levels, produce narcosis. Some have even been used as anesthetics, and are commonly abused (glue-sniffing) because of their narcotic effects. One question for environmental health is whether they are neurotoxic at chronic low levels in workplace settings. Psychological testing supports such a notion. Scandinavian scientists pioneered this research, which began in the late 1960s and has been confirmed in other countries (see Table 3.10). Such outcomes prompted the Environmental Protection Agency (EPA) to request the chemical industry to undertake extended evaluations of the neurotoxicity of 10 high-volume solvents (EPA, 1991).

TABLE 3.10
Chronic Neurotoxic Effects of Solvents

• Cognitive Variables	• Motor Variables
—Intelligence	—Coordination
—Memory	—Response Speed
—Vigilance	• Sensory
—Acquisition	—Color Vision
—Coding	• Personality
—Concept Shifting	—Mood Changes
—Spatial Relations	
—Categorization	

FOOD ADDITIVES

A pediatric allergist from San Francisco published a book entitled, *Why Your Child Is Hyperactive* (Feingold, 1975). He hypothesized that a significant proportion of such children were excessively sensitive to certain dietary constituents and recommended that parents try a diet that eliminated several classes of foods and additives. He especially singled out synthetic colors and flavors because of their lack of nutritional qualities. His claims attracted copious publicity, led to congressional hearings, inspired the formation of parents groups organized as the Feingold Association, and evoked glacial skepticism and outright hostility from the medical community. Feingold's assertions were rooted in his own practice and observations, supplemented by a surprisingly extensive allergy literature, but lacked the support of controlled clinical trials. Public and legislative pressures eventually compelled a reluctant FDA to fund such trials.

Close to 3,000 agents are approved for use as additives in food. None has been subjected to thorough neurobehavioral testing. A study commissioned by the FDA and published in 1977 urged testing for psychotoxicity but to no avail. The development of the discipline of behavioral toxicology, however, seems to have encouraged FDA, in its proposed new protocols, to acknowledge the importance of behavioral testing. At the time that Feingold enunciated his hypothesis additives seemed an unlikely source of behavioral aberrations because the issue had not been examined.

Together with colleagues in the Department of Nutritional Sciences at the University of California at Berkeley and pediatricians in the Kaiser-Permanente system, I participated in a controlled clinical trial of the hypothesis. The experiment focused on synthetic food colors because there are so few, compared to 1,500 artificial flavors, so that a manageable blend could be made to use as a challenge.

Parents who thought that an elimination diet had helped their children were enrolled in the Kaiser system. An experiment was designed in which the child consumed a soft drink every day at the same time (Weiss et al., 1980). On eight occasions during an 11-week period, the drink contained a blend of seven artificial food colors rather than the caramel and cranberry coloring in the control drink. The drinks were indistinguishable either by taste or by color, and children with clinically diagnosed attention deficit disorder (ADD) signs were excluded.

For each of the 22 children, 15 boys and 7 girls between 3 and 7 years of age, the parent selected 10 items, specific for the child, from a large sample of items that was drawn from several child behavior inventories. Two responders were found. Subject 73 was a 34-month-old girl who turned out to be a spectacular responder. On days she drank the challenge, she showed marked elevations of behaviors such as "short attention span" and "acts as if driven by motor." These results are depicted in Fig. 3.1.

These are not isolated data (Swanson & Kinsbourne, 1980; Weiss, 1982). Kaplan, McNicol, Conte, and Moghadam (1989) conducted the most logistically complex study of additives and controlled all elements of the diet. They saw adverse responses in ADD boys to many dietary ingredients and improvements when these ingredients were eliminated. These maneuvers did not cure ADD—the children still manifested disturbing behaviors—but did demonstrate a significant role for food sensitivities in the syndrome.

The FDA sets acceptable daily intakes (ADIs) for humans based typically on 2-year feeding studies in rodents. They then divide the highest dose

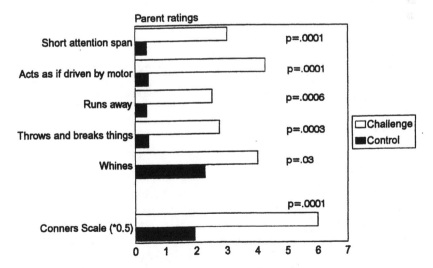

FIG. 3.1. Parent ratings of responses by a 34-month-old girl to a blend of food colors (based on Weiss et al., 1980). The p values are based on randomization tests.

TABLE 3.11
Comparison of Food Dye Doses Producing Behavioral
Disturbances in Children With ADIs

Color	Behavior[a]	ADI[b]
Yellow 5	9.07	300
Yellow 6	10.70	300
Red 40	13.80	420
Red 3	0.57	150
Blue 1	0.80	200
Blue 2	0.15	37
Green 3	0.11	150

[a]Based on Weiss et al. (1980).

[b]ADIs are based on doses in animals producing no statistically significant adverse effects (NOAELs, or no observed adverse effect levels). These doses are then divided by 100 (a factor of 10 for species differences and a factor of 10 to account for variations among individuals in sensitivity) to calculate the ADI, which presumably will not affect humans.

that produces no adverse effects by 100 to provide a safety factor for humans. The food color doses used in our California study (and other studies) are about 50 times lower than the ADIs. Table 3.11 contrasts the ADI levels with what several researchers have determined to be levels evoking behavioral disturbances in children. The FDA still seems unwilling to recognize this body of literature.

Young children are not the only susceptible group. Adults are susceptible as well, as noted in the following passage (Shader & Greenblatt, 1985):

Within two days of substituting 25 mg of desipramine for 25 mg of imipramine (to reduce dry mouth), the patient began to complain of reddened eyes . . . rhinitis, lethargy . . . muscle aching . . . head pressure. The desipramine contained tartrazine (FD&C Yellow No. 5). When discontinued, the symptoms subsided within 36 hours. A desipramine . . . not containing tartrazine provoked no reaction. (p. A16)

DEVELOPMENTAL NEUROTOXICITY

Behavioral teratology describes the outcome of toxic chemical exposures during early brain development. The vulnerability of the developing brain is universally recognized (Needleman & Bellinger, 1994). Fetal alcohol syndrome (Streissguth, Clarren, & Jones, 1985) is a striking example. The lead literature is another (Bellinger, Leviton, Waternaux, Needleman, & Rabinowitz, 1979; Needleman et al., 1979; Needleman, Schell, Bellinger, Leviton, & Allred, 1990). These papers, and many others from different parts of the world, provide convincing evidence that even relatively low levels of lead exposure threaten brain function and development. The most worrisome questions arise from clinically unobservable consequences, not from overt brain damage. Is intellectual potential diminished? Are behavioral disorders created?

David Rall, former director of the National Institute of Environmental Health Sciences (NIEHS) put this fear in the form of a question about thalidomide, which was prescribed for pregnant women because it seemed to be a safe sedative. At the time it was introduced by a German firm, testing for teratologies (birth defects) was not required for new pharmaceuticals. The children who were victimized because of this oversight, and because the company squelched adverse reports, suffered missing limbs and other disabilities. Rall posed the following question at a scientific meeting. The answer has to be disquieting. "Suppose that thalidomide, instead of causing the birth of children with missing limbs, had instead reduced their intellectual potential by 10%. Would we be aware, even today, of its toxic potency?"

A relatively small decline in average intellectual potential poses a significant societal dilemma. Mean IQ for the most common tests was standardized at 100 with a standard deviation of 15. In a population of 100 million, 2.3 million individuals will score above 130. A shift of 5% to a mean of 95 places only 990,000 individuals in that superior range and inflates the number scoring below 70 (Weiss, 1988b). But not only intellectual performance is in jeopardy. The population of habitual criminals tends to score about 5% to 10% below those who do not engage in antisocial behavior.

Another reason for disquiet is the possibility that fetal brain damage can emerge as psychiatric illness many years later. The implications extend far beyond what we conventionally define as toxicity and have secured the attention of some psychiatrists (Waddington, 1993):

> . . . the neurodevelopmental hypothesis [of schizophrenia] takes as the primary event changes in utero that disrupt the development of fundamental aspects of brain structure and function and that might produce the typical symptoms some two decades later, perhaps only after functional maturation of other, associated, symptoms or processes—for example, myelination or synaptic pruning. (p. 536)

A further example of silent damage might be the emergence of neurodegenerative disease late in life, when the diminished reserve capacity of the brain is no longer sufficient to compensate for damage inflicted years earlier. We have no more than a tentative grasp of the possible contribution of environmental poisons to these diseases (Spencer, 1990). Longitudinal research is tedious and expensive, and funding agencies are often reluctant to support them. No one doubts, however, that long before the clinical symptoms of Parkinson's disease, Alzheimer's disease, and others erupt, the underlying processes have been active for many years, perhaps decades. Perhaps they even began, as Waddington postulated for schizophrenia, with abnormal fetal development (Calne, Eisen, McGeer, & Spencer, 1986).

Sexual function is surely an aspect of brain development with enormous implications for psychiatry. It, too, it turns out, is a pawn of toxic exposure. Dioxin, known more precisely as 2,3,7,8-tetrachlorodibenzoparadioxin (TCDD) and to the public as a notorious contaminant of Agent Orange, is the most potent known poison apart from biotoxins such as venoms. Until fairly recently, its primary health threats had been viewed through the lens of cancer. Now, however, behavior has mounted to the summit of concerns. Cancer appears in rodents exposed to doses in the microgram range. In contrast, male offspring of rats treated during gestation and lactation with nanogram quantities of TCDD display aberrations in mating behavior (Mably, Moore, Goy, & Peterson, 1992) and other aspects of sexual development. These responses provide the most sensitive endpoints so far documented for TCDD exposure. They have stirred a lively debate about chemicals with similar properties, such as some of the polychlorinated biphenyls, that have been labeled environmental estrogens or endocrine disrupters. One question lurking at the borders of the debate is the extent to which these agents may modify other, much more subtle, sexually dimorphic behaviors and brain development in general. A recent book (Colborn, Myers, & Dumanoski, 1996) offers an extensive review of these issues.

Behavioral toxicology is still a relatively young discipline. Few of its practitioners are psychiatrists. But no other medical specialty is so closely allied with its aims, techniques, and content. Psychiatric training and textbooks would profit by acknowledging its contributions and perspectives.

ACKNOWLEDGMENTS

Chapter preparation was supported in part by grants ES01247 and ES05433 from the National Institute for Environmental Health Sciences, grant DA07737 from the National Institute on Drug Abuse, and by a grant from the International Life Sciences Institute.

REFERENCES

Ahlqwist, M., Bengtsson, C., Furunes, B., Hollender, L., & Lapidus, L. (1988). Number of amalgam tooth fillings in relation to subjectively experienced symptoms in a study of Swedish women. *Community Dentistry and Oral Epidemiology, 16*, 227–231.

Albers, J. W., Kallenbach, L. R., Fine, L. J., Langolf, G. D., Wolfe, R. A., Donofrio, P. D., Alessi, A. G., Stolp-Smith, K. A., & Bromberg, M. B. (1988). Mercury workers study group. Neurological abnormalities associated with remote occupational elemental mercury exposure. *Annals of Neurology, 24*, 651–659.

Andersen, A., Ellingsen, D. G., Morland, T., & Kjuus, H. (1993). A neurological and neurophysiological study of chloralkali workers previously exposed to mercury vapour. *Acta Neurologica Scandinavica, 88*, 427–433.

Anger, W. K., & Johnson, B. L. (1985). Chemicals affecting behavior. In J. L. O'Donoghue (Ed.), *Neurotoxicity of industrial and commercial chemicals* (pp. 51–148). Boca Raton, FL: CRC Press.

Bellinger, D., Leviton, A., Waternaux, C., Needleman, H., & Rabinowitz, M. (1987). Longitudinal analyses of prenatal and postnatal lead exposure and early cognitive development. *New England Journal of Medicine, 316*, 1037–1043.

Benning, D. (1958). Outbreak of mercury poisoning in Ohio. *Industrial Medicine and Surgery, 22*, 354–363.

Calne, D. B., Eisen, A., McGeer, E., & Spencer, P. (1986). Alzheimer's disease, Parkinson's disease, and motoneurone disease: Abiotrophic interaction between ageing and environment? *Lancet, 2*, 1067–1070.

Cannon, S. B., Veazey, J. M., Jackson, R. S., Burse, V. W., Hayes, C., Straub, W. E., Landrigan, P. J., & Liddle, J. A. (1978). Epidemic Kepone poisoning in chemical workers. *American Journal of Epidemiology, 107*, 529–537.

Colborn, T., Dumanoski, D., & Myers, J. P. (1996). *Our stolen future.* New York: Dutton.

Coleman, P. D., & Flood, D. G. (1987). Neuron numbers and dendritic extent in normal aging and Alzheimer's disease. *Neurobiology of Aging, 8*, 521–545.

Cox, C., Clarkson, T. W., Marsh, D. O., & Amin-Zaki, L. (1989). Dose-response analysis of infants prenatally exposed to methylmercury: An application of a single compartment model to single-strand hair analysis. *Environmental Research, 48*, 318–322.

Drasch, G., Schupp, I., Hofl, H., Reinke, R., & Roider, G. (1994). Mercury burden of human fetal and infant tissues. *European Journal of Pediatrics, 153*, 607–610.

Duffy, F. H., & Burchfiel, J. L. (1988). Long term effects of the organophospate sarin on EEGs in monkeys and humans. *Neurotoxicology, 1*, 667–689.

Echeverria, D., Heyer, N. J., Martin, M. D., Naleway, C. A., Woods, J. S., & Bittner, A. C. (1995). Behavioral effects of low-level exposure to Hg° among dentists. *Neurotoxicology and Teratology, 17*, 161–168.

Ecobichon, D. S., & Joy, R. M. (1993). *Pesticides and neurological diseases* (2nd ed.). Boca Raton, FL: CRC Press.

Environmental Protection Agency. (1991). Multi-substance rule for the testing of neurotoxicity. *Federal Register, 56*, 9105–9119.

Feingold, B. F. (1975). *Why your child is hyperactive.* New York: Random House.

Gamberale, F. (1985). The use of behavioral performance tests in the assessment of solvent toxicity. *Scandinavian Journal of Work, Environment and Health, 11*, 65–74.

Glass, R. I. (1975). A perspective on environmental health in the USSR. *Archives of Environmental Health, 30*, 391–395.

Gottschalk, L. A., Rebello, T., Buchsbaum, M. S., Tucker, H. G., & Hodges, E. L. (1991). Abnormalities in hair trace elements as indicators of aberrant behavior. *Comprehensive Psychiatry, 32*, 229–237.

Kaplan, B. J., McNicol, J. R., Conte, A., & Moghadam, H. K. (1989). Dietary replacement in preschool-aged hyperactive boys. *Pediatrics, 83*, 7–17.

Kishi, R., Doi, R., Fukuchi, Y., Satoh, H., Satoh, T., Ono, A., Moriwaka, F., Tashiro, K., & Takahata, N. (1993). Subjective symptoms and neurobehavioral performances of ex-mercury miners at an average of 18 years after the cessation of chronic exposure to mercury vapor. Mercury workers study group. *Environmental Ressearch, 62*, 289–302.

Levin, H. S., Rodnitzky, R. L., & Mick, D. L. (1976). Anxiety associated with exposure to organophosphate compounds. *Archives of General Psychiatry, 33,* 225–228.

Mably, T. A., Moore, R. W., Goy, R. W., & Peterson, R. E. (1992). In utero and lactational exposure of male rats to 2,3,7,8-tetrachlorodibenzo-p-dioxin: 2. Effects on sexual behavior and the regulation of luteinizing hormone secretion in adulthood. *Toxicology and Applied Pharmacology, 114,* 97–107.

Mergler, D., Huel, G., Bowler, R., Iregren, A., Belanger, S., Baldwin, M., Tardif, R., Smargiassi, A., & Martin, L. (1994). Nervous system dysfunction among workers with long-term exposure to manganese. *Environmental Research, 64,* 151–180.

Molin, M., Bergman, B., Marklund, S. L., Schutz, A., & Skerfving, S. (1990). Mercury, selenium, and glutathione peroxidase before and after amalgam removal in man. *Acta Odontologica Scandinavica, 48,* 189–202.

Morgan, J. P. (1982). The Jamaica ginger paralysis. *Journal of the American Medical Association, 248,* 1864–1867.

National Research Council. (1992). *Multiple chemical sensitivities: Addendum to biologic markers in immunotoxicity.* Washington, DC: National Academy Press.

Needleman, H. L., & Bellinger, D. (Eds.). (1994). *Prenatal exposure to toxicants: Developmental consequences.* Baltimore: Johns Hopkins University Press.

Needleman, H. L., Gunnoe, C., Leviton, A., Reed, M., Peresie, H., Maher, C., & Barrett, P. (1979). Deficits in psychological and classroom performance of children with elevated dentine lead levels. *New England Journal of Medicine, 300,* 689–695.

Needleman, H. L., Schell, A., Bellinger, D., Leviton, A., & Allred, E. N. (1990). The long-term effects of exposure to low doses of lead in childhood. An 11-year follow-up report. *New England Journal of Medicine, 322,* 83–88.

Nelson, K., Golnick, J., Korn, T., & Angle, C. (1993). Manganese encephalopathy: Utility of early magnetic resonance imaging. *British Journal of Industrial Medicine, 50,* 510–513.

Newland, M. C., Ceckler, T. L., Kordower, J. H., & Weiss, B. (1989). Visualizing manganese in the primate basal ganglia with magnetic resonance imaging. *Experimental Neurology, 106,* 251–258.

Newland, M. C., Cox, C., Hamada, R., Oberdorster, G., & Weiss, B. (1987). The clearance of manganese chloride in the primate. *Fundamental and Applied Toxicology, 9,* 314–328.

Rieke, F. E. (1969). Lead intoxication in shipbuilding and shipscraping. *Archives of Environmental Health, 19,* 521–539.

Roels, H. A., Ghyselen, P., Buchet, J. P., Ceulemans, E., & Lauwerys, R. R. (1992). Assessment of the permissible exposure level to manganese in workers exposed to manganese dioxide dust. *British Journal of Industrial Medicine, 49,* 25–34.

Savage, E. P., Keefe, T. J., Mounce, L. M., Heaton, R. K., Lewis, J. A., & Burcar, P. J. (1988). Chronic neurological sequelae of acute organophosphate poisoning. *Archives of Environmental Health, 43,* 38–45.

Shader, R. I., & Greenblatt, D. J. (1985). User unfriendly drugs-fillers, additives, excipients. *Journal of Clinical Psychopharmacology, 5,* A15–A16.

Spencer, P. S. (1990). Chemical time bombs: Environmental causes of neurodegenerative diseases. In R. W. Russell, P. E. Ebert, & A. M. Pope (Eds.), *Behavioral measures of neurotoxicity* (pp. 268–284). Washington, DC: National Academy Press.

Streissguth, A. P., Clarren, S. K., & Jones, K. L. (1985). Natural history of the fetal alcohol syndrome. *Lancet, 2,* 85–91.

Swanson, J. M., & Kinsbourne, M. (1980). Food dyes impair performance of hyperactive children on a laboratory learning task. *Science, 207,* 1485–1487.

Waddington, J. L. (1993). Schizophrenia: Developmental neuroscience and pathobiology. *Lancet, 341,* 531–537.

Weiss, B. (1982). Food additives and environmental chemicals as sources of childhood behavior disorders. *Journal of the American Academy of Child Psychiatry, 21,* 144–152.

Weiss, B. (1988a). Behavior as an early indication of pesticide toxicity. *Toxicology and Industrial Health, 4,* 351–360.

Weiss, B. (1988b). Neurobehavioral toxicity as a basis for risk assessment. *Trends in Pharmacological Sciences, 9,* 59–62.

Weiss, B., & Clarkson, T. W. (1982). *Mercury toxidity in children: Chemical and radiation hazards to children* (pp. 52–59). Columbus, OH: Ross Laboratories.

Weiss, B., & Cory-Slechta, D. A. (1994). Assessment of behavioral toxicity. In A. W. Hayes (Ed.), *Principles and methods of toxicology* (3rd ed., pp. 1091–1155). New York: Raven Press.

Weiss, B., & Reuhl, K. (1994). Delayed neurotoxicity: A silent toxicity. In L. Chang (Ed.), *Handbook of neurotoxicology* (pp. 765–784). New York: Dekker.

Weiss, B., Williams, J. H., Margen, S., Abrams, B., Caan, B., Citron, L. J., Cox, C., McKibben, J., Ogar, D., & Schultz, S. (1980). Behavioral responses to artificial food colors. *Science, 207,* 1487–1488.

Wood, R. W., Weiss, A. B., & Weiss, B. (1973). Hand tremor induced by industrial exposure to inorganic mercury. *Archives of Environmental Health, 26,* 249–252.

Chapter 4

The Psychiatric Evaluation of Patients With Suspected Toxic Exposure

Alice Armstrong Rahill
University of Rochester Medical Center

Ante Lundberg
Washington, DC Commission on Mental Health Services

Chemicals in the environment can affect cognition, mood, and behavior and they are thought to be the main cause of environmental illness (EI). The symptoms are often vague and insidious. This chapter focuses on the neuropsychiatric work-up of patients with suspected toxic exposure and on the manifestations and diagnosis of toxic encephalopathy.

Psychiatrists and psychologists are trained to be aware of their subjective bias; need to remember this part of their training when approaching these patients. Environmental illness is poorly defined and it does not lack for stereotypes and preconceptions. Chemicals seem to be either presumed innocent or presumed guilty. In cases of suspected occupational exposure questions of disability compensation and litigation may cause the patient to exaggerate his or her symptoms. On the other hand, a worker may resist revealing sources of exposure in order to keep his or her job. A patient's personality or presentation may interact with the physician's bias to heighten the suspicion of nonorganic disorder, that is, a histrionic patient claiming exceptional sensitivity.

Patients who maintain that they are sick from chemical exposure are often sent to psychiatrists and neuropsychologists after internists and neurologists have failed to find signs of organic disease. Referring physicians almost always raise the question of secondary gain. It is particularly important that the examination of these patients be rigorous, considers all possible alternative explanations, and methodically supports the final interpretation. The patient must be informed that distinguishing between environmentally related disorders and other possible causes of distress will require time and cooperation.

Some EI patients attribute their distress to other factors. When subtle symptoms with insidious onset (e.g., mental sluggishness and fatigue, dysphoria, dissatisfaction, irritability) gradually build into a pattern of dysfunction that eventually commands attention, the role of chemical exposure, perhaps in interaction with other life factors, is easily overlooked. White, Feldman, and Proctor (1992) provided a useful description of symptoms shared between neurotoxic syndromes and primary neurologic disease, but many neurology textbooks do not include environmental chemicals in their differential for symptoms of dementia or other nervous system disorders.

Neurotoxic pollutants interfere with neurotransmission causing changes in perceptions, cognition, behaviors, and affect. Symptoms can occur in any of the four domains, but it is often disturbances in affect that prompt the referral to the psychiatrist. Weiss (chapter 3, this volume) illustrated how mood changes can signal early cognitive changes caused by chemical exposure. Other chapters reviewed the overlapping syndromes resulting from environmental trauma and stress, which in turn can mimic primary psychiatric disorders. It is important to remember that humans are able to process some amounts of toxins and other foreign substances; when symptoms appear they are the result of a breakdown in one or more aspects of a very complex process.

PREEXAMINATION

Important information may be obtained before meeting with the patient. Suspected chemical exposure calls for a comprehensive psychiatric history with extra attention devoted to the following areas:

- *academic history*: grades repeated or advanced, possible learning disability
- *employment history*: job changes, gaps
- possible *chemical exposures* during work, leisure activities, or at home
- *personal habits*: diet, exercise, alcohol, coffee, tobacco, and other drug use
- current *medications*, alternative therapies
- *medical history*: past head injury, loss of consciousness, systemic disorders such as high blood pressure, diabetes, and so on.
- previous *psychiatric history* and family psychiatric history (with attention to cluster disorders)
- sources of *stress* in recent years, life changes

- past *legal* involvement and possible legal implications of the current evaluation

The exposure history can be deduced from current and past employment, leisure and avocational interests, and place of residence. The clinician would be well advised to become familiar with the local industries most likely to provide exposure (White et al., 1992). It is important to estimate the duration and level, as well as the nature of chemical exposure. Extensive information about toxic chemicals that may be encountered is available in data bases maintained by government agencies and other groups (see appendix). The Environmental Protection Agency (EPA) maintains the Toxic Release Inventory (TRI) that contains detailed release data for more than 650 toxic chemicals. The information can be found in public libraries and on the World Wide Web at http://www.epa.gov.

A comprehensive questionnaire focusing on exposure history and the other items just listed is a useful tool. White et al. (1992) provides tables (Tables 2A–C) of exposure that could easily be incorporated into existing patient information forms. A checklist of symptoms is also useful to determine if symptoms are organized in clinically meaningful clusters, or if a patient indiscriminately endorses all symptoms. Family relationships and sexual history are best reserved for the interview itself, where nonverbal communication can also be assessed.

EXAMINATION

The interview should include a review of past history and current complaints on the basis of previously obtained information and completed questionnaires. Among additional areas to be explored are family situation, sexual history, coping, and precipitating events ("why now?").

Initial impressions are important: the individual's stature and gait; apparel; the condition of skin, fingernails, and hair; the paraphernalia brought into the interview (personal supplies such as drinking water, special tissues, masks, etc.); and interview behavior can offer important information. Does the presentation fit with the patient's complaints?

Neuropsychiatric evaluation of a case of suspected toxic encephalopathy requires a detailed mental status with assessment of cognitive functions and soft neurological signs. It is usually more important to focus on cognition and behavior control than on neuroanatomical localization of lesions. The following should be assessed:

- *motor functions* (activity, gait, involuntary movements, perseveration, ability to tap fingers sequentially, to demonstrate the use of simple objects such as a hammer, to copy a simple figure, to dress)

- *language* (spontaneous speech, fluency, naming, reading, writing, prosody)
- *memory* (rote memory, immediate recall, short-term retention, visual memory)
- *frontal lobe functions* (expressive language, concentration, attention, similarities, reasoning)
- *soft neurological signs* (palmar-mental reflex, snout reflex, simultaneous stimulation discrimination)

The Mini-Mental Status Examination (MMSE; Folstein, Folstein, & Mc-Hough, 1975) is a widely used screening test that assesses orientation, attention, calculation, immediate and short-term recall, visuospatial ability, language, reading and writing, and the ability to follow simple commands. This instrument is not designed to detect subtle disorders, thus absence of negative findings is not proof of absence of pathology, but impaired performance is of considerable diagnostic importance. Repeated testing is useful in following the course of disease and the response to treatment. Visual-manipulative tasks are particularly significant, as they often reveal early neuropsychological disorder. The MMSE score is somewhat affected by age and educational level, but norms have been published taking this into account (Crum, Anthony, Bassett, & Folstein, 1993). A more serious limitation may be that the MMSE has been found insensitive to white matter impairment in multiple sclerosis (MS; Swirsky-Sacchetti, Field, Mitchel, & Sewar, 1992), which suggests insensitivity also to the white matter effects of solvents and other toxins.

Any difficulties on this screening measure warrant further questioning. The first step would be a more intensive evaluation of the suspected area of difficulty. For clinicians experienced in testing, the subsets of the Wechsler Adult Intelligence Scale–Revised (WAIS–R) can give important diagnostic information (Weiss & Cory-Slechta, 1994). The WAIS–R digit span test for short-term memory has been modified and scores from the adapted versions have been found to approximate levels of exposure to lead and mercury in groups of individuals at risk. Tests of motor functions found indicative of neurotoxic effects include finger and toe tapping rate and dexterity in manipulating pegs on a peg board. Tests of reaction time and vigilance are also widely used to measure neurotoxicity. The focus of neurotoxicological research has traditionally been public health. Computerized versions of traditional tests are being validated for clinical use. The most widely used is the Neurobehavioral Evaluation System (Letz & Baker, 1988; White, Diamond, Krengel, Lindem, & Feldman, 1996).

Repeated testing may illustrate the nature and course of the deficits, and of the response to treatment. If the problem is verified with a repeat

MMSE or a more precise test, referral to a neuropsychologist should be considered.

Evaluation

Common neurobehavioral effects of toxic exposure include headache, transient disturbances in awareness, forgetfulness, moodiness, changed behavior, slowed motor movement, weakness, loss of position sense, and muscle weakness or peripheral neuropathy. These signs and symptoms should raise the question of toxic encephalopathy even when no exposure is reported. Soft neurological signs may be the first manifestation of toxic encephalopathy. There is a small but growing literature regarding the neuropsychiatric effects of individual toxins. Extensive reviews are available in texts by White and Procter (1997), Hartman (1995), Bleecker and Hansen (1994), and White et al. (1992). There are also other resources to assist in determining if the symptoms fit the established pattern. For instance, the Agency for Toxic Substances and Disease Registry (ATSDR) publishes Case Studies in Environmental Medicine and other informative material that is increasingly available on the Internet (see appendix). Unfortunately, more than one chemical is usually involved. Although multiple occupational exposures are common in real life, they are uncommon in epidemiological studies, and even more uncommon in experimental studies. Very little is known about the combined effects of neurotoxic substances. This is an important area for continued research.

Complicating the diagnosis, a coexisting medical problem can lower the threshold for symptom formation from toxic exposure and its symptoms can overlap with those caused by the toxin. Examples of such situations are an alcoholic with liver disease exposed to solvents, and a heavy smoker or asthmatic exposed to solvents or fine particle pollution. A history of trauma, such as head injury, or loss of consciousness for any reason can also be a confounding factor.

The insidious but often disabling sequelae of closed head injury are increasingly recognized by clinicians (Lezak, 1995). Head injury is dominant risk factor for adult onset of epilepsy. Even mild closed head injuries or whiplash injuries can damage the vulnerable olfactory nucleus; complaints of loss or change of sense of smell are common after a head injury. Many mild head injuries produce no immediate symptoms, but subtle deficits masked by automatic compensatory mechanisms that make demands on available cognitive resources. The interaction of head injuries with normal aging is not well studied, but is also thought to limit the cognitive reserve of the individual (Satz, 1993). A history of attention deficient disorder (ADD), hyperactivity, or learning disabilities should alert the clinician to the possibility of a developmentally altered brain that may respond in an atypical manner when challenged.

Coexisting psychiatric disorders causing mood disturbance, cognitive impairment, and delusions present diagnostic challenges. A patient with toxic encephalopathy may demonstrate deficits in short-term memory and executive function, with irritability and disinhibited behavior. It is important to establish what the individual's behavior was like prior to the suspected exposure. A complete structured clinical interview can be of great use in identifying preexisting personality disorders and other psychiatric conditions. Drug abuse (including alcohol, solvents, illegal substances, and tobacco) tax the physiological processing mechanisms for toxins and confound the evaluation of neuropsychiatric effects. The extensive physiological changes related to stress are likely to modify responses to chemical exposure; stress may be a cofactor for chemical sensitivity (Hartman, 1995). Traumatic stress can cause posttraumatic stress disorder (PTSD)and contribute to other psychiatric morbidity (Mazure, 1995).

REFERRALS

The diagnosis of EI requires integration of data from multiple sources; referrals to specialists are the standard of care. Patients must be educated about the fact that these complex conditions are not the result of any single etiological factor. Many people have become skeptical or even cynical about traditional medicine and therapy (Arnetz, chapter 9, this volume) and are especially unwilling to accept a psychological component (Hartman, 1995). When appropriate, they should be told that allowing for psychological or interpersonal factors may give them access to beneficial treatment.

Consultation with an occupational health physician or nurse is helpful to establish exposure. Other medical specialists may also be consulted. A neurologist can rule out conditions with symptoms in common with toxic encephalopathy such as movement disorders, epilepsy, and dementia. MS and leukodystrophy, as well as solvent exposure, have erratic presentations due to the variability of the white matter changes they represent. Infections can present with acute or subtle behavioral effects (meningitis, herpes, fungal diseases, mononucleosis). Numerous medical conditions can have an indirect effect on cognitive and psychological functioning, including cardiovascular disorders, respiratory disorders (asthma, chronic obstructive lung disease, and sleep apnea), liver disease, diabetes, and so on. An indication of any of these needs to be considered in the differential diagnosis.

Consultation with a clinical neuropsychologist is recommended to determine if a change in cognitive functioning has occurred and to characterize and quantify neurotoxic effects on cognition and behavior. Records from school and past employment performance should be requested in all cases. Cognitive test results must be interpreted against premorbid level of performance and compared to normative data corrected for age and ability (Agnew & Masten, 1994; Hartman, 1995; White et al., 1992). Clinical neuropsychologists can also administer objective personality measures such as the MMPI2 and interpret the interaction between cognitive and behavioral features. Discriminating between types of chemical exposure and other neurological and affective disorders is a complex and difficult task as different exposures produce different patterns of neuropsychiatric deficit. It is important to select a neuropsychologist who is interested in this type of work.

An ophthalmologist may be consulted in some cases, particularly for testing contrast sensitivity. This is a test of the brightness required for the patient to differentiate between alternating light and dark bars of varying widths. It describes visual function more fully than visual acuity, and has proven useful in the detection of early or subtle neural dysfunction in diseases such as pseudotumor cerebri, optic neuritis, diabetic retinopathy, and MS (Bleecker & Hansen, 1994; Verplanck, Kaufman, Parsons, Yedavally, & Kokinakis, 1988). Contrast sensitivity has also been found to be abnormal in some cases of solvent-induced chronic toxic encephalopathy (Donoghue, Dryson, & Wynn-Williams, 1995).

DIAGNOSIS

The term *organic mental disorder* has been eliminated in the *Diagnostic and Statistical Manual of Mental Disorders* (4th ed. [*DSM–IV*]; American Psychiatric Association, 1994) to avoid the implication that other disorders are not biologically based. The *DSM–IV* acknowledges that exposure to environmental toxins or environmental stress can cause a range of psychiatric syndromes that may meet the criteria for any of the following diagnoses (for details see *DSM–IV*):

- *Substance-Induced Delirium* is characterized by a disturbance of consciousness and a change in cognition that develop over a short period of time.
- *Substance-Induced Persisting Dementia* is characterized by multiple cognitive deficits that include impairment of memory.
- *Substance-Induced Persisting Amnestic Disorder* is characterized by memory impairment in the absence of other significant cognitive impairments.
- *Substance-Induced Psychotic Disorder* is characterized by prominent hallucinations or delusions.

- *Substance-Induced Mood Disorder* is characterized by a prominent and persistent disturbance of mood that may involve depressed mood, or markedly diminished interest or pleasure, or elevated, expansive or irritable mood.
- *Substance-Induced Anxiety Disorder* may involve prominent anxiety, panic attacks, phobias, obsessions, or compulsions.

When the presumed etiology is an environmental or occupational toxin, the code for "other substance" should be used. Examples of toxins possibly causing these syndromes include heavy metals, carbon monoxide, organophosphate insecticides, industrial solvents, fuel, and paint.

The primary differential diagnosis is against primary mental disorders and disorders due to general medical conditions. The effects of illegal drugs and medications given for coexisting conditions also need to be considered.

Delirium. Delirium is most likely to occur during the acute stage of high-level exposure. Symptoms include impairment of attention and cognition, and often hallucinations and agitation, and tend to fluctuate during the day. Repeated and systematic mental status examination is often the conclusive clinical test. Delirium can be mistaken for acute primary psychotic disorder. Among general medical conditions associated with delirium are systemic infections and metabolic disorders, electrolyte imbalances, hepatic or renal disease, thiamine deficiency, and hypertensive encephalopathy.

Dementia. The multiple cognitive deficits of dementia are often accompanied by impaired judgment, disinhibited behavior, anxiety, mood symptoms, delusions, and hallucinations, particularly visual hallucinations. The patterns of neuropsychological deficit may be similar for Substance-Induced Dementia and other white matter disorders, but repeated testing generally indicates that progressive decline is more common in nontoxic disorders (White et al., 1992). More localized cognitive findings, although occasionally consistent with the patterns demonstrated by specific toxins (e.g., visuospatial disorders with solvent exposure), are unusual and may be more suggestive of cerebrovascular disease or MS. The most common cause of dementia is Alzheimer's disease (AD). The pattern of cognitive deficiencies can sometimes help in distinguishing toxic encephalopathy from AD as language disorders are more likely to be found in AD than in solvent exposure. An aging patient who has a history of toxic exposure poses the question of whether he has AD, a frontal dementia, or a toxic encephalopathy. Whereas neuropsychological patterns of performance can discriminate between the two types of dementia, a clear discrimination between past toxic encephalopathy and AD is sometimes more difficult, even with repeated testing. The interaction of toxic exposure with the aging process is not well known. Exposure to toxins may reduce an individual's cognitive reserve, perhaps leading to earlier onset of dementia (Satz, 1993; Weiss & Cory-Slechta, 1994; White et al., 1992). Medical conditions associated with dementia include, in addition to vascular disorder, a long list of neurological conditions as well as infectious, endocrine, hepatic, metabolic and immune disorders, and vitamin deficiencies. Among psychiatric disorders, Schizophrenia can be associated with multiple cognitive deficits and decline in functioning. Major Depressive Disorder can sometimes mimic dementia.

Psychotic Disorders. These disorders can give rise to delusional beliefs involving environmental poisons, somatic delusions about bodily changes and paranoid delusions about being poisoned. Psychotic features including delusions about toxic exposure can be part of both depressive and manic episodes. Primary psychotic disorders need to be considered in the differential diagnosis as well as psychosis due to a general medical condition. Among the latter are a wide range of disorders including endocrine, metabolic, autoimmune, hepatic, and renal diseases.

Mood Disorders. Depressed mood has been reported with a wide array of low level exposures including lead, mercury, carbon disulfide, and some solvents. It can be the presenting symptom of toxic exposure. Bleecker and Hansen (1994) indicated that although many of the psychomotor symptoms are the same, a sense of worthlessness and suicidal ideation are less common following neurotoxic exposure than in primary mood disorder. The Substance-Induced Mood Disorder is generally distinguished only by the presence and timing of toxic exposure. General medical conditions associated with mood symptoms include several neurological conditions, metabolic, autoimmune and endocrine conditions, viral or other infections, and certain cancers. Examples are Vitamin B12 deficiency, thyroid, parathyroid and adrenal cortical abnormalities, mononucleosis, AIDS, and carcinoma of the pancreas.

Anxiety Disorders. Worry about toxic exposure can be a feature of General Anxiety Disorder, Specific Phobia, Obsessive-Compulsive Disorder, Acute Stress Disorder or Posttraumatic Stress Disorder. The last two diagnoses require the presence of an extreme psychosocial stressor. Anxiety and other symptoms following a less severe stressor may signify an Adjustment Disorder. Many general medical conditions can cause anxiety symptoms and need to be ruled out. Among them are endocrine, cardiovascular, respiratory and metabolic conditions.

Somatoform Disorders. Multiple physical symptoms that cannot be fully explained by physical or laboratory examination point to Undifferentiated Somatoform Disorder or, if the symptoms have lasted less than 6 months, Somatoform Disorder Not Otherwise Specified. These diagnoses imply that the symptoms are not intentionally produced or feigned; the patients truly believe that they are impaired due to chemical exposure. They can be distinguished from malingerers with the assistance of a neuropsychological examination, close observation of qualitative signs, and the examiner's perception of intent (White et al., 1992). Intent can be assessed during the interview, and by examining the consistency of responding to questions of personal history and cognitive performance. When the patient's preoccupation with the idea of being seriously ill due to toxic exposure causes clinically significant distress or impairment, the proper diagnosis may be Hypochondriasis.

Adjustment Disorder. This type of disorder may be the proper diagnosis when significant emotional or behavioral symptoms develop within 3 months of a stressful experience. It is not used if the condition meets the criteria for another Axis I diagnosis or if the symptoms last more than 6 months after the end of the stressful situation.

CASE HISTORIES

Ms. S. is a 43-year-old married woman who was referred for an independent medical examination following her report that she is permanently disabled due to a sensitivity to the multiple chemicals to which she is exposed in a factory setting. Ms. S. provided a claim for this condition based on an examination that she paid for herself at an out-of-state environmental health center.

Medical history indicated a back injury 6 years prior to this claim, with a re-injury 3 years later. She was unable to obtain disability status due to her back injuries. A letter from a local chiropractor (whom she had seen since the first injury) supported her current claim, indicating that her work-related exposure to chemicals increased her stress and injured her musculoskeletal system, aggravating her back injury each time she tried to return to work.

Other medical conditions include a hysterectomy at the age of 34, high blood pressure, and a mild closed head injury in an automobile accident about 20 years earlier. She reported a history of treatment for bronchitis and allergies, now attributed to her chemical sensitivity. She denied the use of alcohol or caffeine, never smoked, and never used recreational drugs. She was presently taking about eight prescription medications and supplements.

Ms. S. is a 20-year employee of a large industrial company, where her assignment for the past 11 years has been in a "crib" area within the factory.

Her function was to check out and in various pieces of specialized equipment. As she described it, this job has changed considerably over the 11 years, from an equipment delivery service giving her mobility around the total facility, to a centralized service based in the "cage" to which employees came to obtain their equipment. Once a group of about five workers performed the function that she now performs alone. The physical setting of the cage has also changed, becoming enclosed by brick walls housing new machinery with reduced ventilation and visibility. Ms S. reported that the position involved heavy responsibility, a service attitude and multiple functions without clear performance guidelines. She had sought a transfer from this position, but was ineligible due to her lack of seniority. Although she is eligible to retire, she is concerned about benefit reduction, especially with her large medical needs. Following her return to work from her second back injury and about a year prior to initiating the current claim, a chemical spill of an undefined substance was reported in the workplace.

Ms. S. described herself as previously outgoing and a sports participant, with several social activities, all of which have been curtailed due to her inability to tolerate chemical exposures. Ms. S. has been married for 16 years to her second husband. She had two children from her previous marriage, one child was killed in a traumatic accident about 4 years prior to her first back injury. Her parents are both deceased, and although she had more than seven siblings, several living locally, she does not maintain a relationship with them.

Psychologically, Ms. S. reported several psychomotor symptoms of depression, including disturbed sleep (due to periods of "chemical overload"), and decreased energy, concentration, and pleasure. She denied thoughts of suicide or homicide, and denied depression except as a reaction to her illness. She also endorsed 10 of the 13 symptoms commonly associated with panic disorder. On an objective personality instrument, she produced a valid profile of a naive individual attempting to present a favorable impression. Two major patterns of elevations were noted: a prominent pattern of an individual with a psychophysical reaction (frequently seen in individuals who convert stress and difficulties into physical complaints) and a secondary clinical pattern of chronic feelings of insecurity with difficulty taking assertive roles.

Impression. Ms. S. was considered to have a significant level of psychological distress best characterized as Undifferentiated Somatization Disorder (300.81). There was no indication of posttraumatic stress due to the chemical spill. Although she endorsed many symptoms that co-occur with both depression and anxiety, she attributed these changes in her behavior to her chemical sensitivity. Our recommendations included:

1. Continued full temporary disability pending the completion of the following recommendations.
2. Based on her personal physician's diagnosis of toxic encephalopathy, a neuropsychological evaluation to determine if Ms. S. had the cognitive capacity to meet the current job performance requirements.

3. Individual therapy by behavioral therapist to reduce generalized sensitivity to environmental stimuli, to be done in coordination with her
   treating environmental physician.

CASE 2

Ms. B. is a 35-year-old, married, right-handed woman who had been a laboratory worker for a local research facility. She was referred to a neuropsychologist from a retraining service, having been diagnosed with symptoms
consistent with toxic exposure. Her symptoms were paralysis on the left side,
with left-sided numbness and lower extremity weakness, headaches, dizziness,
and an inability to swallow. Her right eye shuts spontaneously. She reported
additional cognitive and personality changes such as short-term memory
problems, decreased information processing speed, and susceptibility to distraction.

Her job as a laboratory worker required her to perform a series of intricate
tests and calculations on chemicals and to maintain detailed and precise
laboratory records. Her performance had been highly rated in this function.
Although born in the continental United States, she lived in Puerto Rico
between the ages of 5 and 18. She is bilingual, with English as her primary
language. She has a high school diploma and completed a secretarial course
before becoming a laboratory technician. She described exposure to trichlo-
rophosphate, among other chemicals, for several years.

Ms. B. was given a full neuropsychological battery, and was found to be
functioning at the low average range of ability. She demonstrated difficulties
in concentration, sequencing, visual scanning, and memory problems. However, her frank depression was seen as significantly influencing her test
performance, and pharmacologic treatment for depression was recommended.

When records of Ms. B.'s past academic performance were obtained, they
indicated a decline particularly in her mathematical skills. There was also
an atypically wide range of performance within the current tests, with skills
ranging from deficient to above average. Preserved language function tests
indicated a possible premorbid ability level in the average to high average
range, more consistent with previous academic performance. Additionally,
Ms. B. was found to have deficits in visual contrast sensitivity consistent with
solvent exposure. Resolution of this case is pending, but retraining has been
granted and reassignment to work without chemical exposure is recommended.

MANAGEMENT

The multidimensional nature of environmental illness must be recognized
in both diagnosis and treatment. It is essential to share this perspective
with the patient from the onset of the clinical process and to intervene
on several fronts. In cases of established toxic exposure the first step is to

remove the individual from the source. This is not a simple task, when livelihood or home is involved. Next, other risk factors such as smoking, alcohol, and medications should be reduced as much as possible. Behavior therapy and biofeedback have been shown effective for reduction of anxiety (Hartman, 1995). The therapist should also explore the meaning of the illness for the patient and assess his personal resources and coping style in order to help him deal with feelings of helplessness, victimization, grief, and fear.

At times, the clinician may need to be willing to work with a patient who is also pursuing other, nontraditional health initiatives. Many patients, especially those who may have been made ill by environmental sensitivity and exposure, are dissatisfied with traditional medical care. Their forays into alternative medicine are attempts at self-help and self-care. It behooves clinicians to be open-minded supportive of the patient's efforts.

Patients with significant neuropsychological deficits need to be monitored by a team including a neuropsychologist and other specialists and they must be offered rehabilitation aiming to train compensatory functions. Those with subtle neuropsychological findings should be followed with repeated evaluations, 12 to 24 months apart, to determine the course of progression. The limited data available suggest that subtle deficits can improve after exposure ceases.

REFERENCES

Agnew, J., & Masten, V. L. (1994). Neuropsychological assessment of occupational neurotoxic exposure. In M. L. Bleecker & J. A. Hansen (Eds.), *Occupational neurology and clinical neurotoxicology* (pp. 113–160). Baltimore: Williams & Wilkins.

American Psychiatric Association. (1994). *Diagnostic and statistical manual of mental disorders* (4th ed.). Washington, DC: Author.

Bleecker, M. L., & Hansen, J. A. (Eds.). (1994). *Occupational neurology and clinical neurotoxicology.* Baltimore: Williams & Wilkins.

Crum, R. M., Anthony, J. C., Bassett, S. S., & Folstein, M. F. (1993). Population-based norms for the Mini-Mental Status Examination by age and education level. *JAMA, 269,* 2386–2391.

Donoghue, A. M., Dryson, E. V., & Wynn-Williams, G. (1995). Contrast sensitivity in organic-solvent-induced chronic toxic encephalopathy. *Journal of Occupational and Environmental Medicine, 37,* 1357–1363.

Folstein, M. F., Folstein, S. E., & McHugh, P. R. (1975). Mini-mental state: A practical method for grading the cognitive state of patients for the clinician. *Journal of Psychiatric Research, 12,* 189–198.

Hartman, D. E. (1995). *Neuropsychological toxicology* (2nd ed.). New York: Plenum Press.

Letz, R., & Baker, E. L. (1988). *NES2 Neurobehavioral Evaluation System.* Winchester, MA: Neurobehavioral Evaluation Systems.

Lezak, M. D. (1995). *Neuropsychological assessment* (3rd ed.). New York: Oxford University Press.

Mazure, C. M. (Ed.). (1995). *Does stress cause psychiatric illness.* Washington, DC: American Psychiatric Press.

Satz, P. (1993). Brain reserve capacity on symptom onset after brain injury: A formulation and review of evidence for threshold theory. *Neuropsychology, 7*, 273–295.

Swirsky-Sacchetti, T., Field, H. L., Mitchell, D. R., & Sewar, J. (1992). The sensitivity of the Mini-Mental State Examination in the white mater dementia of multiple sclerosis. *Journal of Clinical Psychology, 49*, 779–786.

Verplanck, M., Kaufman, D. I., Parsons, T., Yedavally, S., & Kokinakis, D. (1988). Electrophysiology versus psychophysics in the detection of visual loss in pseudo-tumor cerebri. *Neurology, 38*, 1789–1792.

Weiss, B., & Cory-Slechta, D. A. (1994). Assessment of behavioral toxicity. In A. W. Hayes (Ed.), *Principles and methods of toxicology* (3rd ed., pp. 1091–1155). New York: Raven Press.

White, R. F., Diamond R., Krengel, M., Lindem, K., & Feldman, R. G. (1996). Validation of the NES2 in patients with neurologic disorders. *Neurotoxicology and Teratology, 18*, 441–448.

White, R. F., Feldman, R. G., & Proctor, S. P. (1992). Neurobehavioral effects of toxic exposures. In R. F. White (Ed.), *Clinical syndromes in adult neuropsychology: The practitioner's handbook* (pp. 1–47). New York: Elsevier.

White, R. F., & Proctor, S. P. (1997). Solvents and neurotoxicity. *Lancet, 349*, 1239–1243.

Chapter 5

Psychiatric Aspects
of Technological Disasters

Ante Lundberg
Washington, DC Commission on Mental Health Services

Azara L. Santiago-Rivera
State University of New York at Albany

Disasters can be natural, such as floods, earthquakes, and hurricanes, or caused by people, like nuclear plant accidents and toxic spills. The distinction is not always clear because we live in a complex, interdependent world whose natural rhythms affect us and are in turn affected by our activities in sometimes unpredictable ways (UNEP, 1994). For instance, the number of casualties and amount of destruction caused by an earthquake depend on the number of people living nearby, on the strength of the buildings, bridges, and freeways in an affected area, and so on. Natural disasters can also lead to technological accidents: The 1993 Mississippi River floods dislodged and released buried hazardous waste. But disasters that are primarily technological are different in important ways from natural ones and their psychological impact is different as well. Technological disasters can be local, for example, toxic spills from railway accidents or leaking stores of hazardous substances in some poorly designed disposal site (Green, 1993). Or they can be regional such as the Chernobyl accident and even global, such as the thinning of the ozone layer caused by the use of ozone depleting chemicals.

Some people who have been exposed to fires, hurricanes, and floods develop psychological sequelae such as major depression, chronic anxiety, and posttraumatic stress disorder (PTSD). Current thought among disaster relief workers holds that most people will suffer only transient effects from a natural disaster or "people reacting normally to an abnormal situation" (Flynn, 1995). Appropriate intervention usually consists of outreach and crisis counseling that combines psychological support and information with practical relief like food and shelter. Only those who show more severe reactions are referred to local mental health professionals for continued care. In a meta-analysis of disaster studies, Rubonis and Bickman (1991) found an overall 17% increase in clinical psychopathology among survivors. For excellent summaries on the psychological sequelae to natural disasters, see also Bromet and Dew (1995) and Green (1993).

Common to all disasters is that individual experience determines psychological sequelae. For example, did the individual suffer first- or second-hand from the disaster? Did the individual suffer personal losses or injury, or see others suffer? Social response to a disaster also influences its psychological impact. Was the social support network severely disrupted? Did outside support and aid arrive quickly? The social network can be a great source of support or a great source of secondary stressors due to inefficient or uncaring responses.

CHARACTERISTICS OF TECHNOLOGICAL DISASTERS

In addition to direct health effects technological disasters tend to cause uncertainty and worry about future health effects. There are two broad classes of technological disasters: acute events such as a chemical spill, and chronic events such as living near a leaking hazardous waste site. Acute spills produce quick, noticeable effects much like a natural disaster; however, in contrast to a natural disaster, a chemical spill can leave in its wake an exposed community at risk for latent health effects. At Bhopal, the methyl isocyanate release happened suddenly as the result of an acute systems failure at a pesticide plant and resulted in immediate deaths and injuries. Lingering morbidity and excess mortality continue to affect people who were subjected to exposures at the site (Dhara, 1992).

The social and psychological impact of a chronic technological disaster, (CTD) is quite different from that of a natural disaster. An earthquake begins suddenly and ends within hours or days. There is a clear distinction between before and after the event. At a certain point the danger is over and healing can begin. A CTD often has no clear beginning, not even the authorities know when it all started, nor can they say with certainty when it will end (Edelstein, 1995). The danger often existed before the community became aware of it. Health risks may last for many years and affect future generations. Social conflicts often arise in the wake of a CTD and residents who want to move may find that the value of their property has drastically declined. Cleanup may take years or decades and determination of final costs may be years away. Whereas victims of a flood can get on with their lives, the insidious character of a CTD, its lurking, ongoing threat makes it much harder to cope with and escape from (Robertson, 1993).

RESEARCH ON THE EFFECTS OF TECHNOLOGICAL DISASTERS

Psychological research on stress and technological accidents was discussed by Baum and Fleming (1993). Data consistently show that the threat and long-term uncertainty associated with toxic exposure can affect both physical and mental health and well-being. A series of studies was carried out by Baum and his coworkers in the aftermath of the Three Mile Island (TMI) accident in 1979. The accident was caused by a combination of human and mechanical failures that led to some release of radioactive material and the threat of a deadly disaster. The immediate response by officials and media was confused and contradictory and led to a loss of the public's trust in the available information. People living within 5 miles of TMI (initially 54, later 80 individuals) were studied together with several control groups for up to 10 years after the accident. As a group they consistently manifested chronic stress in self-report measures of symptoms, impaired performance on stress-sensitive tasks, and elevated blood pressure and endocrine levels (norepinephrine, epinephrine, and cortisol). The effects were still present after 6 years. At 10 years, the difference between groups was no longer significant. Observed symptoms included manifestations of PTSD such as hyperarousal, bothersome intrusive thoughts about the accident and avoidance of reminders. Some TMI area residents did not manifest the stress symptoms. They seemed to differ from the others in social support, perceived control, and coping style. Subsequently, the investigators used a similar protocol to study people exposed to a hazardous landfill and other human-caused toxic accidents, and repeatedly found the same response patterns.

Several other researchers have reported similar results. Among more recent studies: Dayal, Baranowski, Yi-hwei, and Morris (1994) interviewed 2,509 persons 2 years after a highly toxic chemical spill, employing a symptom inventory derived from the Symptom Checklist-90 (Derogatis, 1977). Self-reported physical symptoms were also recorded. The study found a linear relationship between the level of exposure to the chemical and the amount of psychological stress 2 years after the accident. Bowler, Mergler, Huel, and Cone (1994) performed a randomized case-controlled study of the psychological and physiological sequelae in a community exposed to a chemical spill and found higher levels of depression, anxiety, and somatic symptoms (possibly connected to chronic arousal) in exposed than in nonexposed people.

Following a theft of radioactive cesium from a medical facility in Brazil, Collins and de Carvalho (1993) investigated the manifestations of stress in 23 persons exposed to radiation, 23 persons living near a low-risk nuclear waste site and normal controls. Three and one half years after the accident

both study groups reported significantly higher scores on the Cornell Inventory inadequacy/helplessness scale, had elevated systolic blood pressure, and elevated levels of catecholamine metabolites in their urine. A
maze test revealed loss in speed and accuracy.

Green, Lindy, and Grace (1994) studied the reactions of people in
Fernald, Ohio, some time after they had been informed that their community had for years been contaminated by radioactive material leaking
from a nuclear weapons factory. They interviewed and tested 50 individuals
involved in a lawsuit against the plant. The results showed relatively high
levels of anxiety, depression, belligerence, impairment of daily routines,
somatic concerns and symptoms, obsessive thoughts, as well as suspicion
and mistrust of others. Although anxiety, depression, and impairment of
daily routine decreased over time, somatic concerns, suspicion, and social
isolation remained high. The residents of Fernald reported psychological
functioning and distress symptoms at rates higher than a comparison group
of nonpatients. However, when comparing the Fernald group with a standardized outpatient sample, the scores were lower.

In 1989, an accident involving the supertanker Exxon Valdez resulted
in the release of 11 million gallons of crude oil into the waters of Prince
William Sound, Alaska. Palinkas, Pettersen, Russell, and Downs (1993) and
Palinkas, Russell, Downs, and Pettersen (1992) studied 599 men and
women in the area 1 year after the Exxon Valdez accident. They found
elevated levels of depression, anxiety, and PTSD in the exposed population.
Alcohol and drug abuse, and domestic violence also increased.

Equally important, the Palinkas studies are an example of the recent
interest in examining the effects of environmental contamination on the
well-being of ethnically and culturally diverse communities. The social and
cultural upheaval associated with this accident was significant. The oil spill
disrupted the normal subsistence activities essential to the economic and
cultural integrity of 13 Native Alaskan communities in the area. Palinkas
and colleagues have argued that the traditional cultural practices of hunting, fishing, and gathering so central to their subsistence way of life were
dramatically altered. Residents reported a loss of identity as a Native people
whose cultural heritage is tied to the land. Paralleling this view, Curtis
(1992) stated that among the risks associated with environmental contamination in Native American communities, one must consider its impact on
the culture: It may result in destruction of cultural traditions and have a
negative impact on overall quality of life.

The fire in the Chernobyl nuclear power plant in 1986 was the largest
accident of its kind with consequences for the region and for the world.
It caused the release of large amounts of radioactive material in the air,
resulting in deposits of radioactive cesium and iodine and other radionuclides in the surrounding regions as well as in more distant areas and

other countries. Millions of Soviets and other Europeans were exposed to measurable levels of radioactive fallout. Among the long-term health effects are an estimated 60,000 excess cancer cases worldwide, one half of whom will die from their disease. The increase is too small to show up in health statistics, except among the groups that received the highest doses. An increase in pediatric thyroid cancer has been reported in Belarus. No other medical consequences have yet been demonstrated; reported increases in infant deaths and birth defects have not been verified.

The public was not immediately informed about the accident or any risks involved, nor were other countries warned. Only after 2 weeks was the extent of the problem made public in a speech by Gorbachov. People in some isolated villages at risk were not informed until 1988. The lack of reliable official information increased the public's distrust and allowed exaggerated and anxiety-producing rumors to thrive. Many studies of the medical and psychosocial consequences of the disaster are still ongoing. The drastic changes in the former Soviet Union taking place during subsequent years, causing dislocations and economic hardship, complicate the picture of these consequences. So far, extensive interview studies have revealed that people in the region, especially those who were evacuated, continue to worry every day about the health effects of radiation. To a lesser extent they worry about their standard of living. Parents worry about their children's future; each illness and death in the vicinity increases their fear. Financial aid and compensation paid to some people in the affected area has brought up questions of fairness and introduced an incentive for victimization (Drottz-Sjöberg, 1997; Drottz-Sjöberg, Engstedt, Hall, Lewensohn, & Valentin, 1995).

EVALUATING SURVIVORS OF TECHNOLOGICAL DISASTERS

The psychosocial consequences of technological disasters are not fully understood, but exposed people need to be helped. It is difficult to distinguish the effects of psychosocial stress from the effects of exposure to toxic and other hazardous substances. It may be expedient to make a psychosomatic rather than a toxicological diagnosis, in effect ruling out any health effects of exposure to toxins, but it may not be of much help to the patient.

Before deciding on diagnosis and treatment the clinician must obtain an exposure history. Community exposure data and public health assessments are available from the state health department or from the Agency for Toxic Substances and Disease Registry (ATSDR; see Appendix). The public health assessment provides information about the source and transport medium of the toxins, the possible route of contamination, and the location of exposed people (ATSDR, 1992). Exposures to hazardous substances at work usually involve higher doses than at home.

Neurotoxic substances can cause psychiatric symptoms. Lead can cause clinical depression, learning disability, and hyperactivity in children. Exposure to elemental mercury can result in erethism: depressive mood, listlessness, irritability, and shyness. Thallium poisoning can cause psychosis. When neurotoxic or other health effects from toxic exposure cannot be ruled out, it may be advisable to refer the patient to a specialist in occupational and environmental medicine. A careful psychiatric evaluation is essential (see also chapters 3 and 4).

PSYCHOLOGICAL ASPECTS OF EXPOSURE TO HAZARDOUS SUBSTANCES

Clinicians working with CTD victims must be familiar with the particular characteristics of their experience. Two types of stressors have been identified in communities coping with a technological disaster. Primary stressors involve visible injuries attributable to the disaster and the risk of exposure to hazardous substances leading to future health effects. Social reactions to technological disasters contribute secondary stressors that people in these communities must also contend with (Kroll-Smith & Couch, 1993). Erikson (1990) pointed out the emotional reactions and deep-seated fear that radioactive and poisonous chemicals provoke in most people. Likewise, Vyner (1988) discussed the lingering uncertainty among residents in a community that has been exposed. The fact that such toxicants are invisible and people cannot be sure if and how much they have been exposed to creates great concern. Because of possible delayed health effects from hazardous exposures, they cannot be sure whether a new symptom is a herald of an exposure related disease. If they do develop a disease, they cannot be sure whether it is related to the invisible exposure and what will be the prognosis of any newly acquired disease. The uncertainty inherent in exposures to hazardous substances is thought to be the source of much of the psychological distress it causes. It becomes difficult for an exposed person to understand and take positive action in response to the danger.

The scientific uncertainty felt by the experts adds to the problem. Tosteson (1995) pointed out that environmental health communication differs from other health communication: The field is new and growing rapidly, it challenges entrenched belief systems and is subject to strong political and social influences. Scientists often deal with uncertainty and unrealistic expectations by insisting on professional doubt and detachment. They don't see it as their role or competence to deal with social context or the reasonable concerns of worried people. The result is deepening public distrust of the experts, who may be seen as incompetent and irresponsible. Without scientific proof, the official response is usually a reluctance to attribute harm to low levels of environmental contaminants. The exposed public understandably is concerned and doesn't want to take any chances.

Social conflict is not limited to disputes between scientists and communities. Many communities will suffer internal division in the face of a chronic technological disaster (Couch & Kroll-Smith, 1991). The causes for social conflicts are numerous. People who live close to a hazardous facility frequently have views of their exposure and its health effects that are different from those who live farther away and who do not believe themselves to be affected. Economic factors such as loss of property values, dependence on a polluting industry for jobs, and the stigma associated with environmental contamination, can create intense conflicts within a community. The result of these conflicts often is a lack of support for people who see themselves as victims. They already tend to feel alienated from their community and believe that "no one else can understand what we have gone through unless they have been contaminated too."

Psychotherapy With Survivors of Technological Disasters

We accept that natural events are largely outside our control. We have no say in the weather, and cannot manage thunderstorms or earthquakes. But we generally believe that we have tamed our technology. Consequently it is our—or at least someone's—responsibility to oversee and master. When this technology fractures, when our inventions behave in unpredictable and harmful ways, our sense of confidence breaks down. We are overwhelmed by our vulnerability and ultimately our mortality: Things don't work as planned. The sophisticated power plant and the tanker carrying heating oil turn into monsters that would destroy us. The suddenness and unpredictability of most technological accidents reinforces the sense of lost control.

Many survivors of technological disasters feel betrayed. When it turns out that the accident was caused by a lack of concern for others, by a drunken pilot or by a careless government bureaucracy the hurt becomes much deeper. We find it hard to believe that another person would harm us by sheer negligence, and when someone can be directly blamed for a disaster, it becomes a base act of injustice. Trauma caused by hurtful betrayal by another is among the most difficult to work through and heal (Lifton & Olson, 1976).

The experience of those exposed to toxins or radioactivity resembles what Lifton calls the "death immersion syndrome" of survivors from Hiroshima and Nagasaki (Lifton, 1967). Victims of CTD must cope with long-term health effects. They may have sustained a genetic injury and future children could be harmed. Any death or illness in the community may be the result of toxins or radiation. CTD is indeed chronic. Its effect may linger for years and people in a contaminated community cannot put the disaster behind them.

Like other victims of severe traumatic stress, many CTD victims have lost their basic sense of security and trust, they feel different, alienated, stigmatized. At times they seem inclined to resolve uncertainty by believing the worst about exposure and actively accept their role as contaminated. This attitude can be prudent and rational and at the same time both relieve their doubt and inaction and validate their view of reality. Such a belief may prompt them to take a more active role in dealing with the consequences.

Clinicians sensitive to these issues can help their aggrieved clients develop better ways to cope. They may be instrumental in explaining the views of scientists whose purposes in studying a contaminated community may be different from those of individuals living in that community. Thus, clinicians may help foster more realistic expectations. Knowledge and understanding also strengthen the patient's sense of competence and control. In particular, physicians are well positioned through their training and experience to explain the uses and limitations of science. They are trained in the scientific tradition and honor it as best they can in the social reality of clinical practice. But any good psychotherapist will always attempt to understand and respect the patient's perceptions and values.

It is well recognized that low-income and minority communities are disproportionately exposed to environmental risks (Adeola, 1994; Bryant & Mohai, 1992; Bullard & Wright, 1992; Santiago-Rivera, Morse, Hunt, & Lickers, in press). Individuals may be predisposed to conceptualize a technological accident in a certain way depending on their background, life experiences, and world views. Reactions to environmental contamination are governed, in part, by beliefs and values that lead to fundamental differences in the way in which individuals cope.

Clinicians should also be aware that exposure may affect men, women, and children differently. For example, Gutteling and Wiegman (1993) found significant gender differences in a sample of 513 men and women who were asked questions regarding the hazards of living in an area contaminated by toxic substances. Women reported that the hazards were more unacceptable and threatening and felt more insecure than men. Thus, clinical intervention strategies may be more effective if tailored to the particular needs of men and women.

Elliot et al. (1993) provided a useful framework for clinicians in which they advised that exposed individuals become involved in a local community group taking action, and build social networks as effective ways of coping with the experience of environmental stress. Along this line of reasoning, clinicians can argue for disclosure of information from responsible officials, thus empowering individuals and their communities. Members of a community exposed to environmental contamination need to see that clinicians also can serve as advocates for social change.

Our technology is growing ever more powerful and difficult to control, while feelings of distrust, insecurity, and alienation appear to become widespread. Technological accidents and exposure to insidious threats can be expected to become an even bigger problem in the future.

REFERENCES

Adeola, F. O. (1994). Environmental hazards, health, and racial inequity in hazardous waste distribution. *Environment and Behavior, 26*, 99–126.

Agency for Toxic Substances and Disease Registry. (1992). *Public health assessment guidance manual.* Chelsea, MI: Lewis.

Baum, A., & Fleming, I. (1993). Implications of psychological research on stress and technological accidents. *American Psychologist, 48*(6), 665–672.

Bowler, R. M., Mergler, D., Huel, G., & Cone, J. E. (1994). Aftermath of a chemical spill: Psychological and physiological sequelae. *Neurotoxicology, 15*, 723–729.

Bromet, E., & Dew, M. A. (1995). Review of psychiatric epidemiology research on disasters. *Epidemiologic Reviews, 17*(1), 113–119.

Bryant, B., & Mohai, P. (Eds). (1992). *Race and the incidence of environmental hazards: A time for discourse.* Boulder, CO: Westview Press.

Bullard, R. D., & Wright, B. (1992). *Confronting environmental racism.* Easthaven, CT: South End.

Collins, D. L., & de Carvalho, A. B. (1993). Chronic stress from the Goiania ^{137}Cs radiation accident. *Behavioral Medicine, 18*, 149–157.

Couch, S. R., & Kroll-Smith, J. S. (1991). Patterns of victimization and the chronic technological disaster. In E. C. Viano (Ed.), *The victimology handbook.* New York: Garland.

Curtis, S. A. (1992). Cultural relativism and risk-assessment strategies for federal projects. *Human Organization, 51*(1), 65–70.

Dayal, H. H., Baranowski, T., Yi-hwei, L., & Morris, R. (1994). Hazardous chemicals: Psychological dimensions of the health sequelae of a community exposure in Texas. *Journal of Epidemiology and Community Health, 48*, 560–568.

Derogatis, L. R. (1977). *The SCL-90 Manual I: Scoring, administration, and procedures for the SCL-90.* Baltimore: Johns Hopkins University School of Medicine, Clinical Psychometrics Units.

Dhara, R. (1992). Health effects of the Bhopal gas leak: A review. *Epidemiologia e prevenzione, 52*, 22–31.

Drottz-Sjöberg, B. M. (1997). *The social and psychological consequences of the Chernobyl accident.* Paper presented at the European Conference on Nuclear Safety and Local/Regional Democracy, Göteborg, Sweden.

Drottz-Sjöberg, B. M., Engstedt, L., Hall, P., Lewensohn, R., & Valentin, J. (1995). Från Hiroshima till Tjernobyl: Sena dödsfall i cancer ökar. *Läkartidningen, 92*, 4100–4105.

Edelstein, M. (1995, September). *The superfund process.* Paper presented at the Expert Panel Workshop on the Psychological Responses to Hazardous Substances, Atlanta, GA.

Elliot, S. J., Taylor, S. M., Walter, S., Stieb, D., Frank, J., & Eyles, J. (1993). Modeling psychosocial effects of exposure to solid waste facilities. *Social Science and Medicine, 37*(6), 791–804.

Erikson, K. (1990, January/February). Toxic reckoning: Business faces a new kind of fear. *Harvard Business Review,* 118–126.

Flynn, B. (1995, September). *The SAMSHA approach to natural disasters.* Paper presented at the Expert Panel Workshop on the Psychological Responses to Hazardous Substances, Atlanta, GA.

Green, B. L. (1993). Identifying survivors at risk, trauma and stressors across events. In J. P. Wilson & B. Raphael (Eds.), *International handbook of traumatic stress syndromes* (pp. 135–144). New York: Plenum Press.

Green, B. L., Lindy, J. D., & Grace, M. C. (1994). Psychological effects of toxic contamination. In R. J. Ursano, B. G. McCaughey, & C. S. Fullerton (Eds.), *Individual and community responses to trauma and disaster: The structure of human chaos* (pp. 154–176). Cambridge, England: Cambridge University Press.

Gutteling, J. M., & Wiegman, O. (1993). Gender-specific reactions to environmental hazards in the Netherlands. *Sex Roles, 28*(7–8), 433–447.

Kroll-Smith, J. S., & Couch, S. R. (1993). Technological hazards, social responses as traumatic stressors. In J. P. Wilson & B. Raphael (Eds.), *International handbook of traumatic stress syndromes* (pp. 79–91). New York: Plenum Press.

Lifton, R. J. (1967). *Death in life: Survivors of Hiroshima.* Los Angeles: S & S Enterprises.

Lifton, R. J., & Olson, E. (1976). The human meaning of total disaster. *Psychiatry, 39,* 1–18.

Palinkas, L. A., Pettersen, J. S., Russell, J., & Downs, M. A. (1993). Community patterns of psychiatric disorders after the Exxon Valdez oil spill. *American Journal of Psychiatry, 150,* 1517–1523.

Palinkas, L. A., Russell, J., Downs, M. A., & Pettersen, J. S. (1992). Ethnic differences in stress, coping, and depressive symptoms after the Exxon Valdez oil spill. *Journal of Nervous and Mental Disease, 180,* 287–295.

Robertson, J. S. (1993). Chemical disasters, real and suspected. *Public Health, 107,* 277–286.

Rubonis, A. V., & Bickman, L. (1991). Psychological impairment in the wake of disaster: The disaster-psychopathology relationship. *Psychological Bulletin, 109*(3), 384–399.

Santiago-Rivera, A. L., Morse, G. S., Hunt, A., & Lickers, H. (in press). Building a community-based research partnership: Lessons from the Mohawk Nation of Akwesasne. *Journal of Community Psychology.*

Tosteson, H. (1995, June). *Communication and negotiation at hazardous waste sites: Some psychological and sociological influences on scientific debate.* Paper presented at the International Congress on Hazardous Waste: Impact on Human and Ecological Health, Atlanta, GA.

UNEP/WHO Information Unit on Climate Change (IUCC). (1994, December). *Understanding climate change: A beginner's guide to the UN framework convention.* New York: Author.

Vyner, H. (1988). *Invisible trauma: Psychosocial effects of invisible environmental contaminants.* Lexington, MA: DC Heath & Co.

Chapter 6

Environmental Influences on Illnesses in Persian Gulf War Veterans[1]

Michael J. Roy
Uniformed Services University of the Health Sciences

The United States deployed 697,000 troops to the Persian Gulf for Operations Desert Shield and Desert Storm in 1990 to 1991. Battle-related morbidity and mortality were remarkably low, and the incidence of nonbattle injuries and illnesses was far lower than has been seen in other military conflicts ("Medicine in the Gulf War," 1991). However, subsequent to the war, some veterans have reported common, nonspecific symptoms such as headaches, fatigue, rashes, and joint or muscle aches. Concerns were expressed about the possibility of environmental exposures unique to the combat arena having an etiologic role. To address this, the Departments of Veterans' Affairs (VA, 1992) and Defense (DoD, 1994) established registries for the comprehensive, standardized evaluation of Persian Gulf War (PGW) veterans. A national hotline was established and concerned veterans were encouraged to call to arrange evaluations. By June 1996, more than 70,000 had registered with the VA and more than 30,000 with the DoD (it should be noted that some individuals are on both registries).

The DoD's program is known as the Comprehensive Clinical Evaluation Program (CCEP), which has two phases. Phase I, available at all military medical treatment facilities, begins with a series of questionnaires requesting demographic information, chief complaint, presence and duration of

---

[1]The opinions or assertions contained herein are the private views of the author and are not to be construed as official or as reflecting the view of the Department of the Army or the Department of Defense.

15 common symptoms, self-report of 20 different deployment-related exposures and 5 potentially traumatic combat experiences, and number of days' work missed due to illness. The Phase I evaluation consists of a basic history and physical examination, with additional laboratory studies and consultations as clinically indicated. Patients who warrant more detailed evaluation (about 10%) are referred to Phase II at 1 of 14 tri-service regional medical centers. Phase II evaluations are coordinated by an internist or family practitioner, who repeats the history and physical examination, reviews the results of approximately 20 predetermined laboratory tests and several subspecialty consultations (including infectious diseases and psychiatry), and orders additional tests and consultations as indicated (Roy, Chung, Huntley, & Blanck, 1994). The results of the CCEP have been continuously updated centrally, and periodically released to the public (DoD, 1994, 1995, 1996). External review has been provided by the Institute of Medicine (1995, 1996) and the Presidential Advisory Committee on Gulf War Veterans' Illnesses (1996). These and other expert panels have not found evidence for a new syndrome or illness (Defense Science Board, 1994; NIH, 1994). Hospitalization and disease-related mortality has been found to be no higher than in comparison groups (Gray et al., 1996; Kang & Bullman, 1996; Writer, DeFraites, & Brundage, 1996). However, a variety of common symptoms are more prevalent, and interest in the possibility of a unique syndrome or mystery illness persists. Many hypotheses have been generated regarding the significance of various exposures, either alone or in combination, to which troops were subject during their deployment.

INFECTIOUS DISEASES

Infectious diseases have been given prominent attention, largely due to the identification of 13 cases of viscerotropic leishmania during and shortly after the war (Magill, Grogl, Gasser, Sun, & Oster, 1993). During the conflict, diarrhea was the most common manifestation of infectious diseases (Hyams et al., 1991). However, infectious diseases have been most remarkable for their rarity and for the banality of those that have been identified. Only 2% of CCEP participants have had a primary diagnosis that is coded as an infectious disease, and of these, the majority were tinea (athlete's foot and jock itch), with the remainder consisting primarily of other skin infections such as scabies and warts, as well as Hepatitis C (DoD, 1996). Nonspecific markers of infection such as white blood cell counts, erythrocytes sedimentation rates, and C-reactive proteins, have almost uniformly been normal. Serologies for zoonoses such as Brucella (no cases identified) and Q-fever (three cases, all identified prior to the CCEP; Ferrante &

Dolan, 1993; Richards et al., 1991) that are known to be endemic in the Persian Gulf had so little utility that they were eliminated from the CCEP Phase II protocol after 7 months.

Several individuals have proposed novel infectious etiologies. Mycoplasma fermentans (incognitus) and a human endogenous retrovirus (HERV; perhaps a spumavirus or related foamy virus) have received the most attention. Mycoplasma fermentans was initially identified in HIV-infected individuals in the 1980s by Lo, Buchholz, Wear, Hohm, and Marty (1991). In the immunocompromised, it appeared to be associated with organ necrosis and failure, although a causal relationship has not been clearly established (S. C. Lo & A. M. Marty, personal communication, May 1996). More recently, Nicolson and Nicolson (1995a, 1995b) suggested it could be a cause of illness in PGW veterans, and they have reported successful treatment with the antibiotic doxycycline. However, there appear to be significant methodologic problems with the Nicolson's studies. They did not standardize their unconventional diagnostic assay by performing blinded testing with controls, and have been reluctant to collaborate with, or have independent review by, investigators such as DoD or the Centers for Disease Control (Blanck, 1996). The preliminary results of a continuing study by S. C. Lo (personal communication, May 1996) show a similar, low prevalence of antibody to this species of mycoplasma in PGW veterans compared to the general population, and evidence of the live organism has been almost uniformly absent.

The endogenous retrovirus hypothesis is that most or all humans may have a virus that remains latent until its expression is facilitated by an alteration to the immune system, perhaps induced by psychological or environmental stress. HERV would then be a potential mediator for some of the untoward health consequences of stress. At Walter Reed, we are involved in collaborative research to attempt to find measures of retroviral presence in PGW veterans, in blinded comparison with healthy controls and patients with documented connective tissue diseases. Although it is an intriguing theory, to date we have observed no apparent differences between the three groups of patients, and even if one were found it would represent an association rather than causation.

CHEMICAL AND BIOLOGICAL WARFARE

Great concern has been expressed about the possibility of exposure to agents of chemical or biological warfare (CW/BW). There was evidence that Iraq had the capability to use such agents, and in fact they had demonstrated a willingness to do so in trying to suppress a Kurd rebellion in preceding years. Biological warfare has been used for thousands of years, but no nation has ever admitted to its use, and it is considered more difficult to prove use of BW as compared to CW or nuclear warfare (Robertson & Robertson, 1995). Although there has been no evidence to suggest that any troops were exposed to BW agents during the PGW, 5 years after the war evidence was uncovered of the detonation of the chemical agents sarin and GF at Khamisiyah (U.S. Central Intelligence Agency [USCIA], 1996). This could have resulted in the widespread dispersal of low levels of the agents, exposing thousands of troops. Although no acute illness consistent with exposure was identified, the chronic effects, if any, of low-level exposure are unknown.

Concern regarding possible CW exposure was heightened by several events that occurred during the war. First, dead animals were seen on the battlefield, which troops had been warned could be evidence of CW use. However, dead animals had been seen on initial deployment in August 1990, and their presence was related to the practice of nomadic herders rather than CW agents (Persian Gulf Veterans Coordinating Board, 1995). A second source of concern was the chemical agent sensor alarms that sounded frequently during the war. The alarms are designed to be quite sensitive, resulting in frequent false positives, due to activation by stimuli such as vehicle emissions, Patriot missile propellant, cigarette smoke, and pesticides. Although thousands of alarm soundings were carefully investigated without identification of a CW agent, the Khamisiyah revelation suggests that at least some of them may have been true positives. In fact, Czech chemical detection units working with the Saudi Arabian Army did detect very low levels of sarin and a mustard agent in two separate instances (NIH Technology Assessment Workshop Panel, 1994). Neither was in an area where U.S. forces were located, there was no associated illness, and the agents were no longer detectable within a few hours when U.S. chemical detection teams were dispatched to the areas (Defense Science Board, 1994). The detections could represent fallout from bombing of Iraqi CW storage facilities that took place in that timeframe, although one would have expected high morbidity and mortality in more proximal populations if this had been the case. In a separate incident, after entering a deserted Iraqi bunker, a soldier noticed blistering on his arm, consistent with exposure to a nitrogen mustard agent.

The Khamisiyah disclosure in particular has fueled numerous research efforts to explore the potential health consequences of exposure to low levels of CW agents. Exposure to even minute quantities of nerve agents such as sarin have been documented to cause acute toxicity and mortality, which was not seen during the war. Again, the association of chronic symptoms in the absence of acute symptoms is a tenuous hypothesis stretching biologic plausibility. However, Haley and colleagues attempted to correlate chronic symptoms with wartime organophosphate exposure in one unit of PGW veterans. Using factor analysis, they identified six syndromes that represented clusters of symptoms in 63 veterans, or about 10% of the unit they studied (Haley, Kurt, & Horn, 1997). Neurologists could not distinguish Haley's cases from controls, and "concluded that the clinical and laboratory findings were nonspecific and not sufficient to diagnose any known syndrome" (Haley, Horn, et al., 1997). Nevertheless, Haley concluded that the symptomatic veterans were "more neurologically impaired . . . compatible with generalized nervous system injury from exposure to cholinesterase-inhibiting chemicals" (Haley & Kurt, 1997). In fact, Haley's work can be considered hypothesis-generating rather than confirming that this or any other etiology may be responsible for symptoms. Haley did not apply factor analysis to symptomatic individuals who were not deployed to the Gulf, who may well have had similar results, discrediting chemical exposures as the etiology.

During the deployment, the possibility of CW/BW exposure was taken seriously enough that all possible measures were taken to protect soldiers. In addition to highly sensitive alarms and the use of gas masks and MOPP gear, vaccinations and chemoprophylaxis were provided. Anthrax and Botulinum were considered the most likely biologic agents to be used, for which prophylaxis might be feasible. Botulinum vaccine was administered to 8,000 troops, all of whom were deployed to advance positions early in the conflict; close follow-up of these individuals has not demonstrated unusual illnesses (Persian Gulf Veterans Coordinating Board, 1995). Anthrax vaccine is approved by the Food and Drug Administration (FDA), and is usually given in a series of shots over the course of a year, but by the time it was available in the field, so little time remained before the end of the war that only 150,000 troops received either one or two shots of the regimen. Administration of the shots was not recorded in medical records, and the nature of the vaccines were often not disseminated, in order to prevent knowledge of their administration from reaching the Iraqis. Unfortunately, this has subsequently limited the ability to ascertain which individuals were vaccinated, particularly for Anthrax, which was more widely distributed than Botulinum. It also caused consternation in some troops, accustomed to having their vaccinations carefully recorded in their shot records, leading them to wonder whether they were being experimented on, and, ironically, whether the immunizations could have resulted in chronic illness. The evaluation of tens of thousands of troops has provided no evidence of association between vaccination and subsequent illness.

CW prophylaxis was attempted with pyridostigmine bromide (PB), given to troops in packs of twenty-one 30-mg pills, with instructions to take one pill three times daily when the risk of CW was felt to be significant. PB has been used for more than 40 years, at up to 30 times this dosage, for the FDA-approved treatment of myasthenia gravis. The FDA provided a waiver for PB as a wartime nerve agent prophylaxis, after it was demonstrated to provide pretreatment protection against soman, another nerve agent, when combined with postexposure atropine. PB is a quaternary amine, which inhibits it from crossing the blood–brain barrier. However, Friedman and colleagues have done animal and human studies demonstrating that under conditions of severe stress, PB can cross the blood–brain barrier, resulting in central nervous system effects (Friedman et al., 1996). Normally, PB acts at peripheral neuromuscular junctions to reversibly inhibit acetylcholinesterase, preventing irreversible binding by nerve agents. Although PB does not protect against the nerve agents sarin and VX, a wide variety of clinical experts feel it is essential to use in combat conditions where nerve agent exposure is anticipated (Dunn, Hackley, Sidell, 1997). Considerable evidence supports its safety and lack of significant adverse effects (Cook, Wenger, Kolka, 1992). During the PGW, some troops experienced minor gastrointestinal and urinary side effects, and rarely bronchospasm resulted (Keeler, Hurst, & Dunn, 1991). There is little evidence or biologic plausibility to suggest chronic side effects—the altered biokinetics reported by Friedman are quite interesting, but PB still has a very short half-life, rendering chronic effects unlikely. Moreover, anticholinesterases such as tacrine and donepezil are being used to treat memory impairment in Alzheimer's disease, so that memory impairment attributable to an anticholinesterase would be unexpected.

Some researchers have postulated that although PB or other exposures alone may not cause difficulty, in combination they might produce chronic ill effects. In particular, the combination of PB, permethrin, and diethyltoluamide (DEET) has been cited. Abou-Donia and colleagues administered high doses of the three agents to chickens (known to have greater sensitivity to pesticides than other species) 5 days per week for 2 months (Abou-Donia, Wilmarth, Jensen, Oehme, & Kurt, 1996). PB was given orally at approximately five times the dose prescribed to troops, and for a much longer duration than that for most, if not all, soldiers. The permethrin and DEET were administered subcutaneously at a dosage that has been estimated to be equivalent to the daily use by a soldier of 15 and 6.5 cans, respectively (USCIA, 1996). It is difficult to estimate exactly how much DEET may have been used by troops, but it was certainly far less than 6.5 cans daily, because an average of 2 cans per service member were given out during the entire deployment. The few troops who had exposure to permethrin were instructed to use it only on their uniforms to assist prevention of insect bites—not directly on or under their skin. It is estimated that less than 2% of troops self-treated their uniforms with permethrin (Perkins, 1995). Thus, although Abou-Donia reported neurologic effects and mortality in treated chickens, it is difficult to extrapolate from this study to the symptoms of PGW veterans. In fact, our analysis of the self-reported exposures of CCEP participants fails to show evidence of synergistic adverse health effects with the use of PB and personal pesticides.

DEPLETED URANIUM

Depleted uranium (dU) was used to enhance the ability of munitions to penetrate armor. Exposure to high levels of dU can result in nephrotoxicity. Sixteen PGW veterans have been confirmed to have urinary dU levels above acceptable U.S. standards, all associated with having been hit with friendly fire that left residual shell fragments in their bodies. All of the identified individuals have been closely followed by the VA, and none have had adverse health effects. All have had dU levels return to acceptable ranges with removal of the fragments, with the exception of two individuals for whom the location of the fragments poses too much of a risk to allow removal (Presidential Advisory Committee Presentation, 1996). Kidney damage has been extremely rare in CCEP participants, and when seen, has been attributable to a medical condition such as hypertension or diabetes.

OIL WELL FIRES

Some troops were exposed to smoke from oil well fires set by Iraqi soldiers. Although visually dramatic, and associated with unpleasant soot that rained down upon troops, there is extensive evidence to refute an association between exposure to the smoke and chronic adverse health effects. Numerous organizations, including the U.S. Environmental Protection Agency, studied environmental conditions while the fires burned (Persian Gulf Veterans Coordinating Board, 1995). It was concluded that the two factors that prevented air quality from being worse than an average American city were (a) most of the smoke was carried above and (b) the heat of the fires was so great that hydrocarbons were largely combusted, leaving elemental carbon, or soot. Although this had the effect of blocking out the sun, and covering soldiers and their environment in a layer of blackness, it posed far less of a health risk than complex hydrocarbons. Also comforting in this respect is the lack of unexplained illnesses in the American civilian firefighters who had high levels of exposure to the oil well fires.

BIRTH DEFECTS

The specter of unusual birth defects in the offspring of PGW veterans has engendered particular media attention. Numerous studies indicate no association between service in the Persian Gulf and birth defects, miscarriages, or infertility. A perceived cluster of birth defects in two Mississippi National Guard Units was the initial source of concern. A collaborative investigation by the Centers for Disease Control and Prevention, the Mississippi State Department of Health, and the Jackson VA found that the rate of major and minor birth defects in the 54 children they studied was consistent with the incidence in the general population (Penman, Tarver, & Currier, 1996). Since then, larger studies have yielded similar results. A study at Robins Air Force Base in Georgia reviewed 620 pregnancy outcomes, identifying miscarriage and congenital malformation rates that were at or below those for the general U.S. population. Two studies that involved a total of nearly 8,000 pregnancies before and after Gulf deployment found identical rates for both time periods, which were lower than that seen in the general population. A study of more than 75,000 infants born at 135 military hospitals from 1991 to 1993, found no difference in the rate of birth defects between those born to Gulf War veterans and those born to nondeployed veterans (Cowan, DeFraites, Gray, Goldenbaum, & Wishik, 1997). Several studies are continuing, and if there is a link between any of the described exposures and adverse birth outcomes, it may require a longer follow-up period to be identified. However, at this time there is nothing to suggest such a relationship.

STRESS

Many of the heretofore described exposures were limited to subsets of the deployed population, yet the development of chronic symptoms such as headaches, fatigue, and joint pain do not appear to be limited to, or even more common in, particular services, units, locations, or times. However, there are potentially significant factors that were common to all, or nearly all, deployed troops. They include separation from family and loved ones, rapid deployment to a distant, alien environment, and imminent confrontation with a large army that could result in injury, exposure to CW/BW, or even death. Numerous animal and human studies have documented an association between stress and not only psychological difficulties, but also organic illness such as asthma, hypertension, stroke, and cardiovascular disease.

HISTORICAL PRECEDENTS

More compelling than unique environmental factors is that symptom complexes similar to those of ill PGW veterans have been reported in veterans of previous conflicts. Da Costa (1871) first described this in relation to the

Civil War, but he noted that British forces in India and in the Crimean War appeared to have similar symptoms, which Da Costa felt were functional in etiology, the "irritable heart of soldiers." Symptoms included palpitations, chest pain, shortness of breath, headache, giddiness, disturbed sleep, pruritis, and diarrhea.

Cohn (1919) reported that identical cases were common in both British and American forces during World War I, applying the label of *effort syndrome*, while noting the similarity to neurasthenia, which had been described by MacKenzie (1916) as ". . . the condition from which certain of these soldiers suffer, who are usually understood to have a heart infection, is not, properly speaking, cardiac in origin . . . they often feel miserable, so that there is a mental side to the case which is aggravated by the supposition that there is something amiss with the heart" (p. 119). Evaluating British soldiers in World War II who had identical presentations, Fraser (1940) stated that:

> An essential to success in treatment is to convince the patient that he is not suffering from a "diseased heart." In many instances no amount of reassurance and persuasion will accomplish this. A thorough and authoritative physical examination is a necessary preliminary. Even in favorable cases he may be convinced only after he has discovered for himself that he is capable of considerable exertion without return of symptoms. (p. 461)

He went on to note that "As the mental element in the disorder became more generally accepted, the importance of games and other forms of healthy occupation under skilled instruction and supervision was recognized" (pp. 461–462). He pointed to the importance not only of a detailed history and physical exam, but also psychiatric evaluation. Elements of successful treatment during both World Wars I and II included occupational therapy, graduated exercises, and supervised games. Most recently, Hyams and colleagues reviewed symptom reports from veterans of each of these conflicts, as well as the Korean and Vietnam wars, noting remarkable similarities after each war (Hyams, Wignall, & Roswell, 1996).

Treatment Experience: The Specialized Care Center

In early 1995, the Specialized Care Center (SCC), a program to treat PGW veterans who were disabled by persistent symptoms, was assembled. Health care professionals from across the United States and in the United Kingdom, who had expertise in chronic fatigue and chronic pain, were contacted and visited. The program was modeled to some extent after the Pain Treatment Center at Johns Hopkins, because their patient population appeared to have greater similarity to those the SCC expected to treat than did other centers. However, there are unique features of the SCC's patient population that consequently led to the incorporation of elements into the program that are not found elsewhere. The staff includes internists, psychiatrists, psychologists, social workers, physiatrists, occupational and physical therapists, fitness trainers, nutritionists, and art and recreation therapists. Patients usually are referred by clinicians or other veterans, but rarely are self-referred. A thorough medical evaluation is required, including the CCEP, prior to being accepted into the SCC. Patients are given a written description of the program that includes the following goals identified by the staff: (a) to maximize the level of health and fitness, while minimizing disability, within 6 months of completion of the program; (b) to promote behaviors that will maintain health and fitness; and (c) to improve inter-personal relationships. Participants must also identify personal goals in advance, sign a contract documenting their understanding of the program, and their agreement to participate in all scheduled activities. It is empha-sized that not all problems will be solved within 4 weeks, but that patients will be provided with tools to facilitate continued self-improvement, and to improve their abilities to cope with symptoms that can not be resolved.

Through August 1996, 50 patients entered the program, for 4-week treatment blocks, with an average of 5 patients in each group. The median age of participants is 35, and 72% have been male. Nearly all have been on active duty; 70% have been in the Army, with relatively small numbers from each of the other services.

Evaluation Component. The first week of the SCC program, staff mem-bers individually evaluate each participant, and additional diagnostic stud-ies or consultations are scheduled as warranted. Patients complete ques-tionnaires, including the Minnesota Multiphasic Personality Inventory-2 (MMPI), Toronto Alexithymia Scale, Prime-MD, and Health Status Survey (SF-36) at the start and end of the treatment cycle, as well as at a 6-month follow-up evaluation. Patients are discussed in detail at staff meetings, and individual treatment plans are developed. Of the first 50 patients, 43 were given a primary psychiatric diagnosis: somatoform disorder (16), posttrau-matic stress disorder (10), major depression (5), personality disorder (5), conversion disorder (2), alcoholism (2), anxiety disorder (2), or body dysmorphic disorder (1). Among the seven medical primary diagnoses were obstructive sleep apnea, chronic obstructive pulmonary disease, sar-coidosis, osteoarthritis, thoracic outlet syndrome, and partial complex sei-zure disorder.

Treatment Component. The primary focus of the SCC program is on treatment that begins simultaneous with the evaluation process. Each day begins with fitness trainers leading progressive aerobic conditioning at 6 a.m. and continues into the evening. Daily group therapy is led by mental health professionals, as are a series of interactive classes focused on topics such as stress management, pain management, coping skills, relationship skills, communication skills, self-esteem, and body/mind/spirit connections. Cognitive behavioral therapy techniques are employed in group and individual sessions. Medical specialists provide group discussions to help patients deal with common problems such as sleep disturbances, irritable bowel syndrome, headaches, and musculoskeletal problems. Patients are provided with information about the significance of Persian Gulf exposures and the medical consequences of stress—including the information that is provided in this chapter. Recreation therapy provides instruction on relaxation techniques as well as promoting better use of free time to improve self-esteem and mood. Physical and occupational therapy coordinate a work-hardening program that combines resolving localized musculoskeletal pain with improving muscle tone and conditioning. Nutritionists perform detailed individual evaluations, and provide individual treatment as well as classes on topics such as triglycerides and eating out.

Outcomes. Patients usually report large numbers of troublesome somatic and psychological symptoms at the start of the program, with a small but significant decrease in symptoms in both categories at the end of treatment. In nearly all patients, the SCC staff has seen significant improvement in self-esteem, ability to express themselves and to interact effectively with others, and in understanding of symptoms. Levels of fitness have improved in almost every case, as represented by the number of sit-ups and push-ups, and times on a 2-mile run, at the end of the program compared to the start. Many patients improved their diets greatly, and some have lost as much as 10 to 20 pounds. Art therapy has been particularly successful in helping a relatively alexithymic group of patients to express themselves and their emotions more effectively. Unfortunately, only a few have demonstrated continued self-improvement in the 6 months following the program. Relapses are particularly common in the areas of fitness, weight, smoking status, and depressed mood.

TREATMENT EXPERIENCE OUTSIDE
THE SPECIALIZED CARE CENTER

Given the thousands of symptomatic PGW veterans who have been evaluated, comparatively few have been able to participate in the SCC. In fact, most do not require the intensity of a 4-week treatment program, and can be successfully treated individually, as has been done for hundreds of veterans at Walter Reed. Of particular interest are a number of patients who report a variety of somatic symptoms such as dizziness, headaches, fatigue, and shortness of breath, in association with environmental stimuli such as vehicle exhaust fumes, passive cigarette smoke (in some cases active smoking has not been problematic!), low levels of pesticides, and perfumes. Although they could be classified as having multiple chemical sensitivity, many have met criteria for panic or anxiety disorders, and have been successfully treated with anxiolytics or antidepressants. For example, one veteran with many years of service noted the onset of the symptoms just described for the first time while spraying pesticides at an Air Force base. His symptoms resolved within an hour, but recurred once or twice each month in the ensuing year, often but not always in association with exposure to perfume, smoke, pesticides, or other environmental factors. He provided a history of several episodes of classic panic attacks while in high school, but had no symptoms in the intervening years. He was treated with clonazepam 0.5 mg twice daily, and his symptomatic episodes initially became less severe, and resolved entirely within 6 months, enabling discontinuation of the clonazepam. He has continued on active duty without further difficulty.

For others, certain environmental stimuli seem to have a Pavlovian effect. For example, veterans who were exposed to the oil well fires under generally unpleasant circumstances now report that they no longer enjoy changing their automobile motor oil, or that exhaust fumes from buses are distinctly unpleasant, which had not been the case prior to the war. This sort of individual generally responds well to reassurance and avoidance of the offending stimuli until the symptoms subside with the passage of time.

A small number of patients report symptoms that occur in relation to environmental stimuli, which do not appear to fit into either of the categories just cited. They tend to be unresponsive to all treatment efforts, including anxiolytics, antidepressants, and the multidisciplinary approach of the SCC. Some have been diagnosed with multiple chemical sensitivity by other practitioners. However, in every case of this sort, there have been many somatic symptoms that are not associated with environmental stimuli, and have no identifiable organic basis on detailed medical evaluation. Moreover, there is frequently evidence of underlying characterologic pathology as well as prominent reasons for secondary gain. Therefore, somatoform and/or personality disorders have been felt to be more accurate and comprehensive diagnoses, and there has not yet been a case where it appeared appropriate to invoke a diagnosis of multiple chemical sensitivity.

As has been widely reported, ill PGW veterans do not appear to have a unifying etiology for their symptoms, and there is no evidence of a single diagnosis or set of diagnoses that is shared among the majority of veterans. This is not surprising, given that anyone with any sort of symptoms is invited to come in for a medical evaluation. CCEP participants have ranged from those who are in perfect health and just wanted to "get checked out," to those with severe medical conditions such as cancer and autoimmune diseases that may or may not have been previously diagnosed. Between the two extremes are many individuals with common, benign conditions, as well as a large number who have common symptoms without significant laboratory abnormalities or other objective evidence of an identifiable organic diagnosis that explains most or all of their symptoms. This is not terribly unusual, in that several studies have shown that up to 30% of patients visiting their primary care physician have unexplained symptoms (Kroenke, Arrington, & Mangelsdorf, 1990; Kroenke & Mangelsdorf, 1989; Kroenke & Price, 1993). However, the number of symptoms reported by PGW veterans (a median of three for CCEP participants) has been shown to be greater than in control populations (CDC, 1995; Iowa Persian Gulf Study Group, 1997).

A correlation between symptom count and the likelihood of psychiatric conditions, including depression and anxiety disorders, has been previously described in several populations, including veterans and their dependents (Kroenke, Jackson, & Chamberlin, 1997; Kroenke et al., 1994; Simon, Gater, Kisely, & Piccinelli, 1996). Our analysis of the CCEP data in fact demonstrates a strong correlation between veterans' symptom counts and psychiatric diagnoses that is not seen for well-defined organic conditions. In addition, the average MMPI scores for all CCEP Phase II participants seen at both Walter Reed and Wilford Hall Air Force Hospital demonstrate a Conversion V, with markedly elevated hysteria and hypochondriasis scales. Patients frequently meet criteria for somatoform disorders when the Structured Clinical Interview (SCID) for DSM-III–R and PRIME-MD are administered. Finally, a detailed social work history almost invariably identifies major life stressors, early in life, at the time of the war, and/or currently. The war is one of many identifiable stressors that appear to be associated with symptomatology. Perhaps equally important is the downsizing of the military, which threatens the career plans and livelihoods of many of the symptomatic veterans. For many who experienced childhood abuse, neglect, or abandonment, the military became a surrogate parent, and the downsizing is a painful reminder of their childhood experience. The media attention given to Gulf War Syndrome has also tended to increase the number of symptoms. For example, benign conditions such as eczema or mosquito bites tend to make some concerned that they have developed the rash of Gulf War Syndrome. The publication of the reported symptoms has also had the power of suggestion for some individuals, much like a medical student who studies the pathophysiology of the heart and fears that the twinge of pain he experiences could be a heart attack. This can be best dealt with by reassurance, and by disseminating correct information to combat some of the misleading information that appears in the lay media. Barsky and Borus (1995) commented on Gulf War Syndrome along with a variety of similar symptom complexes such as chronic fatigue syndrome and fibromyalgia, noting that:

> Such conditions often assume prominence in the mass communications media before their scientific dimensions have been established. Portrayed by the media as major public health problems, they emerge suddenly, accompanied by a groundswell of patients, support groups, and national advocacy organizations. Patients with these functional syndromes are often convinced that they have a specific occult disease . . ." (p. 1932)

This is the environment in which Gulf War Syndrome has developed, but individually or in small groups, we have found, like those who have treated similar ailments after previous wars, that patients can often be successfully reassured, treated, and pointed in a more positive direction.

REFERENCES

Abou-Donia, M. B., Wilmarth, K. R., Jensen, K. F., Oehme, F. W., & Kurt, T. L. (1996). Neurotoxicity resulting from coexposure to pyridostigmine bromide, DEET, and permethrin. *Journal of Toxicology and Environmental Health, 48,* 35–56.

Barsky, A. J., & Borus, J. F. (1995). Somatization in the era of managed care. *Journal of the American Medical Association, 274,* 1931–1934.

Blanck, R. R. (1996). Further information about Persian Gulf War illnesses (letter). *International Journal of Occupational Medicine, Immunology, and Toxicology, 5,* 79–81.

Centers for Disease Control and Prevention. (1995). Unexplained illness among Persian Gulf War veterans in an Air National Guard unit: Preliminary report—August 1990–March 1995. *Morbidity and Mortality Weekly Report, 44,* 443–447.

Cohn, A. E. (1919). The cardiac phase of the war neuroses. *American Journal of the Medical Sciences, 158,* 453–470.

Cook, J. E., Wenger, C. B., & Kolka, M. A. (1992). Chronic pyridostigmine bromide administration: Side effects among soldiers working in a desert environment. *Military Medicine, 157,* 250–254.

Cowan, D. N., DeFraites, R. F., Gray, G. C., Goldenbaum, M. B., & Wishik, S. M. (1997). The risk of birth defects among children of Persian Gulf War veterans. *New England Journal of Medicine, 336,* 1650–1656.

Da Costa, J. M. (1871). On irritable heart: A clinical study of a form of functional cardiac disorder and its consequences. *American Journal of the Medical Sciences, 61,* 17–51.

Defense Science Board Task Force on Persian Gulf War Health Effects. (1994). *Report.* Washington, DC: Office of the Under Secretary of Defense for Acquisition and Technology.

Department of Defense Report. (1994). *Clinical evaluation program for Gulf War veterans: Preliminary status report on the first 1000 participants.* Washington, DC: Author.

Department of Defense Report. (1995). *Comprehensive clinical evaluation program for Gulf War veterans: Report on 10,200 participants.* Washington, DC: Author.

Department of Defense Report. (1996). *Comprehensive clinical evaluation program for Persian Gulf War veterans: Report on 18,598 participants.* Washington, DC: Author.

Dunn, M. A., Hackley, B. E., & Sidell, F. R. (1997). Pretreatment for nerve agent exposure. In F. R. Sidell, E. T. Takafuji, & D. R. Franz (Eds.), *Medical aspects of chemical and biological warfare.* Borden Institute, Walter Reed Army Medical Center, Office of the Surgeon General, U.S. Army.

Ferrante, M. A., & Dolan, M. J. (1993). Q fever meningoencephalitis in a soldier returning from the Persian Gulf war. *Clinical Infectious Diseases, 16,* 489–496.

Fraser, F. R. (1940). Effort syndrome in the present war. *Edinburgh Medical Journal, 47,* 451–465.

Friedman, A., Kaufer, D., Shemer, J., Hendler, I., Soneg, H., & Tur-Kaspa, I. (1996). Pyridostigmine brain penetration under stress enhances neuronal excitability and induces early immediate transcriptional response. *Nature Medicine, 2,* 1382–1385.

Gray, G. C., Coate, B. D., Anderson, C. M., Kang, H. K., Berg, S. W., Wignall, F. S., Knoke, J. D., & Barrett-Conner, E. (1996). The postwar hospitalization experience of US veterans of the Persian Gulf War. *New England Journal of Medicine, 335,* 1505–1513.

Haley, R. W., Horn, J., Roland, P. S., Bryan, W. W., Van Ness, P. C., Bonte, F. J., Devous, M. D., Mathews, D., Fleckenstein, J. L., Wians, F. H., Wolfe, G. I., & Kurt, T. L. (1997). Evaluation of neurologic function in Gulf War veterans: A blinded case-control study. *Journal of the American Medical Association, 277,* 223–230.

Haley, R. W., & Kurt, T. L. (1997). Self-reported exposure to neurotoxic chemical combinations in the Gulf War: A cross-sectional epidemiologic study. *Journal of the American Medical Association, 277,* 231–237.

Haley, R. W., Kurt, T. L., & Horn, J. (1997). Is there a Gulf War syndrome? Searching for syndromes by factor analysis of symptoms. *Journal of the American Medical Association, 277,* 215–222.

Hyams, K. C., Bourgeois, A. L., Merrell, B. R., Rozmajzl, P., Fescamilla, J., Thornton, S. A., Wasserman, G. M., Burke, A., Echeverria, P., Green, K. Y., Kapikian, A. Z., & Woody, J. N. (1991). Diarrheal disease during operation desert shield. *New England Journal of Medicine, 325,* 1423–1428.

Hyams, K. C., Wignall, F. S., & Roswell, R. (1996). War syndromes and their evaluation: From the U.S. Civil War to the Persian Gulf War. *Annals of Internal Medicine, 125,* 398–405.

Institute of Medicine. (1995). *Health consequences of service during the Persian Gulf War: Initial findings and recommendations for immediate action.* Washington, DC: National Academy Press.

Institute of Medicine. (1996). *Health consequences of service during the Persian Gulf War: Recommendations for research and information systems.* Washington, DC: National Academy Press.

Iowa Persian Gulf Study Group. (1997). Self-reported illness and health status among Gulf War veterans: A population-based study. *Journal of the American Medical Association, 277,* 238–245.

Kang, H. K., & Bullman, T. A. (1996). Mortality among U.S. veterans of the Persian Gulf War. *New England Journal of Medicine, 335,* 1498–1504.

Keeler, J. R., Hurst, C. G., & Dunn, M. A. (1991). Pyridostigmine used as a nerve agent pretreatment under wartime conditions. *Journal of the American Medical Association, 266,* 693–695.

Kroenke, K., Arrington, M. E., & Mangelsdorf, A. D. (1990). The prevalence of symptoms in medical outpatients and the adequacy of therapy. *Archives of Internal Medicine, 150,* 1685–1689.

Kroenke, K., Jackson, J. L., & Chamberlin, J. (1997). Depressive and anxiety disorders in patients presenting with physical complaints: Clinical predictors and outcome. *American Journal of Medicine, 103,* 339–347.

Kroenke, K., & Mangelsdorf, A. D. (1989). Common symptoms in ambulatory care: Incidence, evaluation, therapy, and outcome. *American Journal of Medicine, 86,* 262–266.

Kroenke, K., & Price, R. K. (1993). Symptoms in the community: Prevalence, classification, and psychiatric comorbidity. *Archives of Internal Medicine, 153,* 2474–2480.

Kroenke, K., Spitzer, R. L., Williams, J. B. W., Linzer, M., Hahn, S. R., deGray, F. V., III, & Brody, D. (1994). Physical symptoms in primary care: Predictors of psychiatric disorders and functional impairment. *Archives of Family Medicine, 3,* 774–779.

Lo, S. C., Buchholz, C. L., Wear, D. J., Hohm, R. C., & Marty, A. M. (1991). Histopathology and doxycycline treatment in a previously healthy non-AIDS patient systemically infected by *Mycoplasma fermentans* (incognitus strain). *Modern Pathology, 6,* 750–754.

MacKenzie, J. (1916). The soldier's heart. *British Medical Journal, I,* 117–119.

Magill, A. J., Grogl, M., Gasser, R. A., Sun, W., & Oster, C. N. (1993). Visceral infection caused by Leishmania tropica in veterans of operation desert storm. *New England Journal of Medicine, 328,* 1383–1387.

Medicine in the Gulf War. (1991). *U.S. Medicine, 27,* 1–113.

Nicolson, G. L., & Nicolson, N. L. (1995a). Diagnosis and treatment of mycoplasmal infections in Persian Gulf War illness-CFIDS patients. *International Journal of Occupational Medicine, Immunology, and Toxicology, 5,* 69–78.

Nicolson, G. L., & Nicolson, N. L. (1995b). Doxycycline treatment and desert storm (letter). *Journal of the American Medical Association, 273,* 618–619.

NIH Technology Assessment Workshop Panel. (1994). The Persian Gulf experience and health. *Journal of the American Medical Association, 272,* 391–396.

Penman, A. D., Tarver, R. S., & Currier, M. M. (1996). No evidence of increase in birth defects and health problems among children born to Persian Gulf War veterans in Mississippi. *Military Medicine, 161,* 1–6.

Perkins, P. (1995, June). *Presentation to the Research Working Group, Persian Gulf Veterans Coordinating Board.* Washington, DC: Armed Forces Institute of Pathology.

Persian Gulf Veterans Coordinating Board. (1995). Unexplained illnesses among desert storm veterans: A search for causes, treatment, and cooperation. *Archives of Internal Medicine, 155,* 262–268.

Presidential Advisory Committee on Gulf War Veterans' Illnesses. (1996). *Final report.* Washington, DC: U.S. Government Printing Office.

Presidential Advisory Committee on Illnesses of Persian Gulf War Veterans. (1996, April). Presentation. Washington, DC: U.S. Government Printing Office.

Richards, A. L., Hyams, K. C., Merrell, B. R., Dasch, G. A., Woody, J. N., Ksiazek, T. G., LeDuc, J. W., & Watts, D. M. (1991). Medical aspects of operation desert storm (Letter). *New England Journal of Medicine, 325,* 970.

Robertson, A. G., & Robertson, L. J. (1995). From asps to allegations: Biological warfare in history. *Military Medicine, 160,* 369–373.

Roy, M. J., Chung, C. Y., Huntley, D. E., & Blanck, R. R. (1994). Evaluating the symptoms of Persian Gulf veterans. *Federal Practitioner, 11,* 13–17.

Simon, G., Gater, R., Kisely, S., & Piccinelli, M. (1996). Somatic symptoms of distress: An international primary care study. *Psychosomatic Medicine, 58,* 481–488.

U.S. Central Intelligence Agency, Office of Weapons, Technology, and Proliferation. (1996). *CIA report on intelligence related to Gulf War illnesses.* McLean, VA: Author.

Writer, J. V., DeFraites, R. F., & Brundage, J. F. (1996). Comparative mortality among US military personnel in the Persian Gulf region and worldwide during operation desert shield and desert storm. *Journal of the American Medical Association, 275,* 118–121.

Chapter 7

Psychological Aftermath of Participation in the Persian Gulf War

Kevin Brailey
Jennifer J. Vasterling
VA Medical Center, New Orleans

Patricia B. Sutker
*Tulane University School of Medicine
and Louisiana State University School of Medicine*

In recent years, a growing literature on reactions to life-threatening trauma has documented the devastating effects of war among prisoners-of-war (POW), political prisoners and victims of torture, and among combat veterans of World War II, the Korean Conflict, and the Vietnam War (cf. Sutker, 1991; Sutker, Uddo-Crane, & Allain, 1991; Yehuda & McFarlane, 1995). Such research has suggested that the extraordinary stresses associated with war-zone exposure lead to increased vulnerability to psychological symptomatology such as negative moods, psychiatric disorders including posttraumatic stress disorder (PTSD), compromised cognitive functioning, and physical complaints (cf. Green, 1990a; Green, Grace, Lindy, Gleser, & Leonard, 1990; March, 1990; Sutker, Vasterling, Brailey, & Allain, 1995; Sutker, Winstead, Galina, & Allain, 1991). However, findings generated by studies among war veterans suggest that there are no simple generalities to describe war stress across individuals or to draw consistent parallels from one military conflict to another. In addition to individual difference factors, the impact of both military and civilian trauma seems to be influenced by the nature and severity of stressful experiences and the unique characteristics of adverse circumstances (Bartone, Ursano, Wright, & Ingraham, 1989; Green, 1991; Kulka et al., 1990). Symptoms have been found to vary in frequency and intensity depending on such factors as exposure to injury, death, and grotesque events, elements of unexpectedness and unpreparedness, and degree of personal involvement with the disastrous event or person affected (Foa, Steketee, & Rothbaum, 1989; Green, 1990b; Smith,

North, McCool, & Shea, 1990; Sutker, Winstead, Galina, & Allain, 1991; Yehuda & McFarlane, 1995).

There have been important gains over the past 15 years in knowledge of the aftermath of war-zone exposure, but most prior research on the psychological residuals of war-related stress has been clouded by methodological constraints inherent to the populations examined and the time of assessment. For example, with World War II, Korean conflict, and Vietnam combat personnel, research exploration of war-related stress and its consequences was typically delayed for years. In some cases, studies appeared in the literature four decades following war exposure (Elder & Clipp, 1988; Sutker, Allain, & Winstead, 1993; Sutker, Winstead, et al., 1991). The time elapsed between war exposure and subsequent investigation has contributed to misunderstanding of stress-related psychopathology, lack of information regarding the acute and chronic expression of such psychopathology, and failure to address the psychological and psychiatric treatment needs of individuals adversely affected. Moreover, few efforts have been conducted to explore and document emotional, physical, and cognitive residuals to war-zone service among the masses of soldiers deployed to battle. Instead, most psychological studies have focused primarily on veterans or soldiers seeking treatment who experienced emotional distress during combat and were withdrawn from military operations (e.g., Davidson, Smith, & Kudler, 1989; Sierles, Chen, Messing, Besyner, & Taylor, 1986; Solomon & Mikulincer, 1988; Sutker, Winstead, et al., 1991). This limits the generalizability of findings.

An exception to this trend was the rapid response of mental health clinicians and researchers to address the emotional concerns and readjustment needs of both treatment-seeking and nontreatment-seeking Persian Gulf War (PGW) veterans (Baker & Strunk, 1991; Hobfoll et al., 1991; Knudson, 1991; Sutker, Uddo, Brailey, & Allain, 1993; Wolfe, Brown, & Kelley, 1993). Operation Desert Storm (ODS), later identified as the PGW, mobilized thousands of troops in a modern, coordinated air–ground war. Among the unique aspects of this conflict were rapid and unexpected troop activation, exposure to SCUD missile attacks, anticipated chemical or biological warfare, austere living conditions, environmental pollution from burning oil fields, and instantaneous news coverage of war activities. For the first time, armed forces personnel included large numbers of women and relied on an all volunteer force drawn in large part from Reservists and the National Guard. Additionally, Vietnam War veterans may have been recalled to duty or witnessed mobilization of family members (cf. Wolfe, Brown, & Bucsela, 1992).

In an attempt to investigate psychological responses to the unique environment of the PGW, a debriefing and psychological assessment was provided to troops mobilized to action in the Persian Gulf and a comparison sample of similar troops who were not exposed to war-zone stress. The three main objectives were: (a) characterization of the war-zone stressors; (b) documentation of acute and chronic psychological sequelae to war-zone participation, including negative mood states, development of mental disorders, physical complaints, and cognitive deficits; and (c) identification of risk factors predictive of subsequent psychological symptoms and psychopathology, including stressor characteristics and individual differences. In this chapter, the findings, conclusions, and treatment recommendations generated by this empirical effort are presented, as well as a description of the procedures for gathering psychological data. Also included are quotations and personal letters obtained with permission from a subset of the troops that were evaluated.

DEBRIEFING AND ASSESSMENT STUDIES

Participants

The New Orleans VA Medical Center ODS Evaluation, Debriefing, and Treatment Team conducted initial psychological assessments with 1,520 military personnel mobilized in the PGW, including 517 Louisiana National Guard and 1,003 Marine, Army, Air Force, and Navy Reserve troops. Deployed troops were interviewed on average 9 months after they had returned from overseas. The sample consisted of caucasian (57%), African-American (30%), Hispanic (12%), and Asian-American (1%) troops; 14% were women. Ranging in age from 18 to 60 years with a mean age of 29, troops reported an average of 13 years of formal schooling. Seventy-four percent were employed prior to mobilization, and 20% were pursuing educational goals full time. The sample was comprised of 92% enlisted troops and 8% officers, and 81% were characterized by middle/lower middle socioeconomic status determined by the Hollingshead and Redlich (1958) criteria. Over one half (57%) were single, 37% were married, and the remainder were separated, divorced, or widowed. Although 39% of troops reported prior military service, only 6% had experienced previous combat. Of the troops who completed initial assessment, data were analyzed for 1,272 military personnel divided into two subgroups: 876 war-zone deployed troops and 396 troops mobilized in support of ODS but not deployed to the Persian Gulf. Data regarding changes in reported distress were obtained from a subset of 349 participants who received a follow-up assessment an average of 16 months after their initial debriefing.

Assessment Procedures

There were three types of assessment procedures: a standard assessment battery, an expanded battery, and a specialized neuropsychological battery. The standard assessment battery tapped five measurement domains: (a) personal characteristics and resource variables such as gender, ethnicity, education, rank, and intellectual sophistication; (b) characterization of the nature and severity of the stressor experiences; (c) negative mood states and traits; (d) psychiatric and physical symptoms; and (e) symptoms of PTSD. Administered to all troops in regularly scheduled drill exercises, whether individuals were deployed to the Persian Gulf or not, the standard battery was used for initial and follow-up assessments. An expanded battery was designed for troops believed to be at higher risk for negative war sequelae and included a structured clinical interview for psychiatric diagnosis in addition to the standard assessment battery. A special neuropsychological battery was administered to subsets of troops diagnosed with PTSD and those exhibiting no evidence of current psychopathology.

Stressor Characteristics

War-zone stressors described by personnel deployed to the Persian Gulf ranged from those judged to be relatively routine (poor living conditions, separation from family) to the extraordinary (participating in graves registration work, preparing for military attack). As might be expected, combat troops stationed at the front lines confronted different concerns and risks than those faced by troops in rear areas. Although units were organized to undertake discrete duties during the PGW, the increased speed and flexibility exhibited by the military in assigning numerous small contingents of personnel to duties far removed from their regular units significantly reduced the homogeneity of duties within original unit detachments (Presidential Advisory Committee on Gulf War Veterans' Illnesses, 1996). To document the potentially broad expanse of stressors encountered by troops, returnees were requested to describe the nature of their wartime experiences.

Summary of War-Zone Stressors. Returnees reported war-zone deployment for periods ranging from 10 to 808 days, with an average of 154 days. Troops were assigned to units that performed a full range of war-zone duties, including a Marine Corps heavy-weapons anti-tank (TOW) unit; Army maintenance, military police, helicopter medevac, mobile hospital (MASH), supply, and graves registration units; Air Force tactical fighter/ground support units; and a Navy hospital unit. Specific war-zone events were measured by an open-ended questionnaire asking respondents to list the three most stressful conditions experienced during war-zone duty. Content analysis of written replies among a subset of 120 deployed troops revealed five major elements of stress: hardships associated with separation from home, family, and friends (17% of responses); fears of military attack, loss of life, or injury (13%); discomfort related to the physical environment (13%); fears of loss of control, uncertainty, and the unknown (8%); and lack of leadership (7%). Seventeen percent of responses were unclassifiable or unique to the respondent (Sutker, Uddo, Brailey, & Allain, 1993).

Examples of War-Zone Stressor Experiences. First person accounts yield information not captured by summary statistics, and reveal greater detail about the personal variability that troops encountered in both their experiences and ability to describe war-zone events. The accounts demonstrate that some troops acknowledged only isolated reactions such as separation ("missing my family") or fear ("being over there and scared and afraid"), whereas other troops volunteered more descriptive information (separation: "knowing my wife was somewhere in Saudi [with another unit] and not knowing where"; fear: "crying myself to sleep at night for the first 2 weeks in Saudi"). Similar variability existed in responses containing actual images of war ("seeing all the blood" vs. "being on the back of a truck with eight bodies after picking them up from the hospital"). Finally, some responses focused more on subjective reactions rather than objective descriptions ("how I know I need to let go of some of my anger because it is not really productive"; "the realization of being in a war and the mission of dealing with death").

Excerpts from letters written by troops while overseas provided more specific articulation of the relationship between subjective and objective elements of the experience. The following comments illustrate the fatalistic response of one Army nurse in describing physical privations:

> I have died and gone to Hell! I don't think anything could be as bad as this place is. . . . Our tents are set on a big sand dune and they have no floor, so they are set on and under a layer of sand. Our tent has 16 women in it smashed together. Today, the tent was 112 degrees on the inside. The water we drink is so hot it tastes like bathwater. The women's bathroom consists of two boxes with three holes apiece. This is for 130 women. Pray every day that I will be home soon. I don't think it will help, but it can't hurt.

Other letters reassure family members, and reflect the importance of strong family ties as mechanisms of coping with the dangers inherent to war:

> January 18 1992; 2:45am
> Mom:
> The war has started. I have been listening to the news from the get-go. I stood and watched a squadron of fighter jets (F-15s) take off from the airport

here. Mom, I love you and everyone in my family. I want all of you to be strong. Really, I'm O.K. I will stay strong because I have a promise to uphold—I promised my family I would come home.

A final letter, describing the musings of an infantryman anticipating his reaction to combat, perhaps best captures the power of war to dominate the perceptions and emotions of its participants:

We spend time writing letters we won't get answered for a month, hauling water, filling sandbags, cleaning our equipment and complaining. We have live rounds which make us drunk with the idea of using them; and we have our protective gas masks on at all times which keeps us sober . . .
And as the crisis escalates, even more deeper probing brings only more questions: Can I handle the emotional stress of watching my friends die? Can I handle the physical stress of trying to save them? Do I have the courage? Can I take a Life? Will I fight or will I run? Am I prepared to give my life so that others may live free?

These spontaneous expressions of feelings only begin to illustrate the dramatic impact that war-time stressors can exert on the psychological well-being of troops. They also reflect the broad range of stressors and individual differences in reactions. Taken together, they suggest that, for all troops in the war-zone, there exists a unique interaction between the nature of the confronting stressors and available personal resources for responding to such stressors. We have hypothesized that it is the nature of this complex interaction that dictates the extent to which adverse adaptations to stress occur, both in the war-zone and in the months and years to come.

Psychological Outcomes

Psychological sequelae to war-zone participation, including the possible development of negative mood states, mental disorders, physical complaints, and cognitive deficits, were explored in a series of complementary analyses. The question of whether PGW participation was associated with elevated levels of psychosocial impairment was examined by comparing war-zone exposed and nonexposed troops. An attempt was made to gauge the severity of impairment in the deployed group by measuring clinically significant levels of psychopathology within deployed troops, along with cognitive impairment associated with such psychopathology. Finally, follow-up evaluations were conducted on a subgroup of war-zone exposed troops to investigate chronicity and longitudinal progression of stress-related psychological symptoms.

Mood States and Somatic Complaints. Samples of 876 war-zone exposed troops and 396 non-Gulf deployed troops were compared on measures of psychological distress and a Health Symptom Checklist (Bartone, Ursano, Wright, & Ingraham, 1989). Results of analyses of variance indicated that groups differed significantly on the Beck Depression Inventory (BDI; Beck, Ward, Mendelson, Mock, & Erbaugh, 1961), State-Anger Inventory (Spielberger, 1980), and Brief Symptom Inventory (BSI; Derogatis & Spencer, 1982) Depression, BSI Anxiety, and Health Symptom scales (see Table 7.1). Troops exposed to war-zone duty showed higher levels of depression, anxiety, and somatic preoccupation, and analyses of covariance revealed that these differences were not associated with significant effects for age or education. Among deployed troops, high frequency somatic complaints included headaches (22%), general aches and pains (20%), lack of energy (18%), sleep disturbances (17%), and common cold or flu (16%).

Stress-Related Psychopathology and Associated Cognitive Impairment. Data obtained from several of the measures just listed were studied to determine if there was evidence of stress-related psychopathology; results revealed psychological distress sufficiently exaggerated as to suggest psychopathology among sizable subsets of troops exposed to war trauma. For example, with scores exceeding 10 on the BDI being judged as indicative of clinically significant depressive symptoms (Beck, Steer, & Garbin, 1988), 23% of troops reported at least mild levels of clinical depression. Diagnoses of PTSD were indicated in 10% of the sample, reflected by scores greater than 97 on the Mississippi Scale for Desert Storm War Zone Personnel (adapted from Keane, Caddell, & Taylor, 1988). Use of an alternative measure, the 17-item *DSM-III-R*-derived PTSD symptom checklist (Weathers, Huska, & Keane, 1991), yielded a prevalence rate for PTSD of 9%; scores in the clinical range

TABLE 7.1
Comparison of Persian-Gulf-Deployed and Non-Gulf-Deployed
Veterans on Mood State and Health Concern Measures

Variable	Deployed (n = 876)		Nondeployed (n = 396)		F
	M	SD	M	SD	
Beck Depression Inventory	5.69	6.68	4.06	6.43	16.78**
State Anxiety	37.05	11.19	36.68	10.83	0.31
State Anger	21.00	9.32	19.49	7.62	7.94**
BSI Depression	54.91	11.32	53.23	10.67	6.15*
BSI Anxiety	53.19	12.36	50.59	11.64	12.52**
BSI Hostility	55.00	12.61	53.79	11.79	2.61
Health Symptom Checklist	8.92	9.02	6.72	7.70	16.30**

Note. $*p < .05$. $**p < .01$.

on either PTSD measure resulted in 14% classified as positive. Finally, in an attempt to examine an important potential area of impairment associated with stress-related psychopathology, neuropsychological testing was conducted with a subset of 42 war-zone exposed troops. Results indicated that returnees meeting criteria for PTSD by structured psychiatric interview performed more poorly on tasks of attention, impulse inhibition, and new learning than returnees judged to be free of psychological disturbances (Vasterling, Brailey, Constans, & Sutker, 1998).

Psychological Symptoms Over Time. Investigation of mental health symptoms at follow-up was undertaken to determine if war-related psychological sequelae had changed during the period. Such information would be pertinent to hypotheses positing stress evaporation (i.e., gradual dissipation in symptoms due to decreasing vividness of the memories associated with a stressor), delayed onset of symptoms, and stress incubation in war-zone exposed troops. Data were available for 349 participants who were evaluated at an average of 16 months after their initial assessment. As Table 7.2 indicates, scores increased significantly over time on the BDI, the State Anxiety (Spielberger, 1980) and Anger scales, and BSI anxiety and hostility scales (Brailey, Uddo, Vasterling, Constans, & Sutker, 1995). Additionally, deployed troops showed increased rates of clinically significant psychopathology from Time 1 to Time 2 for depression (6.9% vs. 13.8%), PTSD (2.3% vs. 10.6%), and hostility (4.9% vs. 13.8%). Thus, findings suggest an intensification of symptoms with time. Similar results were reported by Southwick et al. (1995), who found that PTSD symptoms intensified over the course of a 2-year follow-up period.

TABLE 7.2
Comparison of Persian-Gulf-Deployed Troops at Initial
and 16-Month Follow-Up Assessments on Mood State,
Health Concerns, and PTSD Symptom Measures

Variable	Time 1		Time 2		
	M	SD	M	SD	F
BDI	5.55	6.68	7.13	8.46	17.60**
State Anxiety	38.11	11.11	39.32	12.14	3.86*
State Anger	20.27	8.51	22.08	11.10	9.97**
BSI Depression	54.84	11.43	56.02	12.48	3.72
BSI Anxiety	52.89	12.35	55.20	13.24	11.89**
BSI Hostility	54.49	12.68	57.70	13.54	20.43**
Health Symptom Checklist	8.43	8.87	10.50	11.01	17.70**
PTSD Checklist	9.07	11.69	10.35	13.50	4.89*
Mississippi Scale	70.56	18.31	75.01	21.88	22.85**

Note. $*p < .05. **p < .01.$

Risk Factors: Stressor Characteristics
and Individual Differences

Theoretical conceptualizations of risk factors contributing to poor psychological outcome following stress exposure provide insight into why some individuals appear to show more psychological resilience to war-zone stress than others. For example, in a two-axis model of the effects of war-related stress, Hobfoll et al. (1991) proposed that increasing exposure to threat of loss and actual loss, in combination with decreasing levels of coping resources, lead to greater risk for subsequent negative psychological sequelae. Thus, the nature and severity of the stressor were seen to interact with personal resources to put individuals at risk for, or conversely mitigate against, manifestations of adverse responses to stress. Objective stressor characteristics seen as increasing risk for negative reactions included extent of hazard, threat of chemical exposure, time in the field of operations, exposure to casualties, perceived sense of abandoning family in a time of need, delayed return home, changed social relationships, and financial difficulties. Hobfoll et al. (1991) also focused on individual difference factors, such as personal resources, perceived social support, and coping strategies, which facilitate a sense of mastery over the environment. Other sources have implicated demographic variables such as female gender (Norman, 1988) and minority ethnicity (Kulka et al., 1990) as influencing the development of war-related stress symptoms.

The present research entailed an examination of both types of risk factors. First, the effects of stressor characteristics on psychological outcome were explored by examining the relationship between perceived stressor severity and subsequent psychopathology in three domains: negative mood states, PTSD symptoms, and physical complaints. It was hypothesized that as the severity of war-zone stress increased, the frequency and severity of psychological symptoms would be greater. A more comprehensive evaluation of troops who performed military mortuary duties enabled an examination of a group we postulated to be at especially high risk for stress-related problems. Second, the relationship between individual differences and stress-related symptoms was examined. Again, associations were hypothesized between personal resource variables (e.g., coping style, intellectual sophistication), demographic variables (e.g., ethnicity, gender) and increased vulnerability for development of psychological symptoms subsequent to trauma.

Relationships Between Distress Outcomes and Stress Severity and Nature. Data from returnees were divided into high and low war-zone stress severity subgroups using a median split of scores on a six-item adaptation of the ODS War Zone Stress Exposure Scale (ODS-SE; Wolfe, 1990), a measure reflecting troop perceptions of the stressfulness of war-zone experiences. The six items focus on hardships of the physical environment, separation from family/home, threat of military attack, cohesiveness of military unit, level of national support during the war-zone tour, and preparedness for military deployment. These items were of particular value because they closely reflect the concerns expressed by veterans in the open-ended responses described earlier.

As displayed in Table 7.3, troops deployed to PGW-zone duty who reported higher levels of stress exposure were characterized by significantly greater levels of negative mood states, PTSD symptomatology, and complaints about somatic problems than the low war-zone stress group (Sutker, Uddo, Brailey, & Allain, 1993). Returnees categorized by high stress exposure also endorsed almost twice as many complaints about physical problems than did their low war-zone stress exposure counterparts, particularly focusing on feelings of lack of energy, general aches and pains, nervousness, difficulties in sleeping, disturbed concentration, upset stomach, depressed mood, clammy hands, flu-like symptoms, needing sleep medication, headaches, and loss of interest in daily activities.

The predictive values of the six stressors were examined using multiple regression methods to assess the relative impact of each of the variables on the subsequent development of negative psychological outcome. Findings suggest that discomfort from environmental or physical conditions was the most important predictor of PTSD symptoms, as measured by scores on the Mississippi Scale (adapted from Keane, Caddell, & Taylor, 1988). Perceived lack of preparation for military duties, lack of unit cohe-

TABLE 7.3

Comparison of ODS War-Zone Stress Exposure Subgroups on Mood
State, Health Concerns, and PTSD Symptom Measures

| | War-Zone Exposure | | | | |
| | Low (n = 462) | | High (n = 414) | | |
Variable	M	SD	M	SD	F
BDI	4.17	5.83	7.39	7.16	53.65**
State Anxiety	35.01	10.67	39.33	11.32	33.87**
State Anger	19.33	7.69	22.86	10.56	32.44**
BSI Depression	52.67	10.42	57.40	11.77	39.84**
BSI Anxiety	50.53	11.28	56.16	12.84	47.60**
BSI Hostility	52.30	11.83	58.01	12.78	47.13**
Health Symptom Checklist	6.57	7.06	11.67	10.22	70.00**
PTSD Checklist	6.46	9.21	13.00	12.96	75.43**
Mississippi Scale	67.99	16.37	78.77	19.99	67.51**

Note. **$p < .01$.

sion, and failure to feel national support also significantly predicted PTSD symptoms. In predicting depression as measured by BDI scores, perceived lack of unit cohesion and discomfort from environmental or physical conditions were the two most important factors, followed by separation from home/family and perceived lack of preparation for military duties. Threat of military attack was not a significant predictor of either Mississippi Scale or BDI scores. Thus, both the degree and nature of stressors appear to be important determinants of subsequent distress.

Troops Assigned High-Risk Activities Such as Graves Registration Duty. Graves registration duties involved such gruesome assignments as retrieval of mutilated or disfigured bodies from the field of battle, placing human remains in body bags, matching separated body parts, sorting through human remains and personal effects to establish identities, and readying and embalming bodies for transport to the United States. Prevalence of PTSD was found to be 46% in a sample of 24 quartermaster troops who performed these horrific functions (Sutker, Uddo, Brailey, Allain, & Errera, 1994). There was also high incidence of psychiatric diagnoses comorbid with PTSD, including major depression (25%), alcohol abuse/dependence (13%), depressive disorder (not otherwise specified) (8%), and simple phobia (4%). These findings were replicated in a subsequent study that incorporated subsets of 40 quartermaster troops who served ODS graves registration duties and 20 similarly trained troops from the same units who were not deployed to the Persian Gulf and had no ODS graves registration exposure (Sutker, Uddo, Brailey, Vasterling, & Errera, 1994). Current diagnoses of PTSD were observed among 48% of deployed troops; whereas, none of the non-war-zone deployed troops met PTSD criteria. Current diagnoses comorbid with PTSD included depressive disorder (18%), alcohol dependence (10%), other anxiety disorder (3%), and drug dependence (3%). In both of these samples, all groups reported similar low levels of pre-war psychopathology. Comparable results were obtained by McCarroll, Ursano, and Fullerton (1993), who found that Persian Gulf troops who handled human remains reported significantly more intrusive and avoidance PTSD symptoms than other Gulf troops. Together, these findings point to the powerful impact exerted by exposure to grotesque war-related stimuli, even when such experiences are somewhat removed from the actual experience of combat.

Potential Mediating Effects of Personal Resources on Psychological Outcomes. Examination of personal resources in Gulf-deployed troops revealed several factors that may alter vulnerability to stress, including personality style, characteristic coping strategies, perceived family support, and intellectual sophistication. Among a subset of 775 PGW-exposed troops, discriminant function analysis correctly classified troops as PTSD positive or negative on the basis of personality hardiness commitment (tendencies toward engagement by purposeful action, autonomous control, and perceptions of change as challenge and growth), avoidance coping (the use of diminution and denial in the appraisal of potential stressors and stress responses), and perceived family cohesion (the extent to which family members are seen as regularly helpful and supportive of each other). In this sample, PTSD diagnoses were associated with low personality hardiness, high avoidance coping, and low perceived family cohesion (Sutker, Davis, Uddo, & Ditta, 1995b). In addition, findings from a specialized intellectual assessment battery pointed to the role of intellectual resources, particularly verbal skills, in buffering development of stress-related psychopathology. In a sample of 18 PTSD-diagnosed and 23 psychopathology-free Gulf War-exposed troops who were administered the Wechsler Adult Intelligence Scale-Revised (WAIS-R; Wechsler, 1981), PTSD-diagnosed veterans performed significantly more poorly on tasks of verbal intellectual functioning, including those tasks thought to reflect premorbid functioning, than did the comparison sample (Vasterling, Brailey, Constans, Borges, & Sutker, 1997).

Gender and Ethnicity Impact on Psychological Distress and Physical Symptoms. Previous research has suggested that psychological disturbances, and PTSD specifically, may be relatively high among ethnic minority and women veterans of military service. We examined these issues among a sample of 653 war-zone deployed troops and 259 non-war-zone deployed troops, and found that depression, anxiety, and physical complaints were higher among war-zone-deployed troops than those who remained stateside. Regardless of war-zone assignment, women reported significantly greater somatic distress than men on the Health Symptom Checklist, and minority troops reported significantly greater depression on the BDI than caucasians. Among deployed troops, minorities were at greater risk for developing symptoms of PTSD than Caucasians as reflected by significantly higher scores on the Mississippi Scale and PTSD Checklist. In particular, minority men reported significantly more PTSD symptoms on the PTSD Checklist than caucasian men, with minority and caucasian women exhibiting no significant differences in PTSD symptomatology (Sutker, Davis, Uddo, & Ditta, 1995a).

DISCUSSION

Results of psychological assessment among Persian Gulf returnees are remarkable in pointing to relatively high levels of psychological symptomatology and somatic complaints that appear to be attributable to war-zone exposure. Findings that from 9% to 23% of war-zone exposed troops show clinically significant psychopathology suggest that there is a substantial need for prompt mental health interventions targeting veterans traumatized by their service in a military engagement. Such psychopathology was associated with emotional distress, physical symptoms, and cognitive impairment, problems that do not dissipate with time. Instead, returnees appeared at elevated risk for developing stress-related symptoms for at least 2 years after the cessation of hostilities. These findings are particularly noteworthy because returnees who constituted this sample were neither seeking treatment at the time of evaluation nor active clinical patients; hence, results highlight the potentially broad impact of war stress on the masses of troops deployed.

Findings regarding the relationship between severity and nature of stress exposure and psychological distress symptoms, though largely correlational in nature, nonetheless point to the well-established dose-response relationship between trauma severity and development of stress-related symptoms (cf. Sutker, Uddo-Crane, & Allain, 1991). Troops who perceived themselves as being exposed to relatively high levels of stress while deployed overseas reported significantly more stress-related symptomatology than those troops who reported lower levels of stress exposure. At especially high risk for negative psychological outcomes were troops assigned graves registration functions that involved increased exposure to injury and the gruesomeness of death. Comprehensive psychological assessments conducted among two graves registration Army Reserve units deployed to the war zone revealed prevalence rates for current PTSD at 46% to 48%, accompanied by significantly elevated levels of comorbid psychopathology. These results suggest that as stressors mount to horrific and grotesque proportions, even troops who were in reasonable psychiatric health prior to exposure are at risk of becoming psychologically overwhelmed.

Other, more commonly encountered aspects of Persian Gulf war-zone duty also exerted a negative psychological impact on a substantial subset of those deployed. An open-ended elicitation of stressors revealed that returnees spontaneously volunteered concerns about many of the same constructs examined in a psychometrically-based questionnaire of war-zone stress. Of these questionnaire items, discomfort from environmental or physical conditions, along with a sense that a returnee's unit was at risk due to either poor preparation or lack of cohesiveness, seemed to predict the presence of both depression and PTSD symptoms. Interestingly, fear of combat injury or military attack, although the second most frequently volunteered stressor, was unrelated to either depression or PTSD, suggesting that anticipated but unrealized stressors do not necessarily lead to high levels of subsequent distress. The possible critical role of fears regarding death or injury from combat in potentiating other war-zone stressors remains an important focus for future research.

Although stressor severity and type of exposure have been shown to be critical determinants of PTSD, personal resources and individual differences may moderate vulnerability. We found that the adverse effects of stress may be mitigated in individuals who experience purposefulness in activities, refrain from avoidant coping, perceive their families to be supportive, and demonstrate relatively sophisticated verbal skills. Findings also underscore conclusions generated in the National Vietnam Veterans Readjustment Study (Kulka et al., 1990) that point to increased risk for PTSD in ethnic minorities, but no greater risk for PTSD in women Vietnam veterans. We found a tendency for non-White returnees, especially men, to report greater levels of psychological discomfort, but female Persian Gulf War veterans did not report greater psychological distress than did their male counterparts or score higher on measures of PTSD symptomatology. The latter finding is especially compelling, because the Persian Gulf War was the first United States military operation to place large numbers of women into combat-exposed duty. The lack of gender differences in military samples differs from estimates of PTSD within the general population, which indicate prevalence rates approximately two to four times higher for women than men (Breslau & Davis, 1992; Helzer, Robins, & McEvoy, 1987), despite the finding that women are no more likely to be exposed to traumatic events. The possibility that women are as resilient as men to the stresses of war-zone exposure but more vulnerable to the negative impact of civilian trauma is an intriguing question that requires exploration.

It should be noted that our findings regarding cognitive impairment and somatic complaints in a subset of Gulf War veterans diagnosed with PTSD do not directly address the possible existence of neuromedical abnormalities associated with Gulf War Syndrome. At this time, little evidence exists for Gulf War Syndrome as a multisystemic unitary condition that defines a new disease category (Presidential Advisory Committee on Gulf War Veterans' Illnesses, 1996). Some studies (Haley et al., 1997; Haley & Kurt, 1997; Haley, Kurt, & Horn, 1997) have postulated the existence of a range of neurologically based cognitive deficits that might be due to low-level neurotoxin exposure, interactions between several chemical agents given prophylactically to Gulf War troops, or additional environmental hazards (cf. Roy, chapter 6, this volume). However, other research has provided little evidence of either subjectively (Iowa Persian Gulf Studies Group, 1997) or objectively (Goldstein, Beers, Morrow, Shemansky, & Steinhauer, 1996) defined neurocognitive or health abnormalities independent of psychological distress, leading to suggestions that cognitive deficits found among deployed troops may be secondary to the stressors and stress reactions that have been described. In the absence of enviromental hazards data, the present findings cannot be regarded as directly relevant to this debate.

Treatment Recommendations

A full examination of assessment and treatment options with stress-related psychopathology is beyond the scope of this chapter, and the interested reader is referred to book-length cognitive-behaviorally (Foy, 1992) and biologically (Giller, 1991) oriented treatments of these issues. However, the present findings clearly have specific ramifications for treatment of Persian Gulf returnees, and veterans of all military operations. Beyond issues typically explored in an assessment, clinicians examining Persian Gulf returnees and other veterans are urged to obtain a full military history, with particular attention to the nature of any feared stressors, the extent to which these fears were realized, and the specific emotional responses and coping strategies. Inquiry regarding current symptoms should include broad questions surveying the existence of mood, cognitive, and somatic complaints, as well as more specific questions concerning the existence of PTSD symptoms. Attention should also be given to assessing factors found to mediate the expression of stress-related psychopathology, such as personal hardiness, coping style, perceived family cohesion, and level of verbal sophistication, along with changes in these factors since the beginning of the war.

Unique issues that confront clinicians assessing Persian Gulf veterans include information desired by veterans and judgment regarding the stage of any distress veterans may be experiencing. Returnees may simply want education about the types of psychological reactions common to stressful situations, as well as seek to ventilate emotions related to their specific experiences. Reactions of this type are most common immediately following exposure to a stressor and are best treated with brief supportive interventions such as educational sessions or critical-incident debriefing techniques (Wolfe, 1990). Assessment at a later time may uncover a waxing and waning of symptoms, suggesting a chronic disorder that requires in-depth intervention.

If returnees experience intrusive symptoms of the type defined by *DSM–IV* Criteria B for PTSD (i.e., intrusive trauma-related memories, flashbacks, nightmares, and either subjective distress or physiological reactivity when exposed to trauma-related cues), treatment may involve an exposure component. The available data suggest that there is positive treatment efficacy for systematic exposure to images of a traumatic incident when accompanied by a countervailing relaxation response (Keane, Fisher, Krinsley, & Niles, 1994). The information obtained in the assessment will prove valuable in developing scenarios to be used in the induction of the traumatic image. It is important that exposure-based treatment be undertaken with caution, as temporary periods of increased distress may occur during the early stages of therapy. Contraindications to exposure-based treatment are listed by Keane (1995) and include acute interpersonal crises, comorbid substance abuse, multiple traumatic events, comorbid physical complications (e.g., angina, hypertension, or myocardial infarction), neurological impairment, psychotic thought processes, and extremely poor impulse control. Inexperienced clinicians attempting this type of intervention are urged to seek supervision from a fully qualified peer.

We also urge clinicians dealing with PGW veterans, and in fact veterans of all military conflicts, to give full attention to descriptions of physical symptoms, even those that seem vague or suggestive of psychosomatic manifestations of anxiety. Whereas the present findings suggest that there are high rates of somatic concerns among Persian Gulf returnees, and that these physical complaints are often related to self-reported levels of stress, these data do not disconfirm the existence of a physical etiology to some subset of veterans' health complaints. Current empirical investigations regarding the existence and etiology of a PGW syndrome have proven inconclusive. We echo the reservations expressed in a recent *Journal of the American Medical Association* editorial, which suggests that "the findings on risk factors should instill a sense of etiologic caution in medical practitioners. Clinicians need to recognize that the precise causation of illness in most Persian Gulf War veterans may never be known with certainty" (Landrigan, 1997, p. 260). This state of uncertainty dictates that mental health professionals make special efforts to remain sensitive to Gulf War veterans' fears of the unknown and avoid reaching premature conclusions regarding the nature of somatic complaints.

ACKNOWLEDGMENTS

This research was supported by special funding from Mental Health and Behavioral Sciences Service, Department of Veterans Affairs Headquarters for evaluation, debriefing and treatment of ODS returnees and veterans of other wars affected by this military action, and by a Veterans Affairs Medical Research Award to Jennifer J. Vasterling and Patricia B. Sutker. Special appreciation is expressed to Drs. Paul Errera, Laurent Lehmann and Robert Rosenheck and to Gay Koerber and Robert Murphy for their guidance in project design and implementation. Grateful thanks go to the armed forces personnel who gave of their time to provide us with the information that forms the basis of this chapter.

REFERENCES

Baker, M. S., & Strunk, H. K. (1991). Medical aspects of Persian Gulf operations: Environmental hazards. *Military Medicine, 156*, 381–385.
Bartone, P. T., Ursano, R. J., Wright, K. M., & Ingraham, L. H. (1989). The impact of a military air disaster on the health of assistance workers: A prospective study. *Journal of Nervous and Mental Disease, 177*, 317–328.

Beck, A. T., Steer, R. A., & Garbin, M. G. (1988). Psychometric properties of the Beck Depression Inventory: Twenty-five years of evaluation. *Clinical Psychology Review, 8,* 77–100.

Beck, A. T., Ward, C. H., Mendelson, M., Mock, J., & Erbaugh, J. (1961). An inventory for measuring depression. *Archives of General Psychiatry, 4,* 561–571.

Brailey, K., Uddo, M., Vasterling, J. J., Constans, J. I., & Sutker, P. B. (1995, November). *A preliminary longitudinal study of stress-related symptoms in ODS veterans.* Poster presented at the 11th annual meeting of the International Society for Traumatic Stress Studies, Boston.

Breslau, N., & Davis, G. C. (1992). Posttraumatic stress disorder in an urban population of young adults: Risk factors for chronicity. *American Journal of Psychiatry, 149,* 671–676.

Davidson, J., Smith, R., & Kudler, H. (1989). Validity and reliability of the DSM-III-R criteria for posttraumatic stress disorder: Experience with a structured interview. *Journal of Nervous and Mental Disease, 177,* 336–341.

Derogatis, L. R., & Spencer, P. M. (1982). *The brief symptom inventory (BSI): Administration, scoring and procedures manual - I.* Baltimore: Clinical Psychometric Research.

Elder, G. H., & Clipp, E. C. (1988). Wartime losses and social bonding: Influences across 40 years in men's lives. *Psychiatry, 51,* 177–188.

Foa, E. B., Steketee, G., & Rothbaum, B. O. (1989). Behavioral/cognitive conceptualizations of post-traumatic stress disorder. *Behavior Therapy, 20,* 155–176.

Foy, D. W. (1992). *Treating PTSD: Cognitive-behavioral approaches.* New York: Guilford.

Giller, M. J. (1991). *Biological assessment and treatment of post-traumatic stress disorder.* Washington, DC: American Psychiatric Press.

Goldstein, G., Beers, S. R., Morrow, L. A., Shemansky, W. J., & Steinhauer, S. R. (1996). A preliminary neuropsychological study of Persian Gulf veterans. *Journal of the International Neuropsychological Society, 2,* 368–371.

Green, B. L. (1990a). *Disasters and PTSD* (Review paper for DSM-IV Advisory Committee on PTSD). Washington, DC: American Psychiatric Association.

Green, B. L. (1990b). Defining trauma: Terminology and generic stressor dimensions. *Journal of Applied Social Psychology, 20,* 1632–1642.

Green, B. L. (1991). Evaluating the effects of disaster. *Psychological Assessment: A Journal of Consulting and Clinical Psychology, 3,* 538–546.

Green, B. L., Grace, M. C., Lindy, J. D., Gleser, G. C., & Leonard, A. (1990). Risk factors for PTSD and other diagnoses in a general sample of Vietnam veterans. *American Journal of Psychiatry, 147,* 729–733.

Haley, R. W., Horn, J., Roland, P. S., Bryan, W. W., Van Ness, P. C., Bonte, F. J., Devous, M. D., Mathews, D., Fleckenstein, J. L., Wians, F. H., Wolfe, G. I., & Kurt, T. L. (1997). Evaluation of neurologic function in Gulf War veterans: A blinded case-control study. *Journal of the American Medical Association, 277*(3), 223–230.

Haley, R. W., & Kurt, T. W. (1997). Self-reported exposure to neurotoxic chemical combinations in the Gulf War: A cross-sectional epidemiologic study. *Journal of the American Medical Association, 277*(3), 231–237.

Haley, R. W., Kurt, T. W., & Horn, J. (1997). Is there a Gulf War Syndrome? Searching for syndromes by factor analysis of symptoms. *Journal of the American Medical Association, 277*(3), 215–222.

Helzer, J. E., Robins, L. N., & McEvoy, M. A. (1987). Post-traumatic stress disorder in the general population. *New England Journal of Medicine, 317,* 1630–1634.

Hobfoll, S. E., Spielberger, C. D., Breznitz, S., Figley, C., Folkman, S., Lepper-Green, B., Meichenbaum, D., Milgram, N. A., Sandler, I., Sarason, I., & van der Kolk, B. (1991). War-related stress: Addressing the stress of war and other related events. *American Psychologist, 46,* 848–855.

Hollingshead, A. B., & Redlich, F. C. (1958). *Social class and mental illness.* New York: Wiley.

Iowa Persian Gulf Studies Group. (1997). Self-reported illness and health status among Gulf War veterans: A population-based study. *Journal of the American Medical Association, 277*(3), 238–245.

Keane, T. M. (1995). The role of exposure therapy in the psychological treatment of PTSD. *National Center for PTSD Clinical Quarterly, 5*(4), 1–6.

Keane, T. M., Caddell, J. M., & Taylor, K. L. (1988). Mississippi scale for combat-related posttraumatic stress disorder: Three studies in reliability and validity. *Journal of Consulting and Clinical Psychology, 56,* 85–90.

Keane, T. M., Fisher, L. M., Krinsley, K. E., & Niles, B. L. (1994). Posttraumatic stress disorder. In M. Hersen & R. T. Ammerman (Eds.), *Handbook of prescriptive treatments for adults* (pp. 237–260). New York: Plenum.

Knudson, G. B. (1991). Operation Desert Shield: Medical aspects of weapons of mass destruction. *Military Medicine, 156,* 267–271.

Kulka, R. A., Schlenger, W. E., Fairbank, J. A., Hough, R. L., Jordan, B. K., Marmar, C. R., & Weiss, D. S. (1990). *Trauma and the Vietnam War generation: Report of findings from the national Vietnam veterans readjustment study.* New York: Brunner/Mazel.

Landrigan, P. J. (1997). Illness in Gulf War veterans: Causes and consequences [Editorial]. *Journal of the American Medical Association, 277*(3), 259–261.

McCarroll, J. E., Ursano, R. J., & Fullerton, C. S. (1993). Symptoms of posttraumatic stress disorder following recovery of war dead. *American Journal of Psychiatry, 150,* 1875–1877.

March, J. S. (1990). The nosology of posttraumatic stress disorder. *Journal of Anxiety Disorders, 4,* 61–82.

Norman, E. M. (1988). Post-traumatic stress disorder in military nurses who served in Vietnam during the war years 1965–1973. *Military Medicine, 153,* 238–242.

Presidential Advisory Committee on Gulf War Veterans' Illnesses. (1996). *Presidential Advisory Committee on Gulf War Veterans' Illnesses: Final Report.* Washington, DC: U.S. Government Printing Office.

Sierles, F. S., Chen, J. J., Messing, M. L., Besyner, J. K., & Taylor, M. A. (1986). Concurrent psychiatric illness in non-Hispanic outpatients diagnosed as having posttraumatic stress disorder. *Journal of Nervous and Mental Disease, 174,* 171–173.

Smith, E. M., North, C. S., McCool, R. E., & Shea, J. M. (1990). Acute postdisaster psychiatric disorders: Identification of persons at risk. *American Journal of Psychiatry, 147,* 202–206.

Solomon, Z., & Mikulincer, M. (1988). Psychological sequelae of war: A 2-year follow-up study of Israeli combat stress reaction casualties. *Journal of Nervous and Mental Disease, 176,* 264–269.

Southwick, S. M., Morgan, C. A., Darnell, A., Bremner, D., Nicolaou, A. L., Nagy, L. M., & Charney, D. S. (1995). Trauma-related symptoms in veterans of Operation Desert Storm: A 2-year follow-up. *American Journal of Psychiatry, 152,* 1150–1155.

Spielberger, C. D. (1980). *Preliminary manual for the State-Trait Anger Scale (STAS).* Tampa: University of South Florida Human Resources Institute.

Sutker, P. B. (1991). Introduction to the special section on issues and methods in assessment in posttraumatic stress disorder. *Psychological Assessment: A Journal of Consulting and Clinical Psychology, 3,* 517–519.

Sutker, P. B., Allain, A. N., & Winstead, D. K. (1993). Psychopathology and psychiatric diagnoses of World War II Pacific theater prisoner of war survivors and combat veterans. *American Journal of Psychiatry, 150,* 240–245.

Sutker, P. B., Davis, J. M., Uddo, M., & Ditta, S. R. (1995a) Assessment of psychological distress in Persian Gulf troops: Ethnicity and gender comparisons. *Journal of Personality Assessment, 64,* 415–427.

Sutker, P. B., Davis, J. M., Uddo, M., & Ditta, S. R. (1995b). War zone stress, personal resources, and PTSD in Persian Gulf returnees. *Journal of Abnormal Psychology, 104,* 444–452.

Sutker, P. B., Uddo, M., Brailey, K., & Allain, A. N. (1993). War-zone trauma and stress-related symptoms in Operation Desert Shield/Storm (ODS) returnees. *Journal of Social Issues, 49,* 33–49.

Sutker, P. B., Uddo, M., Brailey, K., Allain, A. N., & Errera, P. (1994). Psychological symptoms and psychiatric diagnoses in Operation Desert Storm troops serving graves registration duty. *Journal of Traumatic Stress, 7,* 159–172.

Sutker, P. B., Uddo, M., Brailey, K., Vasterling, J. J., & Errera, P. (1994). Psychopathology in war-zone deployed and non-deployed Operation Desert Storm troops assigned graves registration duties. *Journal of Abnormal Psychology, 103,* 383–390.

Sutker, P. B., Uddo-Crane, M., & Allain, A. N. (1991). Clinical and research assessment of posttraumatic stress disorder: A conceptual overview. *Psychological Assessment: A Journal of Consulting and Clinical Psychology, 3,* 5.

Sutker, P. B., Vasterling, J. J., Brailey, K., & Allain, A. N. (1995). Cognitive deficits in POW survivors: Contributing biological and psychological factors. *Neuropsychology, 9,* 118–125.

Sutker, P. B., Winstead, D. K., Galina, Z. H., & Allain, A. N. (1991). Cognitive deficits and psychopathology among former prisoners of war and combat veterans of the Korean Conflict. *American Journal of Psychiatry, 148,* 67–72.

Vasterling, J. J., Brailey, K., Constans, J. I., & Sutker, P. B. (1998). Attention and memory dysfunction in posttraumatic stress disorder. *Neuropsychology, 12,* 125–133.

Vasterling, J. J., Brailey, K., Constans, J. I., Borges, A., & Sutker, P. B. (1997). Assessment of intellectual resources in Gulf War veterans: Relationship to PTSD. *Assessment, 4,* 51–59.

Weathers, F. W., Huska, J. A., & Keane, T. M. (1991). *The PTSD checklist - military version (PCL-M).* Boston: National Center for PTSD.

Wechsler, D. (1981). *Manual for the Wechsler adult intelligence scale-revised.* New York: Psychological Corporation.

Wolfe, J. (1990). *Applying principles of critical incident debriefing to the therapeutic management of acute combat stress.* Boston: National Center for PTSD.

Wolfe, J., Brown, P. J., & Bucsela, M. L. (1992). Symptom responses of female Vietnam veterans to Operation Desert Storm. *American Journal of Psychiatry, 149,* 676–679.

Wolfe, J., Brown, P. J., & Kelley, J. M. (1993). Reassessing war stress: Exposure and the Persian Gulf War. *Journal of Social Issues, 49,* 15–31.

Yehuda, R., & McFarlane, A. C. (1995). Conflict between current knowledge about posttraumatic stress disorder and its original conceptual basis. *American Journal of Psychiatry, 152,* 1705–1713.

Chapter 8

Risk Perception and Coping

Sarah E. Spedden
Harvard University School of Public Health

All our knowledge has its origins in our perceptions.

—Leonardo da Vinci

Cognitively, emotionally, and behaviorally, we respond to the conditions that surround us. We notice some aspects of our environment and overlook others, we identify some circumstances as threatening and others as benign, and we elect to take action in some situations but not in others. Our perceptions are not always accurate and our methods of coping are not always effective. As a result, we may ignore probable sources of harm and overrate improbable sources. Furthermore, we may respond to delayed and unpredictable harmful outcomes by becoming sick or anxious. Because environmental factors so profoundly influence our health and well-being, clinicians will benefit from an understanding of the concepts that environmental risk perception and coping studies reveal.

ASPECTS OF RISK

Natural and Technological Risks

Although much of risk perception and coping research focuses on safety and health risks that originate in the physical environment, there are political, social, and economic risks that pose significant threats to well-

103

being and compete for attention and resources. The environment has both natural and technological elements. Risks with technological origins consistently cause greater distress than natural risks (Baum, Fleming, & Singer, 1983). Thus, nuclear power plants and synthetic chemicals generally elicit more concern than hurricanes and residential radon. Because data on hazard and performance of new technologies are sometimes scarce (Slovic, 1993b), there may be no experience to facilitate decisions about prevention, control, and response.

Probabilistic Risk Assessment

Risk assessment addresses the problem of predicting rare and unfamiliar outcomes. Environmental health risk assessment includes identification of hazards and effects, measurement and calculation of exposure levels, determination of who is likely to be exposed, derivation of the mathematical relationship between exposure level and unwanted outcome (the dose-response relationship), and calculation of the probability of an unwanted outcome (National Academy of Sciences, 1983). These risk assessments are primarily quantitative. They rely on quantitative data analyses and on explicit assumptions about causal relationships, statistical relationships, extrapolation of results from experimental conditions to real-life conditions, and treatment of uncertainty.

In scientific risk assessment, risk is defined as the probability of an unwanted outcome. Risk may be reported in various ways: as the annual fatality rate from a specific cause, as the lifetime probability of experiencing a particular illness, as the average number of years of life lost due to a certain cause, or as the expected frequency of a specified event. An estimate of environmental risk can be presented as the lifetime probability of dying from a particular illness resulting from a specified exposure (e.g., a 10^{-6} or 1-in-1-million) individual lifetime probability of dying of cancer caused by continuous exposure to 100 parts per million of some carcinogen in air). An estimate of environmental risk can also be presented as the probable frequency of a certain magnitude event (e.g., a flood occurring, on average, once every 1,000 years).

Intuitive Risk Assessment

People make intuitive assessments of risk all the time (Malmfors, Slovic, & Neil, 1993). These assessments apply a broad connotation of risk in which attributes and preferences are important. Intuitive risk assessments are primarily qualitative. Characteristics of the source, characteristics of the outcome, and personal preferences about the outcome are considered.

In content and in perspective, intuitive risk assessments are more inclusive than probabilistic risk assessments. The riskiness people ascribe to an agent, exposure, or activity depends not only on the probability of an unwanted outcome, but also on the potential severity of the outcome, the degree of control that is perceived possible, the acceptability and familiarity of the hazard, the extent of exposure, the scope of the effect, the judged fairness of the allocation of benefits and risks, the instinctive emotional response, the amount and type of information available, and the detectability of both exposure and effects (Gregory & Mendelsohn, 1993; Slovic 1987; Slovic, Fischhoff, & Lichtenstein, 1980; Starr, 1969).

Psychometric Studies and Perceived Risk

Because the numerical probability of physical harm is not the only component on which people base their evaluations of risk, it is important to understand the other factors that affect such evaluations. Slovic, Fischhoff, and Lichtenstein (1980) pioneered the use of psychometric evaluations to study the elements of risk perception. Respondents evaluated various qualitative characteristics of specific hazards, judged the relative riskiness of each hazard, and assessed the adequacy of current controls.

Psychometric studies indicate that the best predictor of perceived risk is the level of "dread" that a hazard elicits. Dread encompasses characteristics such as fairness, manageability, and instinctive emotional response (Brun, 1992; Slovic, Fischhoff, & Lichtenstein, 1980, 1985). In Slovic's studies, lay people assigned nuclear power a higher dread rating and considered it significantly riskier than medical x-rays even though experts estimate average annual fatalities from x-rays to be over an order of magnitude higher than from nuclear power. At first, it was thought that perhaps the lay respondents were making inaccurate estimates of the numerical probability of harm. However, these studies showed that lay estimates of average annual fatalities agreed with expert estimates. So, although nonexperts and experts may agree on numerical estimates of harm, nonexperts will judge "riskiness" based on attributes that are not included in probabilistic assessments of risk. For example, even though nonexperts may have a fairly accurate idea of the probability of death caused by nuclear power, they rate it much riskier than the experts. The risk presented by nuclear power is characterized by elements that increase the amount of dread it elicits: There is the potential for huge numbers of fatalities, the effects could have global consequences, future generations could be affected, the risks cannot be reduced easily, damage may be uncontrollable, and exposure is not voluntary.

Risk Acceptability

Both quantitative and qualitative properties are important in evaluating risk. For the nonspecialist, riskiness is characterized by both uncertainty and personal preferences and cannot be adequately captured by numerical probability alone. Risk management priorities based only on probability are often not accepted by the public; risk acceptability cannot be predicted completely by the probable outcome. That is, two alternatives posing risks with equal likelihood of an unwanted outcome may not be equally acceptable (Fischhoff, 1989). Cultural perspectives and individual preferences are particularly important in the perception of risks related to pollution and technological accidents and have been found to influence strongly both the social significance (signal potential) of an incident and the lasting characterization (stigma) that is attached to affected individuals and communities (Kasperson et al., 1988).

CULTURAL AND SOCIAL PERSPECTIVES OF RISK

The same technological advances that account for an improvement in quality of life have caused people to feel that they are living in an increasingly more dangerous world (Brun, 1992; Slovic, Fischhoff, & Lichtenstein, 1982). In a widely cited treatise on risk and culture, Douglas and Wildavsky (1982) noted that even though most people can expect greater longevity and healthier lives than their forebears, they are becoming increasingly more frightened for their lives and health.

The Influence of Technology

With the development of modern society, the framework within which people consider environmental risks has changed. New technologies require adaptation. Historical knowledge and familiarity are missing and new knowledge is limited. Because of their complexity and scale, many new technologies are under institutional custody, so control has been taken away from the individual.

Technological disasters signify a loss of control. By contrast, natural disasters represent an intrinsic and expected lack of control (Baum, Fleming, & Singer, 1983). Technological disasters are likely to be perceived as preventable, adequate control of the technology is considered to be a requirement for its use, and responsibility for technological failures is readily assigned to an individual or institution. By contrast, natural disasters tend to be blamed on fate or chance, prevention is often impossible, and the best that can be hoped is that avoidance or prediction might be possible. Earthquakes, tornadoes, and hurricanes exist without human interference or control. Technological disasters occur only because humans create technologies. A (natural) lack of control may be easier to accept than a (technological) loss of control.

Cultural norms are key factors in risk perception and coping. Laird (1989) found that the evolution of technological societies coincides with changes in how people view traditional sources of authority and power. As a society becomes more technologically developed, the public becomes less willing to trust institutions and regulators to provide protection from technological threats. As a result, members of a technological society demand a larger part in decisions that affect their health and safety (see also Jasanoff, 1986). Recent studies have found that the U.S. Environmental Protection Agency (EPA) has typically allocated resources for environmental control and cleanup to problems that the public perceives as most significant rather than to those problems that environmental experts assess as posing the highest risk to health (Breyer, 1993).

Cultural Concepts

Some researchers argue that risk is wholly a cultural construct (Douglas & Wildavsky, 1982). Cultural attributes are thought to determine which risks are acknowledged and which are ignored. Douglas and Wildavsky (1982) postulated that a predominantly sectarian world view is responsible for the emphasis that environmental pollution is currently receiving. From this sectarian cultural viewpoint, risks to safety, health, and the environment, particularly from pollution, take precedence over risks from other sources. When other worldviews predominate, different risks are emphasized. For example, if the worldview is individualistic, threats to a free market structure (mainly economic threats) take great importance. If the worldview is hierarchical, threats to the internal structure and functioning of the hierarchy are most important. Whether or not risk is entirely culturally determined will continue to be debated, but it is apparent that societal influences are important in both perception and coping.

Social Amplification of Risk

Often the public response to an event can cause indirect impacts of greater magnitude and extent than the direct impacts. This is referred to as the *social amplification of risk* (Kasperson et al., 1988). Signal potential and stigmatization are part of the process in which such amplification occurs. The social amplification of either realized risk or perceived risk has significant implications for physical and psychological health.

An event has high signal potential when it is interpreted as an indication that a technology is not sufficiently well understood, that it shows previously undetected flaws that are becoming worse, or that it may not be managed adequately (Fischhoff, 1985; Slovic, 1993b). For example, the reactor leak at Three Mile Island (TMI) in 1979 had high signal potential. It offered evidence that accidents can happen at nuclear power plants and was interpreted as an indication that the technology was not sufficiently safe to be used. The signal overshadowed the fact that the probability of physical harm caused directly by radiation exposure due to this mishap was very low (Kasperson et al., 1988; Slovic, 1992).

Places like TMI, Times Beach, and Love Canal become stigmatized. Their names no longer refer only to geographical locations but are now used to represent technological disasters. Not only do people who live in these places suffer psychological and physical trauma, but they, along with their communities, become stigmatized. Property values may decline because of actual or perceived contamination and residents may become isolated socially (Hallman & Wandersman, 1992; Slovic, 1992; Unger, Wandersman, & Hallman, 1992).

Outrage and Community Response

Individual and community action is, in many cases, motivated by the amount of outrage that a risk evokes (Sandman, 1987). Outrage increases when people feel that a risk has been imposed on them involuntarily and is out of their control, when some people seem to be benefiting at the expense of others, and when the parties considered to be responsible for protecting the public appear to have failed. The public response to Alar-treated apples was outrage. Known carcinogens have been identified in peanut butter, coffee, and mushrooms, yet apples to which Alar had been applied caused an unusually powerful public response. Apples treated with Alar had attributes that increase outrage: Alar does not occur naturally in apples, media coverage highlighted the suspicion that children were being put at risk to make apple harvesting more convenient for the growers, and the EPA had yet to take regulatory action.

The point is not whether there is a health risk from Alar (some studies indicate that there is), but that Alar became an issue while other probable threats of similar nature and similar or greater magnitude were ignored. In the case of Alar, the indirect societal and economic consequences were enormous: The outrage response resulted in social amplification of the risk. Social amplification can be used to advantage when outrage is elicited intentionally to motivate health-protective behavior. Recently, successful efforts have been made to increase outrage against drunk driving and secondhand smoke in order to mobilize public pressure for reform (Sandman, 1987).

COGNITIVE, EMOTIONAL, AND BEHAVIORAL
RESPONSES TO RISK

People function in an environment that is complex, uncertain, and perilous. Cognitive, emotional, and behavioral responses determine the success
of interactions with the surroundings. When faced with complexity and
uncertainty, people use various methods to simplify judgments and decisions. They may use decision rules, construct mental models, or rely on
outside sources of real or perceived expertise. In order to deal with either
potential or realized unwanted outcomes, people make efforts to understand the personal significance of the situation, assess their capabilities for
dealing with the consequences, regulate their emotional responses, and
often try to alter the physical and emotional impacts.

Intuitive Estimates of Risk Probability

Tversky and Kahneman (1982) identified several universal ad hoc decision
rules (heuristics) that are used by both lay people and experts when making
decisions under uncertainty (see also Malmfors, Slovic, & Neil, 1993).
These rules are based on intuition and past experience. Unfortunately,
intuition and past experience can be biased and incomplete and can lead
to conclusions and decisions that are often wrong or certainly less than
optimal. Three important heuristics have been labeled *availability, representativeness,* and *anchoring and adjustment* (Fischhoff, 1985; Tversky &
Kahneman 1982).

Availability implies that the more memorable or imaginable an occurrence is, the more frequently it is judged to occur. That is, if examples are
readily available, the frequency is judged to be high. For causes of death that
are very familiar, many people are able to give quite accurate estimates of
frequency (Slovic, Fischhoff, & Lichtenstein, 1980), but to estimate the
frequency of other fatalities, people depend on heuristics. Researchers asked
lay people to estimate the annual number of deaths from various causes in
the United States. The respondents estimated that in an average year, the
same number of deaths would be caused by tornadoes as by asthma.
However, asthma was actually responsible for more than 1,800 average
annual deaths, 20 times the number of deaths caused by tornadoes (Slovic,
Fischhoff, & Lichtenstein, 1980). A likely cause of this discrepancy is that
tornado deaths tend to make headlines and are more readily recalled, and
therefore more available, than deaths due to asthma.

Representativeness is applied when people judge an event based on
characteristics that are not predictive of either frequency or occurrence.
For example, one or two summers in which the temperatures are above
average may seem to represent a change in global climate. In reality, any

change in climate is not revealed by only one or two unusual seasons and would take years to establish (Read, Bostrom, Morgan, Fischhoff, & Smuts, 1994).

Anchoring occurs when a readily retrievable number is used as a starting point to estimate other unrelated numbers. Insufficient adjustment occurs when the estimated numbers are not as different as they should be from the anchor value. For example, people who are asked to estimate the frequency of other causes of death after being told how many people die of one cause often tend to overestimate the causes that are less frequent than the anchor event and to underestimate the causes that are more frequent than the anchor event. That is, the estimated frequencies for all of the causes of death tend to be clustered around the frequency given for the original cause.

Mental Models and Risk Perceptions

People use mental models to simplify their understanding of complex processes and relationships. Mental models can be elicited and evaluated. Researchers use open-ended interviews in which the respondents are encouraged to describe specific complex processes in as much detail as possible. Using this approach, researchers have examined the accuracy and completeness of understanding about such environmental threats as residential radon and global warming. Mental models of these processes typically have been found to be inaccurate and incomplete (Bostrom, Fischhoff, & Morgan, 1992). The mental constructs people use to make sense of hazardous processes affect how the risk is perceived. In addition, the cognitive, emotional, and behavioral efforts people make to cope with threatening or harmful situations will be shaped by their mental models.

Information, Communication, and Perception

Information about technological risk is made public for various reasons. It may be required by right-to-know legislation, health advisories may need to be issued, or civic and special interest groups may ask for support. Often people either cannot or choose not to learn enough to interpret and make decisions about technological risk. They turn instead to other sources of information. Studies have found that trust in the source of the information is a deciding factor in whether or not the information is believed. Information from a source that is not trusted may be rejected without due consideration; information from a source that is trusted may be accepted without sufficient examination (Slovic, 1993a). Other studies have indicated that when opinions are strongly held, information that is supportive of existing opinions will be remembered, whereas information that contradicts existing opinions will tend to be disregarded. Thus, well-established mental models and perceptions can be difficult to change even with solid data. Conversely, weakly held opinions are subject to change based on the way in which communications about the risk are framed. The source and the tone of the messages may be more important than the content (Slovic, 1993a). Simply providing information does not mean that it is understood, interpreted as expected, or helpful. To assist people who must deal with technological risk, it is important to understand how they appraise potentially harmful events as well as how they try to cope with them.

Stress

Environmental stress is determined by attributes of both the individual and the environment. The individual applies cognitive and behavioral strategies to deal with stress. Cognitive appraisal is used to assess resources, knowledge, options, and personal significance. Coping strategies are used to mediate emotional responses and to manage stressful situations (Folkman, 1984).

Cognitive Appraisal

People employ cognitive appraisal to evaluate and possibly to diminish distress (Folkman, 1984). Initially, a person may appraise a potential or realized harmful event as irrelevant, benign, or stressful. By categorizing the personal significance of a situation, the individual may be better able to make choices about what to attend to and what to ignore. A stressful event can entail harm or loss (e.g., an unwanted outcome that has already occurred), threat (e.g., the potential for an unwanted outcome), or challenge (e.g., an opportunity). A situation that is appraised as a threat to a significant commitment will be viewed as important to control.

Cognitive appraisal also includes an evaluation of one's physical, social, psychological, and material resources and options. An event is stressful if it appears likely to overpower one's resources. The success of coping efforts may affect the cognitive appraisal of an event which may, in turn, operate as a coping function by managing distress. Continual reappraisal of a stressful situation accompanies ongoing coping efforts. An individual's cognitive appraisal of a situation is influenced by his or her general beliefs about control. A situation with high uncertainty will be considered more controllable by a person who considers the locus of control to be internal to self and less controllable by a person who considers the locus of control to be external (Folkman, 1984).

Coping and Control

Most stressful situations elicit both emotion-focused and problem-focused coping. Emotion-focused coping can make a problem seem more manageable. Problem-focused coping is aimed at altering a stressful situation and encompasses problem solving, decision making, and direct action. Effective coping is determined by the individual's ability to evaluate control options as well as to identify the most effective coping style to apply (Folkman, 1984).

Problem-focused coping is generally believed to be more effective than emotion-focused coping at decreasing distress. Problem-focused coping entails direct action, may provide a sense of control, and may eliminate or decrease environmental stressors. However, when actual control or change of the outcome is impossible, this style of coping may result in more distress than emotion-focused coping. In a study of residents living near TMI after the nuclear accident in the late 1970s, emotion-focused coping and self-blame were associated with less distress than were problem-focused coping and denial (Baum, Fleming, & Singer, 1983). The self-blame that is indicative of emotion-focused coping is a defensive reappraisal; it serves to create the perception that future events may be controllable. The result is that the situation is viewed as a challenge and one's coping strategies are viewed as adequate to deal with future threats. In this example, the residents who applied problem-focused coping may have experienced more distress because they did not reassess the significance of the situation and accurately appraise their ability to control it. When the desired level of control is higher than what is reasonable to expect, the threat is viewed as greater. As a result, anxiety and fear may increase and interfere with problem-focused coping (Baum, Fleming, & Singer, 1983).

In another study, emotion-focused coping was associated with increased distress. In a community near a hazardous waste facility, higher levels of both individual and family distress were positively associated with emotion-focused coping. There was no association between distress and problem-focused coping. Problem-focused coping was strongly associated with concern for the welfare of children. In this case, it was concluded that distress was not necessarily decreased by problem-focused coping but that concern for the children's health was associated with greater efforts to resolve the problem. This study found that social support such as participation in community organizations helped people cope with the stressful situation. Where counseling and social services have been provided to educate residents about normal reactions to stress and have offered opportunities for people to discuss their feelings, significant benefits have been observed (Unger, Wandersman, & Hallman, 1992).

Individual Responses to Risk

Risk perceptions and distress are highly dependent on personal frames of reference. An individual's judgments, concepts, and perceptions may be biased and inaccurate. In some instances, the biases and inaccuracies can be classified and predicted because they follow known patterns in which we think about uncertainty. At other times, biases and inaccuracies result from personal knowledge, values, and aptitudes. In either case, people evaluate new information about threats to health and well-being in the framework of their judgments, concepts, and perceptions. New information may enhance personal understanding of our environment, it may be disregarded, or it may reinforce inaccurate ideas and ineffective responses. The environment may present a situation that people believe is beyond their ability to manage. Distress is typically the result. By a change in viewpoint or by direct action, an individual may be able to moderate a stressful situation and thereby, decrease the amount of distress. Mastery over a stressful situation may require considerable work by the individual who will have to examine the judgments, concepts, and perceptions that contribute to his or her distress.

CONCLUSION

Some aspects of our physical environment are more threatening than others and some interactions with our environment are more stressful than others. Many factors influence perceptions of environmental risk and choices of coping strategies. We make judgments and decisions within a framework that is described by cultural and personal values, historical and personal experience and knowledge, and institutional and personal capabilities. Over time, this framework changes. Some risks may increase while others decrease, new risks may appear as others disappear, and some risks may dominate while others become less important. As values, knowledge, and capabilities change, risk perceptions and coping options will change with them. Clinicians who evaluate and assist individuals experiencing distress from environmental interactions are confronted with the complicated, changeable, and yet, essential relationship between people and their world. The theories and findings of this relatively new field of scientific inquiry may be helpful to this process.

REFERENCES

Baum, A., Fleming, R., & Singer, J. E. (1983). Coping with victimization by technological disaster. *Journal of Social Issues, 39*(2), 117–138.

Bostrom, A., Fischhoff, B., & Morgan, M. G. (1992). Characterizing mental models of hazardous processes: A methodology and an application to radon. *Journal of Social Issues, 48*(4), 85–100.

114 SPEDDEN

Breyer, S. (1993). *Breaking the vicious circle.* Cambridge, MA: Harvard University Press.

Brun, W. (1992). Cognitive components in risk perception: Natural versus manmade risks. *Journal of Behavioral Decision Making, 5,* 117–132.

Douglas, M., & Wildavsky, A. (1982). *Risk and culture.* Berkeley: University of California Press.

Fischhoff, B. (1985). Managing risk perceptions. *Issues in Science and Technology, 2*(1, 83–96), National Academy of Sciences.

Fischoff, B. (1989). Risk: A guide to controversy. In National Research Council (Eds.), *Improving risk communication* (pp. 211–319). Washington, DC: National Academy Press.

Folkman, S. (1984). Personal control and stress and coping processes: A theoretical analysis. *Journal of Personality and Social Psychology, 46*(4), 839–852.

Gregory, R., & Mendelsohn, R. (1993). Perceived risk, dread, and benefits. *Risk Analysis, 13*(3), 259–264.

Hallman, W. K., & Wandersman, A. (1992). Attribution of responsibility and individual and collective coping with environmental threats. *Journal of Social Issues, 48*(4), 101–118.

Jasanoff, S. (1986). *Risk management and political culture: Social Research Perspectives* (Vol. 12). New York: Russell Sage Foundation.

Kasperson, R. E., Renn, O., Slovic, P., Brown, H. S., Emel, J., Goble, R., Kasperson, J., & Ratick, S. (1988). The social amplification of risk: A conceptual framework. *Risk Analysis, 8*(2), 177–187.

Laird, F. (1989). The decline of deference. *Risk Analysis, 9*(4), 543–550.

Malmfors, T., Slovic, P., & Neil, N. K. (1993). Intuitive toxicology: Expert and lay judgments of chemical risks. *Comments on Toxicology, 4*(6), 441–484.

National Academy of Sciences. (1983). *Risk assessment in the federal government: Managing the process.* Washington, DC: National Academy Press.

Read, D., Bostrom, A., Morgan, M. G., Fischhoff, B., & Smuts, T. (1994). What do people know about global climate change? 2. Survey studies of educated people. *Risk Analysis, 14*(6), 971–982.

Sandman, P. M. (1987, November). Risk communication: Facing public outrage. *EPA Journal,* 21–22.

Slovic, P. (1987). Perception of risk. *Science, 236,* 280–285.

Slovic, P. (1992). Perception of risk: Reflections on the psychometric paradigm. In S. Krimsky & D. Golding (Eds.), *Social theories of risk* (pp. 117–152). New York: Praeger.

Slovic, P. (1993a). Perceived risk, trust, and democracy. *Risk Analysis, 13*(6), 675–682.

Slovic, P. (1993b). Perceptions of environmental hazards: Psychological perspectives. In T. Garling & R. G. Golledge (Eds.), *Behavior and environment: Psychological and geographical approaches* (pp. 223–248). New York: Elsevier Science Publishers B.V.

Slovic, P., Fischhoff, B., & Lichtenstein, S. (1980). Facts and fears: Understanding perceived risk. In R. C. Schwing & W. A. Albers (Eds.), *Societal risk assessment: How safe is safe enough?* (pp. 181–214). New York: Plenum Press.

Slovic, P., Fischhoff, B., & Lichtenstein, S. (1982). Why study risk perception? *Risk Analysis, 2*(2), 83–93.

Slovic, P., Fischhoff, B., & Lichtenstein, S. (1985). Characterizing perceived risk. In R. Kates, C. Hohenemser, & J. Kasperson (Eds.), *Perilous progress: Managing the hazards of technology* (pp. 91–125). Boulder, CO: Westview Press.

Starr, C. (1969). Social benefit versus technological risk. *Science, 165,* 1232–1238.

Tversky, A., & Kahneman, D. (1982). Introduction. In D. Kahneman, P. Slovic, & A. Tversky (Eds.), *Judgment under uncertainty: Heuristics and biases* (pp. 3–22). Cambridge, MA: Cambridge University Press.

Unger, D. G., Wandersman, A., & Hallman, W. (1992). Living near a hazardous waste facility: Coping with individual and family distress. *American Journal of Orthopsychiatry, 62*(1), 55–70.

Chapter 9

Environmental Illness: Multiple Chemical Sensitivity, Sick Building Syndrome, Electric and Magnetic Field Disease

Bengt B. Arnetz
The Swedish National Institute for Psychosocial Factors and Health

There is increasing concern among scientists and laypeople regarding possible health effects of indoor and outdoor environments. Sick building syndrome, sensitivity to electric and magnetic fields, chronic fatigue syndrome (CFS), and multiple chemical sensitivity (MCS) are some of the most frequently occurring complaints. Recently the Persian Gulf War (PGW) syndrome has been identified in people who participated in the military operation in the Persian Gulf (Persian Gulf Veterans Coordinating Board, 1995).

Initially, the scientific community dismissed the new syndromes as purely psychological. Typically patients were diagnosed as suffering from some kind of somatoform disorder. The most frequently used psychiatric diagnoses are undifferentiated somatoform disorder, somatization disorder, and somatoform disorder, not otherwise specified.

The diagnostic criteria for 300.81 Undifferentiated Somatoform Disorder (American Psychiatric Association [APA], 1994, pp. 451–452) are:

1. One or more physical complaints (e.g., fatigue, loss of appetite, gastrointestinal or urinary complaints).
2. Either (a) or (b):
   (a) after appropriate investigation, the symptoms cannot be fully explained by a known general medical condition or the direct effects of a substance (e.g., a drug of abuse, a medication);

(b) when there is a general medical condition, the physical complaints or resulting social or occupational impairment is in excess of what would be expected from the history, physical examination, or laboratory findings.

3. The symptoms cause clinically significant distress or impairment in social, occupational, or other important areas of functioning.

4. The duration of the disturbance is at least 6 months.

5. The disturbance is not better accounted for by another mental disorder, (e.g., another somatoform disorder, sexual dysfunction, mood disorder, anxiety disorder, sleep disorder, or psychotic disorder).

6. The symptom is not intentionally produced or feigned (as in factitious disorder or malingering).

Typically, the established medical scientific community and patient interest groups have come to sharply diverse conclusions as to possible health risks. Clinical ecologists have entered the arena and offer a number of remedies, supposedly beneficial for the patient. In addition, patients may act as political pressure groups, sometimes bringing about political initiatives, and a number of committees have been established to review present data and reach scientifically reliable conclusions.

Meanwhile, the medical scientific community has moved from being purely skeptical to establishing research programs. One major reason for the adversarial relationship between patients and the medical community may be that patients feel ignored: Their complaints are not taken seriously. But even if complaints are classified as an undifferentiated somatoform disorder, the clinician should keep in mind that the patient *does not fake his or her symptoms*, but believes they are related to the external environment.

Regardless of the actual cause of these new disorders, the medical scientific community should strive to find an explanation for all syndromes and diseases. When faced with a clinical picture attributed to new causes, many physicians unfortunately react with disbelief rather than with respect for the patient and scientific objectivity for his or her symptoms.

A BRIEF HISTORY

Sick building syndrome, sensitivity to electric and magnetic fields, and CFS are rather new entities, but the combination of various symptoms that make up many of these new age syndromes, are not. Thus, fatigue, headache, memory disturbances, dizziness, gastrointestinal, and dermatological symptoms without any real explanation have been commonly reported throughout the medical history (Spurgeon, Gompertz, & Harrington, 1996).

Clinical disorders with mostly somatic symptoms without any identifiable pathology are common. In his thesis *Epidemic Hysteria,* Sirois (1974) identified 78 epidemics during the time period 1872 to 1972.

Saint Veit's Dances. An early example of a syndrome with no accepted medical explanation is the Saint Veit's dances of 14th-century Europe. Those stricken danced intensely until they collapsed from sheer exertion. One theory is that people danced to ward off the bubonic plague that swept through Europe during this time. In Italy, similar dances were called *tarantism.* People believed they had been bitten by a tarantula and danced to distribute the poison in the body. The name of the dancing condition and the spider originate in the southern Italian village of Taranto (Elkins, Gamino, & Rynearson, 1988).

Arsenic Poisoning. Symptoms associated with arsenic poisoning are an example of actual cases of poisoning influencing patients with similar symptoms but with no, or far less exposure to arsenic. The symptoms include fever, anorexia, melanosis, cardiac arrhythmia, upper respiratory tract symptoms, and peripheral neuropathy. Arsenic, of course, is a classic poison that was used to do away with political and other competitors. In the mid-19th century it was also used as an additive in paint and wallpaper and there was general concern that these could be poisonous. Worries spread rapidly through mass media and a number of people sought medical attention for what they considered to be arsenic-related symptoms. In addition, some actual cases of arsenic poisoning, such as the famous beer epidemics in England in 1900, and some well-publicized cases of murder by arsenic further fueled the general concern (Pershagen, 1983).

Patients who believed they had been exposed to low levels of arsenic often complained of fatigue, headache, dizziness, sleep disorders, and eye irritations, symptoms that are not usually attributed to arsenic poisoning. There was no plausible explanation; both chemists and medical scientists were at a loss to explain how arsenic in wallpaper might induce the reported symptoms.

Highly sensitive tests can now detect minute amounts of arsenic and many naturally occurring substances. At these levels the medical implications are not known. But the mere fact that we have the ability today to detect chemicals at ever lower levels is probably one reason for the continuous concern over possible health effects from low level exposure to a variety of substances.

Repetitive Strain Injury. In Australia during the 1970s a growing number of telegraph workers as well as keyboard operators reported discomfort and pain in the neck and shoulder regions and/or arms. Despite similar equipment all over Australia, the prevalence of symptoms varied from a low of 4% in Melbourne to a high of 23% in Sydney (Ferguson, 1971). In 1982, the term *repetition strain injury* (RSI) was accepted by the Australian health authorities. The RSI condition was divided into three distinct stages: Stage I comprises early onset symptoms that are reversible, Stage III is the chronic irreversible form. The diagnosis of RSI spread rapidly. Additional research indicated that there was no clear dose-response relationship between repetitive work and symptoms, and a large discrepancy between symptoms and clinical signs. The diagnosis of RSI was called into question (Hall & Morrow, 1988; Hocking, 1987). Repetitive work is common all over the world. Despite this, the spread and clinical symptomatology in Australia was unprecedented. The RSI epidemics decreased quickly following a decision in a worker's compensation case by the Australian Supreme Court, which rejected the claim.

Copying Paper Epidemic. Another example of somatic symptoms without any plausible medical explanation is the worldwide occurrence of eye, respiratory, and skin irritations purportedly from carbonless copy paper. More than 2 million tons of such paper are used annually. A number of epidemics have occurred around the globe. In most cases, the problems disappeared following factual and straightforward information (Murray, 1991). However, a detailed review of health effects from this form of paper failed to identify any general risk. Rather, other office-related factors such as dust, poor ergonomics, and so on were mentioned, in addition to a few cases of allergic tendencies (Hocking, 1987; Littlejohn, 1989).

Oral Galvanism. This syndrome is characterized by a number of vague symptoms, such as fatigue and memory disturbance, skin reactions, sleep disorders, and mood swings in addition to local effects in the mouth. The original article linking dental amalgam fillings with possible health effects was published in the 1920s (Stock, 1926). Occasional reports concerning this potential new health problem emerged once in a while in the literature, but it was not until the 1970s that there was a drastic increase in the number of patients reporting they had oral galvanism caused by their dental fillings. Sweden was especially hard hit (Molin, 1990, 1992). At first people were concerned about galvanic currents induced by the metals in their dental fillings. Subsequently, the focus of concern shifted to the spread of mercury vapors possibly resulting in systemic toxic effects. The term *micromercurialism* was invented to describe these effects. Mercury released from dental fillings has been implicated in a number of systemic disorders, including multiple sclerosis, rheumatic conditions, thyrotoxicosis, myasthenia gravis, asthma, and allergy in general. In Sweden, special clinics deal with patients suffering from oral galvanism. Elevated levels of mercury in blood or urine has been reported in patients suffering from oral galvanism (Langworth & Strömberg, 1996). In some cases, improvements of symptoms that patients related to dental amalgam fillings have been reported following the removal of the fillings. However, chronic mercury intoxication is usually noticed at urinary mercury concentrations exceeding 1,000 nmol/L, levels far higher than those reported in cases of oral galvanism (amalgam disease). Any reaction due to mercury must therefore be due to a local accumulation, to date unknown biological mechanism, or a sensitivity in certain individuals who react to levels far lower than what is currently accepted as possible (Marcusson, 1996). In double-blind randomized placebo-controlled studies, chelating therapy has been reported to effectively increase urinary excretion of mercury as compared to the group receiving placebo. However, subjective symptoms appeared to improve in both groups.

A recent review by the Swedish Board of Health and Welfare concluded that there was no scientific support for the belief that amalgam fillings caused systemic diseases. Nevertheless, the debate is likely to continue at least until other reasonable explanations for oral galvanism are found. Recent progress in the field of neuroendocrine immune interactions and awareness of the interplay between mental and physical processes may in the future offer a better understanding of oral galvanism (Reichlin, 1993).

MULTIPLE CHEMICAL SENSITIVITIES

The term *multiple chemical sensitivity* was proposed by Cullen (1987) to define a clinical syndrome described as "an acquired disorder characterized by recurrent symptoms, referable to multiple organ systems, occurring in response to demonstrable exposure to chemically unrelated compounds at doses far below those established in the general population to cause harmful effects. No single widely accepted test of physiologic function can be shown to correlate with symptoms" (p. 656).

The proposed research criteria for MCS are a change in health status identified by the patient, symptoms triggered regularly by multiple stimuli, symptoms experienced for at least 6 months, a defined set of symptoms reported by patients, symptoms that occur in three or more organ systems, and exclusion of patients with other medical conditions.

Psychiatric conditions are not exclusion criteria (Cullen, 1987; Rest, 1992).

The diagnosis of MCS does not require a specific event of high-dose chemical exposure. Rather, the patient needs to identify a point in time when he or she felt well and a subsequent time when he or she did not. This subjective change in health status has no time limit but could have occurred recently or decades ago. Symptoms should be triggered most of the time by multiple chemical stimuli. The patient does not have to react all of the time or even to the same chemical.

Complaints can be classified into three groups: central nervous system, irritative, and gastrointestinal. Symptoms typically associated with MCS are headaches, general weakness, loss of concentration, memory disturbances, eye irritations, cough, sore throat, diarrhea, and other unspecific complaints.

The requirement that symptoms should be of at least 6-months' duration or more has been chosen somewhat arbitrarily. However, the same time limit is being used for somatization disorder and CFS. The requirement that patients report a set of symptoms has not been defined more specifically. For a diagnosis of MCS, symptoms do not have to be identical in all patients. In my experience, individual patients' symptoms may also change over time.

The criteria for MCS are still rather broad and vague, which poses an obvious problem. Self-reported illness from low-level exposure to various environmental chemicals has resulted in an intensive scientific and laypeople debate over the existence and nature of the health problems (Ashford & Miller, 1991; Bell, Schwartz, Bootzin, & Wyatt, 1997).

Theories of the pathogenics of MCS are numerous. Clinical ecologists commonly favor a chemical/physical explanation (Randolph, 1978). They believe that MCS is caused by toxic damage to, or other interference with, the immune system from environmental chemicals, foods, and drugs (Bell, 1982; Levin & Byers, 1987; Terr, 1994). In numerous controlled studies, however, researchers have been unable to demonstrate any consistent change, malfunctioning, or disorder of the immune system. MCS thus differs from common allergic conditions both in terms of symptomatology and clinical and immunological findings.

According to toxicological principles, the toxic effects from low doses of chemicals should be the same in hypersensitive patients as those observed in less sensitive patients at considerably higher doses. Formaldehyde, a common culprit for MCS symptoms, is produced during naturally occurring intermediary processes in the body at far higher levels than is the case from inhaling polluted air (Wolf, 1994). Wolf calculated that an adult male daily uses 58,000 mg formaldehyde created in the intermediary metabolism. The same adult breathing ambient air with a formaldehyde concentration of 0.2 ppm would achieve a system load of formaldehyde of approximately 5 mg.

The initial theory, that environmental agents act as haptens and produce immunoglobulin G, has not been confirmed in controlled studies (Rea, Suits, & Smiley, 1978; Wolf, 1994). However, one study (Thrasher, Broughton, & Madison, 1990) reported an activation of the immune system following long-term inhalation of formaldehyde. In one study, patients with MCS were reported to have lower levels of interleukin 1 than controls, but these results, according to the authors themselves, may have been due to methodological problems (Simon, Stockbridge, Claypolle, & Rosenstock, 1993).

The difficulty in establishing a common pathophysiologic basis for MCS or identifying agents that reproducibly initiate symptoms, has resulted in recommendations that chemical provocation tests should be used to a greater extent. However, to design a valid provocation study not only requires meticulously controlled exposure chambers, but also the use of appropriate odors at the right levels and in the proper sequence and combinations. My research group is in the process of setting up a low-level chemical exposure chamber to further assess possible psychophysical and biological effects from such exposures. Effects from concurrent environmental loads, for example, mental stress combined with low levels of chemical odor, will also be studied.

Hypersensitivity to odors has recently been suspected as one possible mechanism behind MCS. Stimulation of the olfactory sense results in sensations that can be characterized by odor and pungency, that is, prickling, irritating, tingling, fresh or burning. The threshold for odor is typically lower than for pungency (Cometto-Muniz & Cain, 1994). Specific threshold levels for pungency have been studied in subjects clinically diagnosed as anosmics (Bell, Schwartz, Peterson, & Amend, 1993). In general, subjects show a pattern of sensitivity, and a person highly sensitive to one specific factor also tends to be more sensitive to other substances. For odors there is a wide variation in the threshold level between individuals. It is not known whether there is an additive effect from a mixture of substances. People are rarely exposed to only one chemical in otherwise pure ambient air, but most provocation studies have not taken this possibility into consideration.

In one study (Bell et al., 1993), more than 600 college-age students rated whether the smell of pesticides, car exhaust, drying paint, new carpeting, and perfume made them "feel ill." Subjects also filled out the 37-item Weinberger Adjustment inventory, which includes scales for depression, anxiety, and repression. In addition, the Marlow Crowne Social Desirability scale, a shyness index, a mastery index, and a brief health and symptoms scale were included in the assessment. As many as 66% reported feeling ill to a moderate or marked degree from the smell of at least one of the five categories. Fourteen percent reported feeling ill from the smell of at least four chemicals. Among the most sensitive group, 98% identified pesticides to be problematic, 90% paint, 70% car exhaust, 69% new carpeting, and 65% perfume. Women were found to be more sensitive than men. Hayfever was also more common among subjects reporting extreme sensitivity to chemicals. The prevalence of asthma, ulcers, or thyroid disease was similar across various sensitivity groups. Symptoms typical of MCS (e.g., irritability, insomnia, difficulty concentrating, memory disturbances, daytime grogginess, and headache), correlated significantly but weakly ($r <$ .2) with symptoms elicited by smelling four of the five chemicals tested. Correlation between symptoms and sensitivity to the smell of new carpeting was not demonstrated. The association between total sensitivity scores and depression, anxiety, and shyness was also significant but at correlation levels of less than 0.2. There was a significant association between the various chemical groups with regard to feeling ill.

The study was done on college students with no history of multiple chemical exposure, but it pointed out a subgroup that reported extreme sensitivity to an array of various chemical smells. Is this the subgroup from which MCS patients are subsequently recruited? Would this group be equally sensitive in real life? Questions such as these will have to be addressed in controlled chemical provocation studies and subjects followed longitudinally over time.

Bell and her coworkers did not find subjects scoring high on the chemical sensitivity rating scale to be more depressed. This is in line with the outcome of another study (Fiedler, Maccia, & Kipen, 1992) of MCS patients that found no support for the notion that MCS cases more frequently have a history of psychiatric disorders.

In a recent study (Bell et al., 1997) elderly individuals classified as having a higher degree of chemical odor intolerance (based on self-rating) were compared to those with a lower degree of intolerance with regard to time-dependent sensitization of heart rate and blood pressure over multiple laboratory sessions. Results indicate increased sympathetic tone in the cardiovascular system at rest over multiple measurements in subjects with higher intolerance to low-level chemical odor. These results are in line with other studies indicating heightened neurosympathetic reactivity to environmental stimuli in individuals suffering from environmental illness. According to the neural-sensitization model, MCS patients have an amplified reactivity to low-level chemicals, mediated via the olfactory-limbic pathway and subsequently impacting on a range of neuroendocrine and immune systems in the body.

A number of clinicians and researchers believe that MCS is one of several syndromes of psychiatric or psychological origin (Gots, 1993; Hotopf, 1994; Simon et al., 1993). MCS is viewed as fulfilling the criteria for undifferentiated somatoform disorder. The support for this belief is mostly based on case studies and on noncontrolled clinical studies (Brodsky, 1983a; Rosenberg, Freedman, Schmaling, & Rose, 1990). In one study of 21 patients considered to have disabilities disproportionate to their chemical exposure history, 11 were reported to fulfill the *DSM–III* criteria for somatoform disorder and another 3 for posttraumatic stress disorder (PTSD; Schottenfeld & Cullen, 1986). However, depression and anxiety disorders are diagnosed in 5% to 45% of traditional medical illness, and as many as 65% to 71% of depressed patients have concomitant chronic medical conditions (Katon & Sullivan, 1990; Wells, Rogers, Burnam, Greenfield, & Ware, 1991).

Depression and anxiety disorders may thus be the result of the MCS condition or occur independently of MCS. It is also known that depression and feelings of not being in control make subjects more susceptible to reporting pain. Depression may consequently make subjects more likely to report symptoms from various organ systems, but not necessarily make them more sensitive to various chemicals.

In their study, Fiedler et al. (1992) used carefully defined diagnostic criteria for MCS. Subjects were screened for possible medical, psychiatric, immunological, and neuropsychological changes. The study differed from many others in that subjects were not part of a cluster being investigated for MCS. None was under treatment by a clinical ecologist nor belonged to a clinical MCS support group. Results did not support the notion of prior psychiatric morbidity, none complained of food intolerance and there were no unusual or unexpected immunological findings. Memory disturbances were not typical unless tasks were demanding, and poor performance was caused more by difficulties learning than by problems retrieving stored information.

The absence of prior psychiatric morbidity contrasts with other studies of MCS. In one study (Simon, Katon, & Sparks, 1990), 7 out of 13 patients had a prior psychiatric history. (Possibly these findings may be due to different selection criteria and different diagnostic work-ups.) MCS patients exhibited more signs of depression and anxiety, although almost all of them considered these symptoms secondary to their MCS. The symptoms were similar to those found among workers exposed to solvents who have a significantly longer history of exposure to much higher concentrations of chemicals. MCS patients also scored higher on the Psychosocial Adjustment to Illness Survey Self-Report, indicating that they have more problems adjusting to the demands of family, friends, and work than do patients with more traditional diagnoses (Fiedler et al., 1992). The absence of any clear medical explanation for the symptoms of MCS, the lack of any effective treatment and a perceived lack of support from the medical establishment may also enhance an individual's tendency to react with anxiety or depression once MCS symptoms have developed (Fiedler, Kipen, DeLuca, Kelly-McNeil, & Natelson, 1996).

A study (Black, Rathe, & Goldstein, 1990) concerning the way medical practitioners view environmental illness (EI) recruited patients believed to suffer from chronic yeast disease (27%), environmental allergy syndrome (69%) and MCS (15%). Subjects were recruited from EI support groups, from psychiatric and occupational medicine clinics, and through a hospital newsletter and a flyer. Thus, the recruitment base was somewhat different from that used in prior studies (Brodsky, 1983; Pearson, Rix, & Bentley, 1983; Stewart & Raskin, 1985; Terr, 1986).

The 26 MCS cases were compared with a community-based reference group of 46. All subjects were evaluated using the Diagnostic Interview Schedule (DIS), which is commonly used to identify current and prior mental disorders, using criteria from the *Diagnostic and Statistical Manual of Mental Disorders* (*DSM–III*; APA, 1980; Robins, Helzer, Croughan, & Ratcliff, 1981) and the Structured Interview for *DSM–III* personality disorders (Strangl, Pfohl, Zimmerman, Bowers, & Corenthal, 1985). Questions were also asked about work, social and family history, education, illness behavior, somatic concerns, and hypochondriacal beliefs. A symptoms checklist was included among a range of other assessments. EI patients typically complained of respiratory problems, neurological symptoms, including headaches, fatigue or weakness, pain, and psychiatric symptoms, mostly depression.

The onset of EI was triggered by a wide array of factors. Most typical were exposure to fumes at home or work, exposure to insecticides or pesticides, hormonal shifts due to oral contraceptives, pregnancy, antibiotics, and psychological stress. Two thirds of the patients were under the care of a clinical ecologist. The most common treatments consisted of avoiding offending substances, special diets, megavitamin doses, oxygen and charcoal filter masks, spending time in chemically "clean" rooms, and symptom neutralization through agents such as histamine. Recommendations for relocation or remodeling of at least one room in the home were also common. Only 12% were satisfied with their prior traditional medical treatment, whereas 73% were pleased with the treatment they received from clinical ecologists.

Compared to controls, patients with the diagnosis of EI had a significantly higher lifetime prevalence of mood disorders, primarily major depression. The odds ratio for mood disorder for EI patients, compared to the reference group, was 6.3:1, which suggests that EI patients were substantially more likely to have suffered from an earlier mood disorder. However, only 30% of EI patients, as compared to 7% of the reference group, actually had a history of lifetime mood disorder. Anxiety disorders were also significantly more common (odds ratio of 3.7:1). No specific subcategory of anxiety disorders stood out, though panic disorder and agoraphobia tended to be more common among EI patients. Somatization disorder occurred in 19% of the EI patients compared to none in the reference group. Any mood, anxiety, or somatoform disorder occurred in 65% of the EI patients as compared to 28% in the reference groups, yielding an odds ratio of 4.8:1. At the time of the investigation, 36% of patients with a history of a mood or anxiety disorder were free of current symptoms. A number of EI patients were reported to be hypochondriacs, a diagnosis not found in the DIS (Robins et al., 1981).

In one double-blind provocation study, using an environmental chamber, the authors failed to demonstrate a "reliable response pattern across a series of challenges" (Staudenmayer, Selner, & Buhr, 1993). Subjects with EI have in some, but far from all studies, exhibited enhanced reactivity to odor or pungency (Kilburn, 1993). One study found that MCS patients have signs of inflammation in the nasal cavity (Meggs & Cleveland, 1993). They also have a higher respiratory rate when exposed to chemicals and exhibit an increased nasal airway resistance compared to controls (Doty, Deems, Frye, Pelberg, & Shapiro, 1988). Whether this is due to a conditioned reflex, that is, subjects have previously been conditioned to react with specific symptoms following exposure to specific odors, or whether it is merely an effect of neurophysiological hyperreactivity, in line with the neural-sensitization model, is unclear.

It has been postulated that MCS is a consequence of kindling, that is, a time-dependent sensitization of olfactory-limbic neurons (Bell, Miller, & Schwartz, 1992). Through repeated low-level chemical exposure, there is increased sensitivity of the olfactory-limbic system so that symptoms develop even at rather low levels. An interesting aspect of involving the limbic system is that psychological stress may function as a facilitator in lowering the kindling threshold. Many MCS patients report psychological stress factors concurrent with the perceived precipitating event. (For further theories surrounding environmental conditioning, see the section on hypersensitivity to electricity and magnetic fields, p. 132).

There is support for the notion that at least a subgroup of EI patients suffer from mood and/or anxiety disorders in addition to somatization disorders. However, there is still a number of patients with no prior or current psychiatric diagnosis. Whether these make up a special subgroup or not needs to be further investigated. Assessment of lifetime cumulative exposure to chemicals has not been attempted for MCS patients either. There are no studies attempting to assess psychiatric health prior to, versus following, the onset of EI. It is not inconceivable that some of the psychiatric symptoms are a consequence of EI rather than its cause. A number of symptoms may also be paraphenomena, that is, they occur both in psychiatric and EI patients. Psychiatric diagnoses are quite common among patients with medical conditions, especially when they are seen in clinical settings (Katon & Sullivan, 1990; Schottenfeld & Cullen, 1986).

In order to come to grips with diagnostic and other problems, better reference groups need to be identified, for example, patients in somatic wards, and EI subjects. They need to be followed over time. A number of the symptoms fluctuate dramatically with time and the focus of a patient's complaints may migrate between different organs. The fact that some EI patients also have greater difficulty in adjusting to psychosocial demands, such as family and work, may make them more sensitive to stress. The clinician who is confronted with EI patients enters into partly uncharted territory. There are no definitive studies to consult and no proven treatment plans. Sensitivity to stress can be attenuated through teaching the patients internal control, stress management techniques, and means to feel more in charge of their daily life.

EI patients are usually highly dissatisfied with traditional medical care and complain about the attitude of physicians to their disorder. It is imperative that their criticism is addressed. With proper respect, active listening, early intervention, and an open-minded discussion about facts and opinions, both those held by the patient and by the clinician, many EI patients recover instead of progressing further into their medical and social handicap.

SICK BUILDING SYNDROME

During the last decade there has been a growing interest in the sick building syndrome. Typically, employees in an office building complain of upper respiratory irritation, eye irritation, dizziness, and fatigue. Litigations are increasing and the U.S. Environmental Protection Agency, state health departments, and the American Society of Heating, Refrigeration and Air Conditioning Engineers (ASHRAE) have put out guidelines for how to achieve healthy indoor air in buildings and prevent the development of sick building syndrome.

Indoor air quality may be compromised by the presence of pollutants, contaminants, and irritants, inadequate ventilation, and other factors. Some of the major environmental contributors are secondary tobacco smoke, organic vapors from carpeting and upholstery, formaldehyde from building materials and furniture, and paint. Fungi, viruses, and bacteria may grow and spread through the air-conditioning system. A striking example is the 1976 outbreak of Legionnaire's disease in Philadelphia. Even though there are a number of factors that should be checked to ensure healthy buildings, it has been difficult to link specific indoor air pollutants to health complaints.

Large groups of clinicians and researchers remain skeptical as to the specificity of the sick building syndrome. Nevertheless, a growing number of workers complain about poor indoor air quality. The World Health Organization (WHO; 1983) expert group defined the sick building syndrome as consisting of a combination of general, mucosal, and skin symptoms. Common symptoms are eye, nose, and throat irritation, sensation of dry mucous membranes and skin, erythema, mental fatigue, headache, high frequency of airway infections, cough, hoarseness, wheezing, itching, nonspecific respiratory hypersensitivity, nausea, and dizziness. It is apparent that a number of the symptoms are nonspecific and overlap with other syndromes, such as MCS and hypersensitivity to electric and magnetic fields (Arnetz, Berg, & Arnetz, 1997).

Reports indicate that in apparent outbreaks of office-associated symptoms, a specific cause can be identified in some 25% of cases. Causes include microbial contamination of the air-conditioning system, insufficient ventilation, and intake of outside air contaminated by car exhaust fumes. In some surveys as many as 50% to 80% of office workers report symptoms characteristic of the sick building syndrome (Norback, Michel, & Widstrom, 1990). In many instances, ventilation systems have been extensively rebuilt. Symptomatic workers are less productive and have higher absentee rates (Menzies et al., 1993). Because most studies of sick building syndrome have been done in a noncontrolled, nonblinded fashion, it is difficult to draw reliable conclusions as to the underlying causes.

The study by Menzies et al. (1993) tested the hypothesis that increasing the supply of air from 20 ft^3 (0.57 m^3) to 50 ft^3 (1.4 m^3) per minute per person would reduce symptoms. The study was a randomized, double-blind crossover trial. Supply of outside air was manipulated over time in four buildings: In each building, at a given time, one area received a higher outdoor air supply (1.4 m^3 per minute per person), while the other received the lower amount (0.57 m^3). More than 1,500 workers responded to detailed questionnaires covering a range of issues, including personal, smoking, medical, and work histories. Their state of mind was tested using the Bradburn (1969) index of emotional well-being. Detailed questions of symptoms characteristic for sick building syndrome were included in questionnaires. The surveys were repeated during a 6-week study period. Males, and subjects with a history of atopic illness, were less likely to participate or complete the study. Subjects who completed all 6 weekly questionnaires ($n = 637$) were more likely to be female, younger, and work in open areas in clerical positions. Indoor air was analyzed for carbon dioxide content, temperature, relative humidity, air velocity, and contamination/pollutant levels (formaldehyde, nitrogen oxides, carbon monoxide, total volatile organic compounds, total and viable airborne fungal spores, and total airborne dust).

In all buildings, reducing outdoor air supply resulted in a measurable increase in formaldehyde and volatile organic substances. Work site carbon dioxide also changed as planned during the two conditions. However, temperature, air velocity, or humidity at the work site did not change significantly. There were no significant associations between air supply and subjective ratings of overall satisfaction with the indoor environment. Subjects with more sick building symptoms were significantly more likely to rate the overall environment as poor and to rate present environmental conditions as worse compared to the previous week, regardless of the actual situation. The overall proportion of subjects reporting symptoms of sick building syndrome declined over the 6-week study period. There was no difference in symptoms associated with the difference in air supply and no statistically significant difference in the number of subjects with mucosal irritation or systemic symptoms. Sick building symptoms were related to relative humidity, but not to temperature or air velocity, nor carbon dioxide concentration. There was a statistically significant association between symptoms and environmental ratings and study week, but not with the concentration of carbon dioxide, humidity, temperature, or air velocity. Females and younger subjects reported more symptoms of sick building syndrome, as did those with a history of atopic illness, and those using computers more than 4 hours a day.

The study's failure to find any significant association between objective measures and symptoms may be due to a number of reasons, detailed in the study in question (Menzies et al., 1993). The study concerned buildings not specifically defined as sick, but that had the characteristics typical of sick buildings. The WHO defined sick buildings as those with an "excess" frequency of symptoms among its occupants (WHO, 1983). There is no established norm for the frequency of sick building symptoms in typical office buildings, and the reported frequency of symptom among workers in buildings defined as sick, is similar to those defined as healthy (Burge, Hedge, Wilson, Bass, & Robertson, 1987; Norback et al., 1990).

One major limitation of studies of sick building syndromes is the lack of reliable clinical endpoints. In a majority of the randomized double-blind studies, symptom ratings done by subjects appear to be one of the few real outcome measures. In contrast, a number of objective measures are used with regard to exposure. There is a need to look at outcome measures using both subjective and objective ratings. In most instances, psychiatric rating scales show no difference between subjects affected with the sick building syndrome and their coworkers in the same building. Rather, buildings diagnosed as sick appear to have a different psychological climate affecting the work force, when compared to buildings considered healthy (Bauer et al., 1992; Skov, Valbjorn, & Pedersen, 1989).

Norback and Edling (1991) reported on risk factors for sick building symptoms in the general population. In a random sample of adults, such factors as childhood exposure to environmental tobacco smoke, urban upbringing, urban residency at present, preschool children at home, history of atopic illness, work with video display units, work dissatisfaction, and climate of cooperation at work were all associated with the occurrence of symptoms. Factors not related to symptoms were age of building, type of building, mechanical ventilation, signs of moisture, and evidence of mold.

A number of factors related to buildings and the quality of indoor air have been shown to correlate with sick building syndromes. Nevertheless, there does not seem to be any systematic difference in indoor air quality between "healthy" and "sick" buildings (Finnegan & Pickering, 1986; Stenberg, 1989). Even in severely affected buildings, the indoor air is usually considered acceptable (Skov et al., 1989). In part, this may be due to the fact that the wrong things are measured, that there is no true correlation with the physical environment, or that most of the symptoms are due to a complex interaction among physical, chemical, and psychosocial factors.

Five major categories of building-related illness are generally recognized (Bardana, Montanaro, & O'Hallaren, 1988). Among these, four are rather well-defined clinically: hypersensitivity pneumonitis, asthma and allergic rhinitis, infectious syndromes, and dermatitis. However, these four categories have been estimated to explain only about one third of outbreaks. As demonstrated earlier, the remainder of the cases consists of mucous membrane irritation and general symptoms like headache, fatigue, sinus problems, itching, burning and/or watery eyes, dry and irritated throat, nausea, dizziness, and abnormal taste and odors (Boxer, 1990). These symptoms are usually transient, worsen as the workday progresses, and improve typically during the weekends or when affected people leave the building. Even though inadequate ventilation has been suggested to be the culprit in as many as 53% of the cases assessed by the National Institute for Occupational Safety and Health (NIOSH; 1989), in 13% the cause was unknown.

The Psychosocial Perspective

Advocates for the theory that sick building syndrome is a form of mass psychogenic illness point out certain characteristics. There is usually a rapid spread of symptoms, one worker or a group of workers becomes ill and blames the disease on some physical factor in the workplace. As anxiety spreads, other workers also fall ill with numerous symptoms. The most common trigger of sick building syndrome appears to be odor and perception of the indoor air as "stuffy." The threshold for detection of odor is mostly well below air concentrations associated with toxic effects.

Most published outbreaks of sick building syndrome appear in office buildings and to a greater than expected extent affect white-collar workers. One study (Colligan & Murphy, 1979) suggested the following working definition for contagious psychogenic illness: "the collective occurrence of a set of physical symptoms and related beliefs among two or more individuals in the absence of an identifiable pathogen" (p. 82). The definition appears to be of relevance for some outbreaks of sick building syndromes, albeit not for all of them.

Odors signal a potential threat to homeostasis and may cause anxiety. Symptoms of anxiety may manifest themselves as hyperactivity of the autonomic system like palpitations, shortness of breath, dizziness, nausea, dry mouth, hot flashes, and diarrhea. Musculoskeletal symptoms such as trembling and fatigue are also common. Central nervous system effects include difficulty concentrating and irritability. For most people these symptoms are transient. For a smaller group, however, the symptoms are chronic, referred to as generalized anxiety disorders. Panic disorders, with shortness of breath, dizziness, palpitations, trembling, and so on, also fall within the group of anxiety disorders.

Despite these findings there is rarely a thorough psychiatric/psychological work-up in cases of sick building syndrome. Various reliable and calibrated instruments are used to assess physical/chemical properties of the indoor air quality. But the use of well-researched, validated, and reliable questionnaires for psychiatric/psychological profiling is quite limited. Furthermore, when it is suggested that psychosocial factors may be a contributing factor, many patients tend to shy away from the subject, even react with outrage, and disregard that avenue of investigation.

Colligan and Murphy (1979) reviewed a number of outbreaks defined as mass psychogenic illness. Affected workers typically were bothered by production pressure and noise, had more sickdays, scored higher on the hysteria subscale of the MMPI, perceived work as more boring and repetitious, and complained more often of temperature variations than did nonaffected controls. Contributing stress factors may include job insecurity and lack of control over work and immediate working conditions.

Mayou (1975) suggested that contagious psychogenic illness appears to be a social phenomenon affecting a certain proportion of the normal population under psychological and/or physical stress. Subjects with poor coping strategy may be more susceptible to reacting with psychosomatic symptoms in times of stress. Poor labor–management relations have also been implicated in some outbreaks (Colligan & Murphy, 1979), as have stressful conditions at work (Arnetz, 1996). Psychophysiological reactions to stressful conditions are well described in the literature. However, in many offices there is an unwillingness to discuss psychosocial aspects of work, as well as individual worker's emotional state. Pent up psychosocial stress, frustration with working conditions and with life in general may then take the form of mass psychogenic illness focusing on an environmental culprit.

If sick building syndrome is partly related to mass psychogenic illness, stress level prior to the outbreak is an important factor (Colligan & Murphy, 1979). Straightforward information and support of individual workers may limit outbreaks. If workers are told what is known about sick building syndrome in general and their workplace in particular, if they perceive support and are able to understand something about mind–body interaction, the spread of the problem may well decrease. In a Swedish study (Keisu, Lille, & Hedström, 1991), workers' concern about possible health effects of video display units (VDUs) decreased after presentation and discussion of state-of-the-art information, compared to a reference group receiving no such structured information. The study also pointed out the importance of the media in influencing workers' beliefs. Health professionals play an important role in providing untainted facts.

In a prospective study, Arnetz (1996) assessed the impact of a controlled stress reduction program on psychosocial well-being, physiological stress measures, and the perception of the indoor air quality. Following baseline assessments, 61 advanced telecommunication systems design engineers participated in a stress management program, while another 50 served as the reference group. Follow-up measurements were sampled immediately after the 3-month program, and after an additional 5 months. The program effectively reduced the stress-sensitive hormone prolactin, as well as perceived mental stress in the intervention group, compared to the reference group. Perception of indoor air quality (temperature, dry air, poor ventilation, draught) did not change significantly over time. The degree of intellectual exhaustion was marginally associated ($p = .06$) with perception of poor indoor air. Enhanced autonomy and influence over work significantly increased satisfaction with indoor air quality, as did perceived social support at work.

Coping style (intellectual, problem-oriented, or emotional) and rating on a scale for moodiness and depressive tendencies were not related to perceived indoor air quality. This suggests that work-related factors, as well as mental energy might covary with the perception of the quality of the indoor air. Reducing stress per se did not impact significantly on the perception, though the intervention group showed a tendency of rating the air quality as somewhat better than the reference group. Thus, the way a person fits into a specific environment may be an important factor to consider, not merely the environment per se. However, the Arnetz (1996) study also warns against explaining all sick building outbreaks as mass psychogenic illness and stress related.

It is of interest to look at the effects of controlled interventions even though the underlying reasons for sick building syndrome are not yet convincingly identified. There have been quite a few experimental interventions focusing on the physical and chemical aspects of the sick building syndrome. Eighteen studies are reviewed in a recent dissertation (Stenberg, 1994). Remedial measures ranged from manipulating the humidity, ionizing the air, changing air flow velocity, varying exposure to n-decane and carbon dioxides, changing temperature, lighting, work week, and the proportion of recirculated air. Significant associations between symptoms and environmental conditions were reported in four out of four open studies. When experimental subjects, although not necessarily the researchers, were blinded for the experiment, some improvement was observed in 9 out of 12 studies. In four double-blind studies, three reported improvement with better environmental conditions. The effects of various remedial measures in real life are reported in reference (Andersson & Stridh, 1991). The sick building cases concerned both office buildings, schools, and residential buildings. In all instances, there were significant complaints with regard to stuffy and foul-smelling air, mucosal irritation, skin symptoms, and general symptoms, such as fatigue. After remedial work, the situation most often improved considerably and in some cases problems disappeared altogether (Cynkier, Söderman, & Kolmodin-Hedman, 1994). In one residential building, where more than $40,000 was spent per apartment, no real improvement was noticed especially with regard to odor and dust. However, in these full-scale interventions there has been no double-blind study.

Obviously, it is difficult to conduct double-blind studies in real life, especially in residential areas. Nevertheless, considering the scope of the problem and the human, social, and economic impact, innovative ways to design double-blind, controlled real-life interventions should be encouraged. Re-analysis of symptoms in air-conditioned office buildings has also indicated a consistent pattern of increased work-related headaches and upper respiratory/mucous membrane symptoms (Mendell & Smith, 1990).

Conclusion

There are supportive data linking the indoor environment to actual symptoms but psychosocial factors, personality factors, and sociodemographic factors appear to be modifiers of such a relationship. The lack of any consistent and systematic differences in indoor air quality in sick versus healthy buildings suggests that there are other contributing factors as well. Some of these appear to be influence over work, social support, and individual predisposition. However, there is to date no scientific support for the notion that sick building syndrome is merely another version of mass psychogenic illness. Among outbreaks the relative importance of indoor air quality versus nonair issues may differ significantly. It is therefore imperative that outbreaks be better defined, that reliable measures to assess both physical/chemical and psychosocial and psychiatric factors be used to a greater extent. Better objective measures of health outcomes, not merely subjective ratings, should be developed. It is also of interest to note the relative lack of psychosocial interventions against sick building syndrome, despite numerous papers indicating an association between the physical/chemical and the psychosocial environment.

HYPERSENSITIVITY TO ELECTRIC AND MAGNETIC FIELDS AND VDUs

Reports of dermatological complaints from people exposed to VDUs first appeared in Norway (Nilsen, 1982) from concerned workers in a telecommunication company. Symptoms subsided following an initial investigation by the Norwegian Occupational Health service that failed to find any clear association to VDU work. Later reports appeared from the United Kingdom (Rycroft & Calnan, 1984), the United States (Feldman, Eaglstein, & Johnson, 1985), Sweden (Berg, 1988; Lagerholm 1986), and Japan (Matsunaga, Hayakawa, Ono, & Hisanaga, 1988). Most patients had rosacea or rosacea-like dermatitis. A large-scale epidemiological study showed that although subjective facial skin symptoms were more common among VDU-exposed workers, there were no significant differences between exposed and nonexposed groups in objective skin signs and skin disease (Berg, Lidén, & Axelsson, 1990).

The literature reports both an association between subjective skin signs and VDU use (Bergqvist, Knave, Voss, & Wibom, 1992; Bergqvist & Wahlberg, 1994; Knave, Wibom, Voss, Hedström, & Bergqvist, 1985; Lidén & Wahlberg, 1985), and no evidence of such a correlation (Frank, 1983; Koh et al., 1991). Only one controlled study found a tendency for an association among seborrhoeic eczema, erythema, and VDU use (Bergqvist & Wahlberg, 1994), but the majority of studies have found no scientific support for a causal link between VDU work and skin disease (Berg, Hedblad, & Erhardt, 1990). Another study found that school teachers and support staff in schools report significantly more skin symptoms than do office workers exposed to VDUs (Koh et al., 1991). In a histopathological study there were no specific histological changes in the facial skin of VDU operators that differed from those of controls (Berg, Hedblad, & Erhardt, 1990).

Epidemiological studies have attempted to link VDU-associated symptoms to electric and magnetic fields. However, most studies have found no correlation, or only a weak one, between symptoms and exposure, and despite much research no clear association between VDU work and skin disorders has been demonstrated. Despite the lack of positive findings there has been a continuous move to equip VDUs with "protective" screens, which only shield against electric and not against magnetic fields. Recently, Swedish courts have ruled that there is no scientific support that VDU exposure per se would be hazardous to the skin.

As a direct outgrowth of VDU-associated skin symptoms there has been an increase in people complaining about general hypersensitivity to electric and magnetic fields. Characteristically, they complain of headaches, fatigue, skin sensations including itching, burning, redness, and swelling, memory disturbance, nausea, and mucosal irritation. In many ways, the array of symptoms overlaps those of multiple chemical sensitivity, sick building syndrome, and CFS. The one clear difference is that symptoms are attributed to electric and magnetic fields, to radio frequency waves, and lately also to cellular phones (Buffler, 1996). Most studies have failed to establish a link between the macroelectromagnetic environment and skin symptoms, one important ingredient in the hypersensitivity syndrome (Arnetz, Berg, Anderzén, & Lundeberg, 1995).

One avenue to enhance our understanding of the possible association between electromagnetic fields and hypersensitivity symptoms is to carry out double-blind electromagnetic provocation studies, using healthy as well as hypersensitive subjects. In these provocations, subjects are exposed to more or less well-defined electric and magnetic fields in a laboratory setting and the development of hypersensitivity symptoms is monitored. To date, the bulk of these studies has been negative, and no statistically significant association between exposure and symptoms has been demonstrated (Andersson et al., 1996; Franzén, Paulson, & Wennberg, 1992; Hamnerius et al., 1992; Sandstrom, Stenberg, & Hansson Mild, 1989; Swanbeck & Bleeker, 1989).

Double-blind provocation tests have also been used as an ingredient in a treatment package for electromagnetic hypersensitivity. Approximately 160 patients were challenged in Swedish studies through the end of 1996. Out of those, one single subject was able to correctly identify the on–off setting four times in a row, a result that requires further testing.

One provocation study is an exception (Rea et al., 1991). Among patients with multiple problems, including MCS and electric hypersensitivity, a subgroup was identified that reacted psychophysiologically in 100% of the provocation tests as compared to a healthy control group that reacted psychophysiologically in 0% of the tests. There are limitations to the study: The experimental situation may not have been completely double-blind; the basis for the conclusion that a patient had a positive reaction was not supported by conventional statistical testing, but by case-by-case descriptions or in the form of a number of positive responses within various psychophysiological categories.

A number of studies support the notion that hypersensitivity to electric and magnetic fields is at least partly attributable to psychophysiological reactions and environmental stress (Berg, Arnetz, Lidén, Eneroth, & Kallner, 1992). Stressful situations at work or at home may result in psychophysiological arousal leading to increased metabolism and increased heat generation with a need for peripheral vasodilatation. In addition, both mental stress and hormonal stress responses in the form of elevated prolactin levels have been reported in patients suffering from VDU-associated skin symptoms and electric hypersensitivity (Berg et al., 1992). A person may then be conditioned to the VDU environment where the initial stress situation was first encountered and the VDU environment consequently may act as the conditioned stimulus. Once the response has been learned, the psychophysiological response is elicited by the conditioned stimuli, that is, the VDU environment. The VDU environment is here defined broadly to encompass both the physical and psychological environment, but to the affected subject the VDU screen has become the focus of interest. Once the conditioned response is learned, the subject will face increasing difficulties approaching other areas known or believed to have electromagnetic fields.

Another similar interpretation postulates that symptoms are not due to the electromagnetic environment, but to the way an individual interprets naturally occurring skin reactions and to the way he copes with any stress factors in the environment. In general, however, there is no support for the notion that subjects suffering from hypersensitivity are more depressed or show more anxiety and somatoform disorders than is common in the general population. Arnetz and Wibom (1991) assessed the number of subjects who purported to be hypersensitive to electric and magnetic fields at a major telecommunications systems design laboratory. There were 236 employees who responded to a questionnaire concerning their occupational and medical history, indoor air quality issues, and present health status. Of these, 13% stated that they were hypersensitive to electric and magnetic fields only at work, whereas another 3.4% stated that they had symptoms of hypersensitivity both at work and at home. There were no statistically significant differences between healthy and hypersensitive employees with regard to family history of depression, allergies, or asthma. Childhood eczema had occurred in 5% of the respondents with no difference between the groups. Hypersensitive employees spent significantly more time using computers. As many as 39% of those who were constantly hypersensitive spent 75% or more of their work day at the computer, as compared to an average of 4.5% for those only hypersensitive at work. Of those, 12% who were always hypersensitive to electric and magnetic fields were too tired to interact with family and friends, as compared to 7% of those hypersensitive only at work and 3% of the healthy controls. Among healthy controls, 1% stated they had oral galvanic symptoms, as compared to 7% of those hypersensitive at work and 38% of those who were constantly hypersensitive. Subjects with hypersensitive symptoms did not differ from healthy controls with regard to somatic complaints, such as musculoskeletal disorders. However, they used more vitamins, supplemental minerals, and so-called free radical scavengers.

There has been no controlled intervention study in real life concerning the effects of modifications of electromagnetic fields on symptoms of electric and magnetic hypersensitivities. However, numerous adaptations of the workplace have been done. Some are reported to be beneficial, whereas others have failed to show any lasting effects. Electromagnetic cleanups in the workplace are similar to improving buildings characterized as sick. A number of changes are usually done simultaneously, involving both physical and indirectly psychosocial factors as well. Under those circumstances it is difficult to ascribe the beneficial results to mere physical changes.

Arnetz, Berg, Anderzén, Lundeberg, and Haker (1995) carried out controlled double-blind treatment studies of patients with hypersensitivity to electricity and magnetic fields and attempted various controlled interventions to improve their situation. In one study the impact on randomly chosen patients of either deep or superficial acupuncture was assessed. Both treatment groups improved significantly following treatment. There were no changes in biological variables apart from a gradual and continuous increase in serum cortisol and a decrease in neuropeptide Y, somewhat more accentuated in those receiving deep acupuncture. It may be that both treatments have a real effect, even though deep acupuncture is supposed to be more useful.

The efficacy of the Andersson et al. (1996) cognitive–behavioral program was also assessed. Treatment consisted of presenting a model to explain how somatic symptoms may interact with an individual's interpretation of the cause of these symptoms. Most patients more or less automatically interpreted their symptoms as warning signals of worse things to come, for example, they would be forced to move to an isolated setting and avoid all sources of electric and magnetic fields. Concrete evidence in support of such conclusions were discussed. Possible alternative interpretations were reviewed, stressing that they did not invalidate the patient's original beliefs. Rather, they offered a look at the symptoms from a different perspective.

Patients were asked to register their symptoms, the situations in which they occurred, and the perceived cause at that particular time. Ways to control stress were explained when indicated. The methods focused on relaxation techniques and means to alter external stress, for example, working out new job routines, managing demands from others, and learning to say no. Results showed beneficial effects: The patients' own rating of how handicapped they felt due to their hypersensitivity decreased significantly in the treatment group. In the reference/control group there were no significant changes. None of the patients had reduced exposure to VDUs or other sources of electromagnetic fields during treatment. In a separate part of the study, possible biological effects from electromagnetic provocations were assessed. Using a double-blind design no exposure-related biological effects were identified, neither absolute nor changes in serum levels of prolactin and cortisol related to real or perceived on/off exposure. However, following treatment, patients rated their postexposure symptoms as less intense, regardless of on–off conditions. When subjects believed the electromagnetic fields were on, regardless of whether that was the case, they reported a significant, time-dependent, worsening of symptoms.

There is support for the notion that exposure to electric and magnetic fields is not sufficient to induce hypersensitivity to electricity. Psychophysiological factors appear to be one important determinant. Our treatment studies, the first controlled studies of hypersensitivity to electricity, point to the beneficial aspects of working with a mind–body axis in dealing with new age disorders.

There have also been reports on possible threats to a fetus from working with VDUs. The use of electric blankets has been reported to increase the risk for spontaneous abortion (Nair, Morgan, & Florig, 1989). Careful studies have not been able to substantiate these risks (Knave, 1994; Schnorr et al., 1991) with one possible exception (Lindbohm et al., 1992). In most studies other occupational factors appear to be at play as well, and stress has been implicated as one risk factor for spontaneous abortion (Brandt & Nielsen, 1992; Homer, James, & Siegel, 1990). Further studies concerning the importance of stress are needed in order to draw any firm conclusions. There are also epidemiological studies linking proximity to high-voltage transmission lines and depression (McMahan, Ericson, & Meger, 1994; Perry & Pearl, 1988).

In addition, there has been a great deal of research concerning the possible links between electric and magnetic field exposure and childhood leukemia (Wertheimer & Leeper, 1979). The link has been recently reexamined by a Swedish study (Feychting & Ahlbom, 1993), but there is still no firm conclusion that electric and magnetic fields actually increase the risk of childhood leukemia, and no plausible and understandable biological mechanism has been proposed.

Conclusion

Hypersensitivity to electric and magnetic fields and VDUs is a growing new age disorder that fulfills the criteria of EI. Work is currently under way to study possible interactions between psychophysiological arousal and electromagnetic exposures. In most cases EI develops when a person is under both physical/chemical and psychosocial stress but despite this well-known clinical fact, studies have been either physical/chemical or psychosocial in design.

**DIAGNOSTIC WORK-UP OF PATIENTS
WITH ALLEGED ENVIRONMENTAL ILLNESS**

In order to better define the various subgroups of patients suffering from different categories of EI, it is important to refine our diagnostic tools. To date, criteria for diagnosing MCS (Cullen, 1987) have been published along with a survey questionnaire (Fiedler et al., 1992; Kipen, Hallman, Kelly-McNeil, & Fiedler, 1996); criteria for diagnosing hypersensitivity to electric and magnetic fields have been discussed elsewhere (see Arnetz et al., 1997). However, for the most part, present diagnostic instruments are focused on merely one or two of a number of EI subcategories with overlapping symptomatology. Thus, it is quite common that patients with electric hypersensitivity also complain of heightened sensitivity to chemicals and odors. Conversely, patients with MCS not infrequently complain of reacting to fluorescent lights, telecommunication equipments, televisions, and computer equipments as well.

In order to get a complete picture, patients with alleged EI are asked to describe what symptoms they believe are elicited by the physical, chemical, indoor, and the psychosocial environments. This is done in a nondiscriminatory fashion. Thus, patients are specifically asked if they react and, if so, to computers, the television, fluorescent light, mobile telephones, sunlight, domestic and office indoor environments, specific chemicals, odor, or smoke. Patients are also asked about possible sensitivities to food stuffs. Initially, however, it is important to let the patient describe his or her own symptomatology and what environmental factors he or she believes elicit symptoms and what the patient does to ameliorate these symptoms.

An international collaborative project is presently being planned to develop and test a comprehensive diagnostic questionnaire for patients with alleged EI. The questionnaire will be as brief as possible but include key symptoms and a broad range of environmental factors, including food stuff. The aim is to sharpen the diagnostic criteria and allow for international comparisons of the prevalence of specific subgroups of EI. A detailed medical, occupational, and environmental history is taken from all of the patients. All patients undergo a thorough physical exam. In addition, in order to rule out possible disease that could elicit similar symptomatology, such as skin sensations, fatigue, memory impairment, fainting spells, and other metabolic neurological, cardiovascular, and skin symptoms, a set of biochemical analyses of blood is carried out. These tests include hemoglobin, erythrocyte sedimentation rate, white blood cell count, electrolytes, serum iron, plasma glucose, liver function enzymes, serum levels of thyroid stimulating hormone (TSH), free thyroxin (F T4), prolactin, and cortisol.

Clinically, patients with electric hypersensitivity commonly have been found to have serum prolactin exceeding 6 µg/l as compared to levels below 6 µg/l in healthy controls. As patients' symptoms decrease serum prolactin also tends to decrease. Patients with visible skin alterations are referred to a dermatologist. Quite a few have been diagnosed as suffering from rosacea and successfully treated. The patients office environments are evaluated by an industrial hygienist.

Finally, all of the EI patients are encouraged to meet with psychologists. The psychologists focus on intra- and interindividual circumstances surrounding the development of EI. They also carry out a traditional psychological work-up, including upbringing, family relationship, and related areas of interest. An important function of the patients meetings with the psychologists is to discuss how the disease has interferred with the patients every day life and to deal with the patients reactions, fears, and thoughts related to suffering from EI.

The patients' work-up is thus multidisciplinary and rather broad. It allows for the fact that not enough of the origin and course of environmental illness is known and that prior work-ups of patients with alleged EI all too frequently have been incomplete. Many times, curable diseases are found among patients referred to our environmental health center. It is important that the diagnosis of EI is not taken as an excuse for not doing a thorough and high-quality diagnostic work-up of patients, including both somatic and mental health indicators.

UNDERSTANDING AND MANAGING ENVIRONMENTAL ILLNESS

Based on the published literature, there is no convincing evidence that the various forms of EI are uniquely attributable to specific environmental factors. Rather, we are dealing with a large group of poorly defined symptoms that are almost completely based on subjective criteria. Patients with EI receive a diagnosis very much based on their own beliefs and experiences. Among this group there are probably cases with real physical/chemical sensitivity and medical conditions that remain unrecognized in the larger pool of unexplained cases. Cases of sick building syndrome probably encompass people with primary disease, as well as those attributing a number of symptoms to poor indoor air quality. Clinicians are rarely used to dealing with new age disorders and may easily distance themselves from these patients. The best way to help patients with new age complaints may be to communicate what is known, recognize the symptoms as real, offer double-blind provocation tests if possible, and alternative treatment models together with more conventional treatments. Patients can benefit substantially, even though the true cause of their complaints is not known.

Considering the fact that EI is such a diffuse entity, based on subjective criteria, the various conditions need to be better defined. In many instances it is purely arbitrary which specific diagnosis of EI a patient receives. Many patients also have a history of other forms of EI and proceed to yet new ones.

A Working Model for the Understanding of Environmental Illness

The limbic system, including the hippocampus and the amygdala, play an important role in psychophysiological reactions. The catecholamine-driven locus coeruleus projects to the limbic system and to higher cortical areas. External stimuli, such as odor and skin sensations, activate the locus coeruleus. Other sensory systems also act on the central nervous systems at different levels. In addition, mental stress acts via higher cortical functions on the limbic system. Modifying factors are coping style, social support, and so on. Subjects who feel in control and have stable social support may react with preponderantly the limbic-catecholaminergic system, whereas subjects who perceive a lack of control react with frustration and the hippocampal-hypothalamo-pituitary-adrenal-cortical axis (Henry, 1993). Subjects under increased stress, either originating in the psychosocial or physical/chemical environment or from increased sensitivity and/or awareness of the external environment, are more likely to develop a chronic change in the limbic system. The elevated arousal level, which could be described as a changed signal-to-noise level in the hypothalamus-pituitary system, results in increased sensitivity to signals from peripheral receptors, more afferent input to the central nervous systems and increased awareness (Gramling, Clawson, & McDonald, 1996). The cascade of neurohormonal changes as well as immunological changes that follow, have fundamental physiological consequences. Immunocompetence can also be modified by the brain. Each of the anterior pituitary hormones is under neuroendocrine control of the hypothalamus, and their secretion can be influenced by suprahypothalamic stimuli, such as environmental, physical, and emotional stressors (Reichlin, 1993). Activation of cytokines in the central nervous system can lead to profound changes in neural function, including behavioral disturbances, fatigue, and other symptoms found in EI. Thus, peripheral cells, immunoactive cells, are not only sensitive to central nervous system input, but to emotional and behavioral factors as well (Ader & Cohen, 1993).

Conclusion

The mind-body interaction has not been sufficiently recognized in dealing with environmental illness. Studies have mainly focused on pure physical/chemical factors, while the mental/mind aspect of new age disorders has been relegated to second place. Patients are hesitant to seek help because of society's view of mental illness. Psychiatrists and psychologists are in a position to offer help, and to support people in their attempts to cope with disorders of unknown origin. There is ample opportunity to enhance our understanding of environmental illness if we take a multidisciplinary approach involving psychiatrists, psychologists, physicians, and industrial hygienists. Controlled intervention studies should be encouraged and efforts made to develop a theoretical concept concerning the etiology of environmental illness.

REFERENCES

Ader, R., & Cohen, N. (1993). Psychoneuroimmunology: Conditioning and stress. *Annual Review of Psychology, 44,* 53–85.

American Psychiatric Association. (1994). Diagnostic and statistical manual of mental disorders (4th ed.). Washington, DC: Author.

Andersson, B., Berg, M., Arnetz, B. B., Melin, L., Langlet, I., & Lidén, S. (1996). A cognitive-behavioral treatment of patients suffering from "electric hypersensitivity." Subjective effects and reactions in a double-blind provocation study. *Journal of Occupational and Environmental Medicine, 38*, 752–758.

Andersson, K., & Stridh, G. (1991). The use of standardized questionnaires in building-related illness (BRI) and sick building syndrome (SBS) survey. In F. Levy & M. Maroni (Eds.), *Epidemiological and medical management of building-related complaints and illnesses. NATA/CCMS pilot study on indoor air quality* (pp. 44–64). Oslo, Norway.

Arnetz, B. B. (1996). Techno-stress. A prospective psychophysiological study of the impact of a controlled stress-reduction program in advanced telecommunication systems design work. *Journal of Occupational and Environmental Medicine, 38*, 53–65.

Arnetz, B. B., Berg, M., Anderzén, I., Lundeberg, T., & Haker, E. (1995). A nonconventional approach to the treatment of "environmental illness." *Journal of Occupational and Environmental Medicine, 37*, 838–844.

Arnetz, B. B., Berg, M., & Arnetz, J. (1997). Mental strain and physical symptoms among employees in modern offices. *Archives of Environmental Health, 52*, 63–67.

Ashford, N. A., & Miller, C. S. (1991). *Chemical exposures: Low levels and high stakes.* New York: Van Nostrand Reinhold.

Bardana, E. J., Jr., Montanaro, A., & O'Hallaren, M. T. (1988). Building-related illness. A review of available scientific data. *Clinical Reviews in Allergy, 6*, 61–89.

Bauer, R. M., Greve, K. W., Besch, E. L., Schramke, C. J., Crouch, J., Hicks, A., Ware, M. R., & Lyles, W. B. (1992). The role of psychological factors in the report of building-related symptoms in sick building syndrome. *Journal of Consulting and Clinical Psychology, 60*, 213–219.

Bell, I. R. (1982). *Clinical ecology: A new medical approach to environmental illness.* Bolinas, CA: Common Knowledge Press.

Bell, I. R., Miller, C. S., & Schwartz, G. E. (1992). An olfactory-limbic model of multiple chemical sensitivity syndrome: Possible relationships to kindling and affective spectrum disorders. *Biological Psychiatry, 32*, 218–242.

Bell, I. R., Schwartz, G. E., Bootzin, R. R., & Wyatt, J. K. (1997). Time-dependent sensitization of heart rate and blood pressure over multiple laboratory sessions in elderly individuals with chemical odor intolerance. *Archives of Environmental Health, 52*, 6–17.

Bell, I. R., Schwartz, G. E., Peterson, J. M., & Amend, D. (1993). Self-reported illness from chemical odors in young adults without clinical syndromes or occupational exposures. *Archives of Environmental Health, 48*, 6–13.

Berg, M. (1988). Skin problems in workers using visual display terminals: A study of 201 patients. *Contact Dermatitis, 19*, 335–341.

Berg, M., Arnetz, B. B., Lidén, S., Eneroth, P., & Kallner, A. (1992). Techno-stress. A psychophysiologcial study of employees with VDU-associated skin complaints. *Journal of Occupational Medicine, 34*, 698–701.

Berg, M., Hedblad, M. A., & Erhardt, K. (1990). Facial skin complaints and work at visual display units: A histopathologica study. *Acta Dermato-Venereologica [Stockholm], 70*, 216–220.

Berg, M., Lidén, S., & Axelson, O. (1990). Skin complaints and work at visual display units: An epidemiological study of office employees. *Journal of American Academy of Dermatology, 22*, 621–625.

Bergqvist, U., Knave, B., Voss, M., & Wibom, R. (1992). A longitudinal study of VDT work and health. *International Journal of Human–Computer Interaction, 4*, 197–219.

Bergqvist, U., & Wahlberg, J. E. (1994). Skin symptoms and disease during work with visual display terminals. *Contact Dermatitis, 30*, 197–219.

Black, D. W., Rathe, A., & Goldstein, R. B. (1990). Environmental illness. A controlled study of 26 subjects with 20th century disease. *Journal of the American Medical Association, 264*, 3166–3170.

Boxer, P. (1990). Indoor air quality: A psychosocial perspective. *Journal of Occupational Medicine,* *32,* 425–428.

Bradburn, N. M. (1969). *The structure of psychological well-being.* Chicago: Aldine.

Brandt, L. P., & Nielsen C. V. (1992). Job stress and adverse outcome of pregnancy: A causal link or recall bias?. *American Journal of Epidemiology, 135,* 302–311.

Brodsky, C. M. (1983a). Allergic to everything: A medical subculture. *Psychosomatics, 24,* 731–742.

Brodsky, C. M. (1983b). Psychological factors contributing to somatoform diseases attributed to the workplace. *Journal of Occupational Medicine, 25,* 459–464.

Buffler, P. A. (1996). Cellular telephones and health. *Epidemiology, 7,* 219.

Burge, S., Hedge, A., Wilson, S., Bass, J. H., & Robertson, A. (1987). Sick building syndrome: A study of 4373 office workers. *Annals of Occupational Hygiene, 31,* 493–504.

Colligan, M. J., & Murphy, L. R. (1979). Mass psychogenic illness in organizations: An overview. *Journal of Occupational Psychology, 52,* 77–90.

Cometto-Muniz, J. E., & Cain, W. S. (1994). Sensory reactions of nasal pungency and odor to volatile organic compounds: The alkylbenzenes. *American Industrial Hygiene Association Journal, 55,* 811–817.

Cullen, M. (1987). Workers with multiple chemical sensitivities. *Occupational Medicine: State Art Review, 2,* 655–806.

Cynkier, I., Söderman, E., & Kolmodin-Hedman, B. (1994). *Indoor environment—Evaluation of results following proposed measures.* St. Petersburg, Russia: Indoor Air International.

Doty, R. L., Deems, D. A., Frye, R. E. Pelberg, R., & Shapiro, A. (1988). Olfactory sensitivity, nasal resistance, and autonomic function in patients with multiple chemical sensitivities. *Archives of Otolaryngology – Head and Neck Surgery, 114,* 1422–1427.

Elkins, G. R., Gamino, L. A., & Rynearson, R. R. (1988). Mass psychogenic illness, trance states, and suggestion. *American Journal of Clinical Hypnosis, 30,* 267–275.

Feldmann, L., Eaglstein, W., & Johnson, R. B. (1985). Terminal illness. [Letter]. *Journal of American Academy of Dermatology, 12,* 366.

Ferguson, D. (1971). An Australian study of telegraphists' cramp. *British Journal of Industrial Medicine, 28,* 280–285.

Feychting, M., & Ahlbom, A. (1993). Magnetic fields and cancer in children residing near Swedish high-voltage power lines. *American Journal of Epidemiology, 138,* 467–481.

Fiedler, N., Kipen, H. M., DeLuca, J., Kelly-McNeil, K., & Natelson, B. (1996). A controlled comparison of multiple chemical sensitivities and chronic fatigue syndrome. *Psychosomatic Medicine, 58,* 38–49.

Fiedler, N., Maccia, C., & Kipen, H. (1992). Evaluation of chemically sensitive patients. *Journal of Occupational Medicine, 34,* 529–538.

Finnegan, M. J., & Pickering, C. A. (1986). Building related illness. *Clinical Allergy, 16,* 389–405.

Frank, A. L. (1983). *Effects on health following occupational exposure to video display terminals.* University of Kentucky: Dept. of Preventive Medicine and Environmental Health.

Franzén, O., Paulsson, L. E., & Wennberg, A. (1992). *Human exposure to electrical and magnetic fields: An experimental detection study.* Berlin, Germany: Abstract to Work with Display Units.

Gots, R. (1993). Medical hypothesis and medical practice: Autointoxication and multiple chemical sensitivities. *Regulatory Toxicology and Pharmacology, 18,* 2–12.

Gramling, S. E., Clawson, E. P., & McDonald, M. K. (1996). Perceptual and cognitive abnormality model of hypochondriasis. Amplification and physiological reactivity in women. *Psychosomatic Medicine, 58,* 423–431.

Hall, W., & Morrow, L. (1988). Repetition strain injury: An Australian epidemic of upper limb pain. *Social Science and Medicine, 27,* 645–649.

Hamnerius, Y., Agrup, G., Galt, S., Nilsson, R., Sandblom, J., & Lindgren, R. (1992). *Provocation study of hypersensitivity reactions associated with exposure to electromagnetic fields from VDUs.* Berlin, Germany: Abstract to Work with Display Units.

Henry, J. P. (1993). Psychological and physiological responses to stress: The right hemisphere and the hypothalamo-pituitary-adrenal axis, an inquiry into problems of human bonding. *Integrative Physiological and Behavioral Science, 28,* 369–387.

Hocking, B. (1987). Epidemiological aspects of repetition strain injury in Telecom Australia. *Medical Journal of Australia, 147,* 218–222.

Homer, C. J., James, S. A., & Siegel, E. (1990). Work-related psychosocial stress and risk of preterm, low birthweight delivery. *American Journal of Public Health, 80,* 173–177.

Hotopf, M. (1994). Seasonal affective disorder, environmental hypersensitivity and somatisation. *British Journal of Psychiatry, 164,* 246–248.

Katon, W., & Sullivan, M. D. (1990). Depression and chronic medical illness. *Journal of Clinical Psychiatry, 51* (Suppl. 6), 3–11.

Keisu, L., Lille, K., & Hedström, L. D. (1991). *Decreased worry over VDU-associated health risks following a fact-based lecture.* Stockholm, Sweden: National Institute of Psycho-Social Factors and Health.

Kilburn, K. H. (1993). How should we think about chemically reactive patients? *Archives of Environmental Health, 48,* 4–5.

Kipen, H. M., Hallman, W., Kelly-McNeil, K., & Fiedler, N. (1996). Measuring chemical sensitivity prevalence: A questionnare for population studies. *American Journal of Public Health, 85,* 574–577.

Knave, B. (1994). Electric and magnetic fields and health outcomes—an overview. [Special issue] *Scandinavian Journal of Work, Environment and Health, 20,* 78–89.

Knave, B. G., Wibom, R. I., Voss, M., Hedström, L. D., & Bergqvist, U. O. (1985). Work with video display terminals among office employees. I. Subjective symptoms and discomfort. *Scandinavian Journal of Work, Environment and Health, 11,* 457–466.

Koh, D., Goh, C. L., Jeyaratnam, J., Kee, W. C., & Ong, C. N. (1990). Dermatological symptoms among visual display unit operators using plasma display and cathode ray tube screens. *Annals of the Academy of Medicine, Singapore, 19,* 617–620.

Koh, D., Goh, C. L., Jeyaratnam, J., Kee, W. C., & Ong, C. N. (1991). Dermatological complaints among visual display unit operators and office workers. *American Journal of Contact Dermatitis, 2,* 136–137.

Lagerholm, B. (1986). Bildskärmar och hudförändringar: Ingående undersökningar motiverade. *Läkartidningen [Journal of Swedish Medical Association], 83,* 60–61.

Langworth, S., & Strömberg, R. (1996). A case of high mercury exposure from dental amalgam. *European Journal of Oral Sciences, 104,* 320–321.

Levin, A. S., & Byers, V. S. (1987). Environmental illness: A disorder of immune regulation. In M. R. Cullen (Ed.), *Workers with multiple chemical sensitivities* (pp. 669–682). Philadelphia, PA: Hanley & Belfus.

Lidén, C., & Wahlberg, J. E. (1985). Work with video display terminals among office employees. V. Dermatologic factors. *Scandinavian Journal of Work, Environment and Health, 11,* 489–493.

Lindbohm, M. L., Hietanen, M., Kyyrönen, P., Sallmén, M., von Nandelstadh, P., Taskinen, H., Pekkarinen, M., Ylikoski, M., & Hemminki, K. (1992). Magnetic fields of video display terminals and spontaneous abortion. *American Journal of Epidemiology, 136,* 1041–1051.

Littlejohn, G. O. (1989). Fibromyositis/fibromyalgia syndrome in the workplace. *Rheumatic Diseases Clinics of North America, 15,* 45–60.

Marcusson, J. A. (1996). Contact allergies to nickel sulfate, gold sodium thiosulfate and palladium chloride in patients claiming side-effects from dental alloy components. *Contact Dermatitis, 34,* 320–323.

Matsunaga, K., Hayakawa, R., Ono, Y., & Hisanaga, O. (1988). Facial rash in a visual display terminal operator (in Japanese, abstract in English). *Annual Reports of the Nagoya University Branch Hospital, 22,* 57–61.

Mayou, R. (1975). The social setting of hysteria. *British Journal of Psychiatry, 127,* 466–469.

McMahan, S., Ericson, I., & Meger, I. (1994). Depressive symptomatology in women and residential proximity to high-voltage transmission lines. *American Journal of Public Health, 139*, 58–63.

Meggs, W. J., & Cleveland, C. H., Jr. (1993). Rhinolaryngoscopic examination of patients with multiple chemical sensitivity. *Archives of Environmental Health, 48*, 14–18.

Mendell, I. M., & Smith, A. H. (1990). Consistent pattern of elevated symptoms in air-conditioned office buildings: A reanalysis of epidemiological studies. *American Journal of Public Health, 80*, 1193–1199.

Menzies, R., Tamblyn, R., Farant, J.-P., Hanley, J., & Nunes, F., (1993). The effects of varying levels of outdoor-air supply on the symptoms of sick building syndrome. *New England Journal of Medicine, 328*, 821–827.

Molin, C. (1990). Oral galvanism in Sweden. *Journal of American Dental Association, 121*, 281–284.

Molin, C. (1992). Amalgam—fact and fiction. *Scandinavian Journal of Dental Research, 100*, 66–73.

Murray, R. (1991). Health aspects of carbonless copy paper. *Contact Dermatitis, 24*, 321–333.

Nair, I., Morgan, M. G., & Florig, H. K. (1989). *Biological effects of power frequency, electric, and magnetic fields: Background paper.* Washington, DC: Congress of the United States, Office of Technology Assessment.

National Institute for Occupational Safety and Health (NIOSH). (1989). *Indoor air quality investigations: 1981 through 1988.* Cincinnati, OH: Author.

Nilsen, A. (1982). Facial rash in video display unit operators. *Contact Dermatitis, 8*, 25–28.

Norback, D., & Edling, C. (1991). Environmental, occupational, and personal factors related to the prevalence of sick building syndrome in the general population. *British Journal of Industrial Medicine, 48*, 451–462.

Norback, D., Michel, I., & Widstrom, J. (1990). Indoor air quality and personal factors related to sick building syndrome. *Scandinavian Journal of Work, Environment and Health, 16*, 121–128.

Pearson, D. J., Rix, K. J. B., & Bentley, S. J. (1983). Food allergy: How much in the mind? A clinical and psychiatric study of suspected food hypersensitivity. *Lancet, 1*, 1259–1261.

Perry, S., & Pearl, L. (1988). Power frequency, magnetic fields and illness in multi-storey blocks. *Public Health, 102*, 11–18.

Pershagen, G. (1983). The epidemiology of human arsenic exposure. In B. A. Fowler (Ed.), *Biological and environmental effects of arsenic* (pp. 199–232). New York: Elsevier.

Persian Gulf Veterans Coordinating Board. (1995). Unexplained illness among Desert Storm veterans. A search for causes, treatment, and cooperation. *Archives of Internal Medicine, 155*, 262–268.

Randolph, T. (1978). *Human ecology and susceptibility to the chemical environment.* Springfield, IL: Thomas.

Rea, W., Bell, I., Suits, C., & Smiley, R. (1978). Food and chemical susceptibility after environmental chemical overexposure: Case histories. *Annals of Allergy, 41*, 101–109.

Rea, W. J., Pan, Y., Fenyves, E. J., Sujisawa, I., Samadi, N., & Ross, G. H. (1991). Electromagnetic field sensitivity. *Journal of Bioelectricity, 10*, 241–256.

Reichlin, S. (1993). Neuroendocrine-immune interactions. Review. *New England Journal of Medicine, 329*, 1246–1253.

Rest, K. M. (1992). Advancing the understanding of multiple chemical sensitivity (MCS): Overview and recommendations from an AOEC workshop. In K. M. Rest (Ed.), *Proceedings of the AOEC workshop on mutiple chemical sensitivity. Toxicology and Industrial Health, 8*, 1–13.

Robins, L. N., Helzer, J. E., Croughan, J., & Ratcliff, K. S. (1981). The NIMH Diagnostic Interview Schedule: Its history, characteristics, and validity. *Archives of General Psychiatry, 38*, 381–389.

Rosenberg, S. J., Freedman, M. R., Schmaling, K. B., & Rose, C. (1990). Personality styles of patients asserting environmental illness. *Journal of Occupational Medicine, 32*, 678–681.

Rycroft, R. J. G., & Calnan, C. D. (1984). Facial rashes among visual display operators. In B. G. Pearce (Ed.), *Health hazard of VDTs?* (pp. 13–15). Chichester, England: Wiley.

Sandborgh Englund, G. S., Dahlqvist, R., Lindelöf, B., Söderman, E., Jonzon, B., Vesterberg, O., & Larsson, K. S. (1994). DMSA administration to patients with alleged mercury poisoning from dental amalgams: A placebo-controlled study. *Journal of Dental Research, 73,* 620–628.

Sandstrom, M., Stenberg, B., & Hansson Mild, K. (1989). *Provocation tests with ELF and VLF electromagnetic fields on patients with skin problems associated with VDT work.* Montreal, Canada: Abstract to Work with Display Units.

Schnorr, T. M., Grajewski, B. A., Hornung, R. W., Thun, M. J., Egeland, G. M., Murray, W. E. Conover, D. L., & Halperin, W. E. (1991). Video display terminals and the risk of spontaneous abortion. *New England Journal of Medicine, 324,* 727–733.

Schottenfeld, R. S., & Cullen, M. R. (1986). Recognition of occupation-induced post-traumatic stress-disorders. *Journal of Occupational Medicine, 28,* 365–369.

Simon, G., Daniel, W., Stockbridge, H., Claypolle, K., & Rosenstock, L. (1993). Immunologic, psychological, and neurophysiological factors in multiple chemical sensitivity. *Annals of Internal Medicine, 19,* 97–103.

Simon, G. E., Katon, W. J., & Sparks, P. J. (1990). Allergic to life: Psychological factors in environmental illness. *American Journal of Psychiatry, 147,* 901–906.

Sirois, F. (1974). Epidemic hysteria. *Acta Psychiatrica Scandinavica, 252* (Suppl.), 1–46.

Skov, P., Valbjorn, O., & Pedersen, B. V. (1989). [The Danish indoor climate study group]. Influence of personal characteristics, job-related factors and psychosocial factors on the sick building syndrome. *Scandinavian Journal of Work, Environment and Health, 15,* 286–295.

Skov, P., Valbjorn, O., & Pedersen, B. [The Danish indoor climate study group]. (1990). Influence of indoor climate on the sick building syndrome in an office environment. *Scandinavian Journal of Work, Environment and Health, 16,* 363–371.

Spurgeon, A., Gompertz, D., & Harrington, J. M. (1996). Modifiers of non-specific symptoms in occupational and environmental syndromes. *Occupational and Environmental Medicine, 53,* 361–366.

Stangl, D., Pfohl, B., Zimmerman, M., Bowers, W., & Corenthal, C. (1985). A structured interview for DSM-III personality disorder. *Archives of General Psychiatry, 42,* 591–596.

Staudenmayer, H., Selner, J. C., & Buhr, M. P. (1993). Double-blind provocation chamber challenges in 20 patients presenting with "multiple chemical sensitivity." *Regulatory Toxicology and Pharmacology, 18,* 44–53.

Stenberg, B. (1989). Skin complaints in buildings with indoor climate problems. *Environment International, 15,* 81–84.

Stenberg, B. (1994). *Office illness: The worker, the work and the workplace.* Unpublished medical dissertation, Umeå University.

Stewart, D. E., & Raskin, J. (1985). Psychiatric assessment of patients with 20th century disease (total allergy syndrome). *Canadian Medical Association Journal, 133,* 1001–1006.

Stock, A. (1926). Die Gefährlichkeit des Quecksilberdampfes und der Amalgame. *Zeitschrift fur Angewandte Chemie, 39,* 984–989.

Swanbeck, G., & Bleeker, T. (1989). Skin problems from visual display units. *Acta Dermato-Venereologica [Stockholm], 69,* 46–51.

Terr, A. I. (1986). Environmental illness: A clinical review of 50 cases. *Archives of Internal Medicine, 146,* 145–149.

Terr, A. I. (1994). Multiple chemical sensitivities. *Journal of Allergy and Clinical Immunology, 94,* 362–366.

Thrasher, J., Broughton, A., & Madison, R. (1990). Immune activation and autoantibodies in humans with long-term inhalation exposure to formaldehyde. *Archives of Environmental Health, 45,* 217–223.

Wells, K. B., Rogers, W., Burnam, A., Greenfield, S., & Ware, J. E. (1991). How the medical comorbidity of depressed patients differs across health care settings: Results from the Medical Outcomes Study. *American Journal of Psychiatry, 148*, 1688–1696.

Wertheimer, N., & Leeper, E. (1979). Electrical wiring configuration and childhood cancer. *American Journal of Epidemiology, 109*, 273–284.

Wolf, C. (1994). Multiple chemical sensitivities. Is there a scientific basis? *International Archives of Occupational and Environmental Health, 66*, 213–216.

World Health Organization (WHO). (1983). *Indoor air pollutants: Exposure and health effects.* (Report and Studies 78). Copenhagen: Author.

Chapter 10

Psychosocial Effects of Urban Environments, Noise, and Crowding

Hugh L. Freeman
Green College, Oxford, United Kingdom

Stephen A. Stansfeld
University College London Medical School

The relationship of physical health to the structural environment is reasonably well understood in terms of water supply, sewage disposal, protection from weather, and so on. But the complex and interrelated causes of the psychological and social pathologies that seem increasingly to plague urban areas have yet to be fully identified.

DEFINITIONS OF SOCIAL ENVIRONMENT AND MENTAL HEALTH

The social environment has been defined as consisting of "the norms, values, customs, fashions, habits (which might include work), prejudices, and beliefs of a society" (Burke, 1990). Although these vary enormously from one society to another, "in each one, their profile will be more or less supportive of health. They are modulated through the mass media . . . and institutionalized in the family, the community (which may be defined ethnically as well as geographically) and the nation" (Burke, 1990).

Mental health can be defined in innumerable ways—most of them too vague or too idealized to be of much value. Practical scientific considerations, however, require it to be used primarily in terms of emotional symptoms such as anxiety or depression that people report; if environmental changes in an area resulted in significant reductions in the levels of these complaints it would be reasonable to say that the mental health of that population had improved.

Social pathology is usually taken to mean significant deviation from prevailing norms of behavior, as delinquency and crime, disordered or broken family relationships, and addiction. Most people who behave badly are not psychiatrically disordered, though the exact proportion of those who are is unknown, but there is evidence that communities with high rates of psychiatric disorder also tend to show high levels of behavioral deviance and of psychiatric sequelae to crime and social disturbance.

On the other hand, there seems to be no firm ground for the view that in psychiatric terms, urban living as a whole is less healthy than life in the country (Webb, 1985), because as units of analysis, urban and rural are now too large and heterogeneous to be meaningful. The characteristics of particular environments therefore need to be specified more clearly, if their possible effects on mental health are to be analyzed in a scientifically useful way.

There may, however, be an optimum size beyond which the costs of cities start to outweigh their benefits, resulting in an escalation of social pathology, particularly crime (Wedmore & Freeman, 1985). The sheer size of today's urban settlements may involve "the destruction of whatever natural order of territoriality was established by historical and social usage" (Cappon, 1975). Mexico City, with an estimated population of 20 million, has passed the size of any previously known metropolitan area.

In many large cities, inner-city malaise has been described in recent decades. Common factors underlying this phenomenon in different places are decayed infrastructure, bad physical conditions, high levels of unemployment, limited job opportunities, and a concentration of people with social problems. Inner cities and public housing have shoddy buildings, a lack of social or shopping facilities, and isolation from employment and civic amenities. Demoralization, substance abuse, family breakdown, crime, and alienation are not surprising in such circumstances. Whether there is an identifiable factor of urbanicity that could be related to an excess of specific psychiatric disorders such as schizophrenia (Lewis, Andreasson, & Allebeck, 1992) remains uncertain; the relationship might be explained by the effects of migration and social class (Freeman, 1994).

THE INTERRELATIONSHIP BETWEEN MENTAL HEALTH AND PLANNING

In industrialized countries, those responsible for development of transport and changes in the pattern of industry and commerce have had a general lack of interest in the human consequences of their actions. Economic considerations have been overwhelming, irrespective of the political ideology with which a society operates.

One of the most important urban processes relevant to mental health is redevelopment and residential relocation. This process began on a large scale after 1918, but gathered momentum after World War II. The density of the new environment was on average about one third that of the old, so that areas exploded in size; the standard of facilities such as bathrooms and hot water systems was, of course, generally much higher. Most of this development was undertaken by private builders, and planning controls were minimal, so that "ribbon development" and "urban sprawl" emerged as widespread phenomena.

A description of "suburban neurosis" (Taylor, 1938) recorded the stress that commonly occurred after people moved from more central areas, for example, higher expenses, social isolation, distance from employment, and loss of familiar surroundings. Such developments were designed on the assumption that the undesirable features of the old communities could be planned away, and that life would be better in an environment consisting only of adequate housing, together with a few essential shops (Hansen & Hiller, 1984). Often, these housing areas are not integrated into the wider community, and even within them, the layout may provoke more suspicion than sociability. Yet hardly any research has been carried out into possible adverse psychological and emotional effects of this process on individuals, or of social effects on the areas they left behind. It is likely that such effects have occurred considering that many of the abandoned areas were long-established communities with a characteristic culture of their own and important social networks that could never be reproduced artificially. It has become increasingly recognized in recent years that the social support derived from these networks is of fundamental importance in the maintenance of social health.

Demolition of a neighborhood is not just the destruction of buildings, but also that of a functioning social system (Gans, 1968). While "slum clearance" was a powerful slogan in Britain, doing away with unsatisfactory old environments, it ignored the fact that most of the social problems found in slums were not directly related to their physical structure. Furthermore, the redevelopment process—from first plans to resettlement of all the residents—proved to be a long one, during which time people were worried about their future, watched the decay of the familiar neighborhood around them, and finally were often moved against their will to a home they did not want (Willmott, 1974). In this process, the boundaries and spatial arrangements that different ethnic or social groups had established over time were wiped out, and with them, often their modus vivendi with society in general—having predictably adverse effects on the social order of cities.

While inner-city areas in Western countries have been largely emptied of their previously established working-class residents, much of the housing that remained has been reoccupied, predominantly by poor members of minorities or by people with socially marginal characteristics, such as alcoholics, drug addicts, or those with severely disordered personalities. During this process, the nature of large urban communities has changed fundamentally, and in such a way as to foster the development in many places of major social problems, particularly as it has coincided with their economic decline and deindustrialization. With a global labor market for routine tasks, including manufacturing, "the cities of every advanced nation are marked by growing disparities between cosmopolitan professionals, linked to worldwide enterprises from desks and computer terminals . . . and unskilled laborers . . . who must now engage in low-wage service jobs" (Reich, 1990).

The move from urban to suburban communities was promoted by an assumed desirability of low population density (though it had never been shown that high density per se is harmful); by a belief in shortage of land (although all cities contained enormous unused or partly used areas); and by the assumption that old houses should be demolished rather than rehabilitated (although no evidence existed that this was in fact preferable or even economical). Grandiose road developments were ruthlessly imposed on (mainly poor) communities, bringing them few if any benefits, but enormous social costs. In tearing apart compact and human-scale environments, highways caused the subdivision of urban areas into artificial and segregated cells. Movement between these areas became more difficult. The conventional wisdom says that there is never enough public investment to undertake changes; this was in fact a case not of too little being spent but far too much. Not for the first time, such policies tended to have the opposite effects of those claimed for them.

In many European countries, one of the foremost urban policies of the last 50 years has been the construction of high-rise residential blocks as a quick technological fix for the housing shortage. This was carried out in the absence of any systematic enquiry as to what kind of accommodation people wanted (Dunleavy, 1981), and often in combination with the use of industrialized building methods, nearly all of which have proved to be disastrous. There has been little systematic research into the effects on mental health of high-rise living, but the balance of evidence suggests that it has been adverse for families with young children, and possibly also for others (Freeman, 1985). Likely explanations include shoddy construction, lack of sound insulation, poor maintenance, difficulty in monitoring the surrounding space, difficulties in informal interaction between residents, inability to make physical changes to the home, lack of opportunity to participate in management of the block, and unpleasant appearance, both inside and out (Freeman, 1993).

Many urban areas lack effective planning authorities or the means to implement their decisions. Yet, as Sherlock (1990) pointed out, even with such planning, "the problems of urban transport and land use will never be solved. As a result, urban living is likely to become even more unattractive and, if this drives people out of urban areas, it will take many of the urban problems, including traffic congestion, to the surrounding countryside."

RACE AND UNEMPLOYMENT

The factors of race and employment are critical to an understanding of the urban environment in older industrial countries, particularly the United States. Since the 1970s, the loss of jobs for men of less education who were previously able to support families through factory work, may well have been one of the strongest forces promoting urban decay. From the early 19th century, the central areas of cities contained a dense amalgam of factories, workshops, warehouses, offices, railways, and public buildings. All employed large numbers of people—mainly men—at every level from management to unskilled laborers, and immigrants could usually find some forms of employment, although it might require starting at the bottom of the heap. More importantly, cities like London, New York, and Paris were the greatest single centers of manufacturing in each country, quite apart from their commercial, financial, administrative, and political functions.

In recent decades, however, it has become more profitable to move many of these economic activities to the peripheries of urban areas, to other parts of each country, or even to another part of the world, where labor costs are lower. As a result, working-class people living in cities find that employment opportunities have either moved away beyond their reach or else have ceased to exist. It is not only money, however, that has been lost through these changes; the economic and related activities that were the raison d'être of industrial age cities created rich networks of interpersonal and group relationships. With the end or reduction of these activities, the associated relationships also wither and the social support is lost.

Like all adverse changes, this loss of economic activity bears most heavily on those who are most disadvantaged to start with, among whom are many from minority races. In this way, the influence of racism has contributed to the degradation of urban environments: whereas equal opportunity laws have served the Black middle class well and have allowed them to leave Black neighborhoods and institutions, the Black lower class have been left even worse off as a result. Although this process has been most marked in the United States, similar tendencies can be found in Britain, France, Germany, Holland, and other countries that have absorbed substantial numbers of immigrants.

Wilson (1987) pointed out that since the mid-1960s, there has been a breakdown in the social organization of U.S. inner-city areas. This has meant a loss of the sense of community, of positive identification with one's neighborhood, and of communal norms and sanctions against aberrant behavior. However, Wilson does not believe that the sharp increase in social dislocation in these areas "can simply be explained by a ghetto culture of poverty." In his view, the key concept applicable to these processes is not a culture of poverty, but social isolation from groups with different class and/or racial backgrounds, which enhances the effects of living in a highly concentrated poverty area.

The term *underclass*, which has become increasingly common, refers to groups that are not only excluded from the main legitimate activities of society but also ecologically separate from it. The phenomenon has emerged in several advanced industrialized countries, since the collapse of the postwar economic boom in the early 1970s. In the United States and to some extent in other countries, the underclass is predominantly non-White.

Wilson also pointed out that once the social institutions of a neighborhood have deteriorated, isolation has occurred from the wider job network system, and the number of marriageable (i.e., employed) young males has been much reduced, a vicious cycle that is perpetuated through the family, community, and schools. The massive unemployment, flagrant lawlessness, and low-achieving schools are all profoundly unattractive to outsiders. An important difference between Black and White populations in America is that increasing male unemployment in Blacks has been related to rising proportions of families headed by females, whereas this has not been so among Whites. There is a strong association between female-headed households and severe, prolonged poverty.

Structural economic changes, with their shift from manufacturing to service industries, have polarized the labor market into high-wage and low-wage sectors. Blacks and other minorities, who tend to be concentrated in central areas, have been hardest hit by the resulting economic dislocation. "Since an overwhelming majority of inner-city Blacks lack the qualifications for the high-skilled . . . segment of the service sector . . . they tend to be concentrated in the low-skilled segment, which features unstable employment, restricted opportunities, and low wages" (Wilson, 1987). The dangers to the wider society of these pockets of social breakdown hardly need to be emphasized.

Unemployment is a loss experience involving both reduced income, loss of the legitimate social role of worker, and loss of opportunities for social interaction, both with colleagues and often those in the immediate community as well (Fryer & Payne, 1986). Levels of psychiatric disorder are twice as high in unemployed as in employed samples (Warr, 1984) and in some studies rise in the suicide rate parallels rise in the number unemployed (Platt, 1984). The direction of causation has not always been clear; are people with preexisting ill health selected into unemployment or does unemployment lead to psychiatric disorder? Nevertheless, there is good evidence now that unemployment leads to higher levels of depression and anxiety (Kasl, 1979; Payne & Hartley, 1984). Anticipation or fear of unemployment is also associated with reduced psychological well-being (Ferrie, Shipley, Marmot, Stansfeld, & Davey Smith, 1995; Iversen & Sabroe, 1988) and obtaining insecure employment after a period of unemployment does not lead to a reduction in psychological distress as is found after re-employment in secure work (Burchell, 1994). This is relevant to Western societies where permanent unemployment and a transition from long-term secure employment to short-term insecure employment is becoming more frequent.

Nevertheless, people adapt to unemployment, the young and the old more than middle-aged people who may have family commitments. Well-being declines sharply immediately after unemployment and stabilizes after about 6 months at a lower level than in employed people. Reduced commitment to getting a new job (Warr & Jackson, 1987), lack of financial difficulty, adequate support from social relationships (Gore, 1978), feeling that time is occupied (Hepworth, 1980) and lack of accompanying physical ill health tend to increase well-being in the unemployed. Expectation of new work that is not achieved seems to have worse effects on mental health than remaining unemployed as planned (Hamilton, Hoffman, Broman, & Rauma, 1993). With the increasing shortage of paid work the development of other types of purposeful activity are a priority in improving the mental health of unemployed people if higher levels of full employment cannot be achieved.

NOISE AND PSYCHIATRIC DISORDER

One of the ubiquitous features of urban, and increasingly, rural environments, is exposure to environmental noise. Noise defined as unwanted sound, usually predominantly aircraft, road traffic, and neighbors' noise, is a type of stressor that might be expected to have a deleterious effect on mental health. It is generally hypothesized that noise will cause disturbance of activities and communication as well as annoyance and that these will lead to stress responses, and hence to symptoms and possibly overt illness (Van Dijk, 1987).

Noise Exposure and Symptoms

Symptoms reported among industrial workers regularly exposed to high noise levels in settings such as weaving mills (Granati, Angelepi, & Lenzi, 1959), schools (Crook & Langdon, 1974), and factories (Melamed, Najenson, Luz, Jucha, & Green, 1988) include nausea, headaches, argumentativeness, changes in mood, anxiety, and sexual impotence. More self-reported illness and illness-related absenteeism (Cameron, Robertson, & Zaks, 1972), social conflicts at work and home (Jansen, 1961), and actual absenteeism (Cohen, 1976) have been found in noisy rather than quiet industries. Many of these industrial studies are difficult to interpret, however, because workers were exposed to other stressors such as physical danger and heavy work demands, which may be more potent than noise in causing symptoms. There may also be differential selection of individuals working in noisy areas. For instance, jobs in noisy areas may be less desirable, may be more difficult to fill, and hence may attract individuals with health problems that have prevented them from attaining more desirable jobs. On the other hand, health factors may operate in the selection of personnel for jobs in high noise-exposure areas that may be dangerous, demanding toughness and resilience not required for those in quieter areas; for example, few symptoms were found among men working in high noise on aircraft carriers (Davis, 1958). Also, choice of coping strategies by individuals may influence whether aircraft noise actually causes symptoms: Passive coping strategies were related to higher scores on the Hopkins Symptom Check List in areas of high exposure to aircraft noise (Altena, 1989).

Environmental noise outside work settings, though less intense, tends to be more difficult for the ordinary citizen to avoid. Community surveys have found that high percentages of people reported headaches, restless nights, and being tense and edgy in high-noise areas (Finke et al., 1974; Kokokusha, 1973; Öhrström, 1989). An explicit link between aircraft noise and symptoms emerging in such studies raises the possibility of a bias toward over reporting of symptoms (Barker & Tarnopolsky, 1978). Notably, a study around three Swiss airports (Grandjean, Graf, Cauber, Meier, & Muller, 1973), did not find any association between the level of exposure to aircraft noise and symptoms. In a West London survey (Tarnopolsky, Watkins, & Hand, 1980), tinnitus, burns, cuts, and minor accidents, ear problems, and skin troubles were all more common in areas of high noise exposure. Acute symptoms like depression, irritability, difficulty getting off to sleep, night waking, skin troubles, swollen ankles, and burns, cuts, and minor accidents—were particularly common in high noise areas. However, apart from ear problems and tinnitus, 20 out of 23 chronic symptoms were more common in low noise environments. Symptoms did not increase with increasing levels of noise. Nevertheless, noise may cause some acute psychological symptoms; many of the effects of noise in industrial and teaching settings may in fact be related primarily to disturbances in communication.

Noise Exposure and Mental Hospital Admission Rates

Early studies found associations between the level of aircraft noise and psychiatric hospital admissions, both in London (Abey-Wickrama, A'Brook, Gattoni, & Herridge, 1969) and Los Angeles (Meecham & Smith, 1977). These results have been criticized on methodological grounds (Chowns, 1970; Frerichs, Beeman, & Coulson, 1980) and a replication study of Abey-Wickrama's study by Gattoni and Tarnopolsky (1973) failed to confirm these findings. Jenkins, Tarnopolsky, Hand, and Barker (1979) found that age-standardized admission rates to a London psychiatric hospital over 4 years were higher as the level of noise of an area decreased, but lower noise areas were also central urban districts, where high admission rates would be expected. In a further extensive study (Jenkins, Tarnopolsky, & Hand, 1981), high aircraft noise was associated with higher admission rates in two hospitals, but in all three hospitals, admission rates seemed to follow non-noise factors more closely; the effect of noise, if any, could only be moderating other causal variables but not overriding them. Kryter (1990), in a re-analysis of the data, found "a more consistently positive relation between level of exposure to aircraft noise and admissions rates." One may conclude that the route to hospital admission is influenced by many psychosocial variables that are more potent than exposure to noise.

Noise Exposure and Psychiatric Morbidity in the Community

In a community pilot study carried out in West London, Tarnopolsky, Barker, Wiggins, and McLean (1978) found no association between aircraft noise exposure and either General Health Questionnaire (GHQ) scores (dichotomized 4/5, low scorers/high scorers; Goldberg, 1972), or estimated psychiatric cases (Goldberg, Cooper, Eastwood, Kedward, & Shepherd, 1970). This was the case even when exposure to road traffic noise was controlled, except in three subgroups: persons aged 15–44 of high education, women aged 15 to 44, and those in professional or managerial occupations. The authors expressed the guarded opinion that noise might have an effect in causing morbidity within certain vulnerable subgroups.

In the subsequent West London Survey of Psychiatric Morbidity (Tarnopolsky & Morton-Williams, 1980), 5,885 adults were randomly selected from within four aircraft noise zones. No overall relationship was found between aircraft noise and the prevalence of psychiatric morbidity either for GHQ scores or for estimated numbers of psychiatric cases, using various indexes of noise exposure. However, there was an association between noise and psychiatric morbidity in two subgroups: finished full time education at age 19 years +, and professionals. These two categories, which had a strong association with each other, were combined and then showed a significant association between noise and psychiatric morbidity ($\chi^2 = 8.18$, df = 3, $p < 0.05$), but only for GHQ scores. Tarnopolsky and Morton-Williams (1980) concluded that their results "show so far that noise per se in the community at large, does not seem to be a frequent, severe, pathogenic factor in causing mental illness but that it is associated with symptomatic response in selected subgroups of the population" (p. 73).

The possible relationship between noise and psychiatric disorder was pursued further in a population unlikely to have been selected by noise exposure, (which may be the case around a well-established airport such as Heathrow), by examining any association among road traffic noise exposure, noise sensitivity, and psychiatric disorder, in a cross-sectional study of the small town of Caerphilly, South Wales (Stansfeld, Sharp, Gallacher, & Babisch, 1993). In the longitudinal results, no association was found between the initial level of road traffic noise and minor psychiatric disorder, even after adjustment for sociodemographic factors and baseline psychiatric disorder. Psychosocial well-being has been shown to be reduced in areas exposed to high traffic noise, but the results have not been especially consistent and may be mediated through disruptive effects on sleep (Öhrström, 1989, 1993).

The use of health services has also been taken as a measure of the relationship between noise and psychiatric disorder. Grandjean et al. (1973) reported that the proportion of the Swiss population taking drugs was higher in areas with high levels of aircraft noise and Knipschild and Oudshoorn (1977) found that the purchase of sleeping pills, antacids, sedatives, and antihypertensive drugs all increased in a village newly exposed to aircraft noise, but not in a "control" village where the noise level remained unchanged. In both studies, there was also an association between the rate of contact with general practitioners and level of noise exposure. In the Heathrow study (Watkins, Tarnopolsky, & Jenkins, 1981), various health care indicators were used—use of drugs, particularly psychiatric or self-prescribed, visits to the general practitioner, attendance at hospital, and contact with various community services—but none of these showed any clear trend in relation to levels of noise.

Effects of Noise on Performance and Sleep

Effects of noise on mental health might be expected, because there is evidence that noise does impair other aspects of human functioning such as performance (Loeb, 1986) and sleep, and causes adverse reactions such as annoyance. In general, it seems that noise increases arousal and decreases attention through distraction (Broadbent, 1953), increases need for focusing or attention to irrelevant stimuli (Cohen & Spacapan, 1978), as well as altering choice of task strategy (Smith & Broadbent, 1981). Even relatively low levels of noise may have subtle ill-effects, and in this respect, the state of the person at the time of performance may be as important as the noise itself (Broadbent, 1983). Individuals' perception of their degree of control over noise may also influence whether it impairs memory (Willner & Neiva, 1987). Noise may also affect social performance: (a) by becoming a stressor that causes unwanted aversive changes in affective state; (b) by masking speech and impairing communication; and (c) by distracting attention from relevant cues in the immediate social environment (Jones, Chapman, & Auburn, 1981). It may be that people whose performance strategies are already limited for other reasons (e.g., through high anxiety), and who are faced with multiple tasks may be more vulnerable to the masking and distracting effects of noise.

There is both objective and subjective evidence for sleep disturbance by noise (Öhrström, 1982; Öhrström, Rylander, & Bjorkman, 1988). Although noise effects on sleep may habituate over time (Vallet & Francois, 1982), small sleep deficits may persist for years (Globus, Friedmann, Cohen, Pearson, & Fidell, 1973) with unknown effects on health.

Noise Annoyance

The most widespread and well documented subjective response to noise is annoyance, which may include fear and mild anger, related to a belief that one is being avoidably harmed (Cohen & Weinstein, 1981). Noise is also seen as intrusive into personal privacy, and its meaning for any individual is important in determining whether that person will be annoyed by it (Gunn, 1987). Annoyance reactions are often associated with the degree of interference that any noise causes in everyday activities, which probably precedes and leads on to annoyance (Hall, Taylor, & Birnie, 1985; Taylor, 1984). In both traffic and aircraft noise studies, noise levels have been found to be associated with annoyance in a dose–response relationship (Griffiths & Langdon, 1968; Schulz, 1978; Tarnopolsky & Morton-Williams, 1980). Annoyance is also dependent on the context in which the noise is heard. Overall, it seems that conversation, watching television, or listening to the radio (all involving speech communication) are the activities most disturbed by aircraft noise (Hall et al., 1985), whereas traffic noise at night is most disturbing for sleep.

Noise Annoyance, Noise, Symptoms,
and Psychiatric Morbidity

Noise annoyance is associated, on the one hand with noise level, and on the other with symptoms and psychiatric disorder. Against expectation, although there was a strong link between noise and annoyance, and those who were highly annoyed showed the greatest number of symptoms, symptoms were not more common in high—rather than low—noise areas. This apparent paradox might be explained by the "Vulnerability Hypothesis" (Tarnopolsky et al., 1980). According to this explanation, noise is not directly pathogenic, but sorts individuals into annoyance categories according to their vulnerability to stress. Tarnopolsky et al. (1978) found that noise and minor psychiatric disorder were the strongest predictors of annoyance and that psychiatric morbidity led to annoyance, rather than vice versa. Moreover, annoyance does not seem to act as an intervening variable between noise and morbidity. At any particular level of exposure, there is wide individual variation in the degree of annoyance that is expressed. Individual variance in annoyance can be explained largely in terms of noise sensitivity and attitudes to the source of the noise (Evans & Tafalla, 1987; Job, 1988).

Noise Sensitivity and Vulnerability to Psychiatric Disorder

Noise sensitivity, based on attitudes to noise in general (Anderson, 1971; Stansfeld, 1992), is an intervening variable that explains much of the variance between exposure and individual annoyance responses (Fields, 1994; Langdon, 1976; Langdon, Buller, & Scholes, 1981; Weinstein, 1978). Individuals who are noise sensitive are also likely to be sensitive to other aspects of the environment (Broadbent, 1972; Stansfeld, Clark, Jenkins, Turpin, & Tarnopolsky, 1985; Thomas & Jones, 1982; Weinstein, 1978). This raises the question whether noise-sensitive individuals are simply those who complain more about their environment. Certainly there is an association between noise sensitivity and neuroticism (Jelinkova, 1988; Öhrström, Bjorkman, & Rylander, 1988; Thomas & Jones, 1982), although it has not been found in all studies (Broadbent, 1972). On the other hand, Weinstein (1980) hypothesized that noise sensitivity is part of a critical–uncritical dimension, showing the same association as noise sensitivity to measures of noise, privacy, air pollution, and neighborhood reactions. He suggested that the most critical subjects, among whom noise sensitive people would be grouped, are not uniformly negative about their environment, but more discriminating than the uncritical group, who comment uniformly on their environment.

    Noise sensitivity has also been related to current psychiatric disorder (Bennett, 1945; Iwata, 1984; Tarnopolsky & Morton-Williams, 1980). Stansfeld et al. (1985) found that high noise sensitivity was particularly associated with phobic disorders and neurotic depression measured by the Present State Examination (Wing, Cooper, & Sartorius, 1974). Noise sensitivity has also been linked to a coping style based on avoidance that may have adverse health consequences (Pulles, Biesiot, & Stewart, 1988). Noise sensitivity may be partly secondary to psychiatric disorder: Depressed patients followed over 4 months became less noise-sensitive as they recovered. These subjective psychological measurements were complemented by objective psychophysiological laboratory investigation of reactions to noise in a subsample of depressed patients. Noise-sensitive people tended to have higher levels of tonic physiological arousal, more phobic and defense/startle responses, and slower habituation to noise (Stansfeld, 1992). Thus, noise-sensitive people attend more to noises, discriminate more between noises, find noises more threatening and out of their control, and adapt to noises more slowly than people who are less sensitive in this way. Through its association with greater perception of environmental threat, its links with negative affectivity, and physiological arousal, noise sensitivity may be an indicator of vulnerability to minor psychiatric disorder (Stansfeld, 1992).

In the Caerphilly study, noise sensitivity did predict psychiatric disorder at follow-up after adjusting for baseline psychiatric disorder, but did not interact with the noise level, suggesting that noise sensitivity does not specifically moderate the effect of noise on psychiatric disorder (Stansfeld et al., 1993). After adjusting for trait anxiety at baseline the effect of noise sensitivity was no longer statistically significant. This suggests that much of the association between noise sensitivity and psychiatric disorder may be accounted for by the confounding association with trait anxiety. Constitutionally anxious people may be both more aware of threatening aspects of their environment and more prone to future psychiatric disorder. It seems possible that these traits might be linked.

Complaints About Noise in the Clinical Setting

In clinical practice it is not uncommon to see patients who complain of considerable disturbance by noise, often noise by neighbors. In some cases, on taking further history it becomes apparent that this is related to persecutory delusions and may be a symptom of paranoid psychosis, schizophrenia, or in the elderly, paraphrenia. In such cases disturbance by noise is often part of a wider system of persecutory ideas about neighbors in which noise is only one of many afflictions that the patient believes the neighbors are causing him. An accurate history and further information from a close relative or friend will often reveal the fantastic nature of the complaint.

On the other hand the clinician should not be too ready to dismiss the reality of complaints about noise. Undoubtedly, prolonged exposure to noise can be very upsetting, and intrusive, interfering with sleep and everyday activities. In poorly built dwellings, especially apartments, even low intensity noises may be clearly audible through walls, floors, or ceilings. In this situation, noise is destructive of privacy, especially for those living alone, may be associated with perceptions of threat or increases in sense of isolation. This may be especially the case among people who are chronically anxious; prolonged noise exposure may make them more anxious and unhappy. Often this leads to arguments with neighbors that lead to a breakdown of neighborly relationships and further isolation that may in itself have a bad effect on mental health. Occasionally, such conflicts may result in violence and homicide. This may occur either in people with overt psychotic illness, or in those with personality disorders.

In summary, community noise exposure is related to noise annoyance, performance deficits, and sleep disturbance and may be responsible for certain psychological symptoms. However, apart from Kryter's (1990) isolated finding on psychiatric hospital admission rates and noise, there is little from community surveys to suggest that noise is an important etiological factor in psychiatric disorder. This does not rule out the possibility that noise acts through moderating other stressors or through its effects being moderated by other factors such as perceived control or coping strategies.

INDICATORS OF THE PSYCHOSOCIAL ENVIRONMENT

Many planning bodies and local governments have had an overwhelming preoccupation for many years with reducing the density of urban population. Choldin (1978) pointed out, however, that "it is more important to recognize that high density is a basic feature of the urban community and to discover ways in which to organize community life and to build satisfying environments." Even more important is the fact that relatively high density is actually essential for the positive qualities of towns and cities, such as cultural life and specialized professional services. Newman (1980) drew attention to the way in which suburban communities endlessly reproduce the same relatively low level of collective amenities, while leaving behind the "decaying remnants of a once rich environment in their flight from the pathology of the inner city. A principal casualty of this endless process is the disappearance of urban lifestyle."

Density-pathology research has mostly assumed that dense living conditions have pathological effects on the inhabitants of urban areas, but Magaziner (1989) pointed out that in fact, no consistent or linear relationship has been demonstrated between the two. Living alone must be viewed as separate from the continuum of low- to high-density environments. His data from Chicago (where the greatest amount of research into this subject has been done) show that density outside the dwelling unit interacts with the in-unit density to promote or prevent psychopathology. If opportunities for social contacts are readily available in the neighborhood, living alone need not cause social isolation. This was more apparent in the older age groups, presumably because they are generally less mobile, whereas younger people can usually obtain their social contacts more widely, unless prevented by poverty or lack of transport. Mitchell (1976) pointed out that density (number of persons per geographical area) is different from crowding (excessive demands on available space in the dwelling unit), which is strongly influenced by psychosocial factors. Except in extreme cases, the amount of space per person appears to be less important for mental health than lack of personal control over it, with the accompanying disordered social relationships.

Housing may be regarded as that part of the physical environment that is most directly relevant to mental health; because it usually contains the immediate family, it also relates to the most significant aspect of the social environment. However, relatively little is known in scientific terms about the direct effects of any specific aspect of housing on psychiatric morbidity. One fact that is clearly established, though, is that there is no simple dichotomy whereby unsatisfactory physical conditions impair only physical health, whereas poor psychological or social conditions impair mental health. In fact, the two constantly interact. Much of the research in this field has focused on residential movement, but this is far from ideal, because moving home tends to be accompanied by changes that were the reasons for the move, rather than its effects. Examples of these factors include changes in economic status and moving into a different age range.

The most important investigation up to now into the psychiatric sequelae of relocation is that of Fried (1963) of people who had been compulsorily moved from the West End of Boston—a long-established, mainly Italian, working-class community. Two years after it occurred, about 25% of the sample still felt significantly depressed about this move, another 20% had such feelings for at least 6 months, whereas less severe response was reported by many others. The two most important components of this grief reaction were a fragmentation of people's sense of spatial identity and the dependence of their group identity on stable social networks. In such a working-class community, the sense of continuity—which is believed to be an important factor for mental health—appears to be strongly related to the external stability and familiarity of places and people. It also seems likely that an integrated sense of spatial identity is fundamental to human functioning and that this is generally related to a specific place.

The bereavement-type reactions that follow such enforced removal from a well-established community would presumably not apply to areas undergoing rapid social change of an adverse kind, or where there has been a breakdown of law and order. Similarly, in the case of people who have marked neurotic or personality problems, a new housing environment may represent little more than a matrix for the projection of longstanding difficulties (Hall, 1966). Unless adverse practical problems become overwhelming, most families eventually adapt to new residential environments, but this still leaves a substantial minority who suffer stress from such changes.

CROWDING AND HEALTH

Stokols (1972) defined that crowding exists when the demand for space exceeds supply. People have differing needs for personal space dependent on gender, personality, and culture. Crowding may be distinguished from density, which is the number of persons per unit of geographical area. High density is associated with perceived crowding. "Social density" may be an issue in conditions of moderate crowding but "spatial density" becomes an important factor at high levels of occupation (Paulus, McCain, & Cox, 1978).

Potentially, the effects of crowding that may impair health include sensory overload, fewer behavior choices, increased unpredictability in the behavior of others, and anxiety caused by invasion of instinctive boundaries (Kellett, 1984). Evans, Palsane, Lepore, and Martin (1989) included the breakdown of social support under high density living conditions. Gove, Hughes, and Galle (1979) described two interrelated concepts involved in crowding, namely excess of stimulation and lack of privacy. They suggested that the subjective experience of crowding intervenes between objective measure of number of persons per room and dependent health measures.

Crowding and Psychiatric Disorder

In a community study of psychiatric disorder in Brighton, United Kingdom, crowding, measured by the percentage of households with more than 1.5 persons per room was associated with a higher prevalence of psychiatric disorder (Bagley, Jacobson, & Palmer, 1973). However, not surprisingly, single person households, representing the risk of social isolation, also had higher rates of psychiatric disorder. In many of these studies crowding is confounded by low income, social class, and education. Gove et al. (1979) in a study of 80 census tracts of Chicago found that the number of persons per room correlated with rates of psychiatric symptoms and rates of nervous breakdown in the previous year. They also correlated negatively with self-esteem and positive affect. These effects remained after adjusting for sex, race, marital status, education, age, and family income. Number of persons per room also showed a relationship to marital quality, lack of sleep, and dissatisfaction with child care. Although Sainsbury (1955) found no association between crowding and suicide both McCulloch, Philip, and Carstairs

(1967) and Bagley et al. (1973) found suicide and parasuicide correlated with crowding. However, isolation was a more important factor.

Higher residential density has been associated with decreased social support and greater psychological distress /on the PERI scale/ in the Indian town of Pune (Evans et al., 1989). Moreover, in regression analyses after adjusting for income and education, when social support was taken into account, density was no longer significant, indicating that the negative effects of residential density on psychological distress were, at least in part, explained by reduced social support. Subjects' appraisal of crowding (not enough rooms in the house) had a similar effect.

Baldessare (1979) stated that crowding is likely to affect the health of those who are unable to find ways to alleviate stress such as children, mothers of young families, and the elderly. In his Isle of Wight study, Rutter et al. (1975) found that large families and crowding were risk factors in the incidence of childhood psychiatric disorder. Large families tend to lead to delayed language development through lack of verbal stimulation from adults, thence to delayed reading and dissatisfaction at school and a greater risk of truancy and delinquency.

PROMOTING MENTAL HEALTH
THROUGH THE SOCIAL ENVIRONMENT

The World Health Organization (WHO) Ottawa Charter states that health promotion actions include the building-up of a social and physical environment that is supportive to health. Supportive environment includes both physical and social aspects, but with particular emphasis on ecological stability and sustainability of resources. Any suggestions for the reform of society by the application of medical (and specifically psychiatric) knowledge have up to now had unimpressive results, probably because they have been too general and too ambitious. Yet more modest efforts to improve psychiatric or social pathology, on the basis of existing knowledge and resources, could be extremely worthwhile for urban communities. Cities do tend to house concentrations of multiply disadvantaged people, who may show poor mental or physical health along with other unfavorable attributes, but it would be unjustified to extrapolate this negative picture to whole city populations (Freeman, 1984).

When prevention of psychiatric disorder is discussed, it is often assumed that it must in some way deal with basic causes; yet this involves a naive and simplistic view of etiology, most of which still remains unknown. The result is a tendency to wait for the millennium, mostly because of entirely unproven beliefs that psychiatric and social pathologies are direct expressions of the harmful structure of society. Furthermore, Leighton and Murphy (1994) pointed out that in the case of affective disorders, because of chronicity, prevalence is on a much larger scale than incidence. Even if primary prevention were possible, it would make relatively little difference for another generation; on the other hand, secondary prevention of chronicity—for which effective methods already exist—could significantly reduce levels of psychiatric morbidity. There is certainly an important social contribution to the causes of these disorders—which includes the influence of the physical environment—but the interrelationship of the various etiological factors is highly complex, often subtle, and still far from understood.

Although the relationship between physical surroundings in general and mental health lacks reliable data, it is reasonable to believe that an attractive environment will tend to make people generally happier than an unattractive one. There is evidence that dimly lit and hostile-looking constructions that lack the human scale of more traditional environments are likely to make many people anxious or afraid. This is not without reason, because the danger of harassment or attack is far greater in these areas.

In a unique experiment, Halpern (1995) assessed the mental health of residents of a public housing development in England; they were found to have a high level of both anxiety and depression. A large program of environmental improvement was then carried out by the city, and the residents were reassessed after this had been completed. Significant improvement was found in both anxiety and depression, which was thought to be due not only to the environmental changes, but to the process of consultation with residents that had taken place before the program began.

It also seems likely that there are human advantages in such traditional forms as arcade streets or enclosed markets. Many agoraphobics feel less anxious if they go around the edge of a large open space, whereas people often experience anxiety on pedestrian bridges over main roads, or when an elevator opens onto a dimly-lit area. Architecturally overdetermined new environments have generally broken away from established patterns of movement, even abolishing such a fundamental scene of human life as the street. In these changes, the formerly rich pattern of interaction around homes, local shops, and cafes or bars—which were an important source of social support—have been largely destroyed. That support is likely to be an important underlying factor in mental health, and Faria (1989) has suggested that mental health promotion should include the reinforcement of social networks that might help individuals to cope with more distressing situations.

It would be reasonable to maintain that mental health is unlikely to be promoted by incomprehensible urban sprawl, severed by dangerous freeways, and full of monotonous blocks, with unwelcoming spaces between them. There are also the likely ill-effects of population dispersal, such as the time and energy wasted by millions of people every day in long-distance commuting, together with the stress that must come from this frustrating activity. As a consequence, city centers are deserted at night and on weekends, whereas suburbs are empty during the weekdays, causing further undesirable social and psychological effects.

This also makes the control of deviant behavior more difficult, because people are constantly on the move (except for the poor and the unemployed), and the unofficial monitoring that neighbors and workmates carry out in less complex societies is no longer possible. In contrast, a concern for people's mental health would suggest the need to restore to large human settlements true benefits of urbanity—of an environmental structure that would provide the social matrix in which a worthwhile quality of life and work could exist.

The International Hearing on Achieving Better Living Conditions in Towns, held in Strasbourg in October 1988, concluded that a mixed-use policy of combining housing, commerce, and business could play a significant role in reducing levels of urban delinquency and vandalism. It condemned housing policies based on demolition and rehousing of the inhabitants elsewhere, which tend to create a climate of tension and insecurity and to provoke a breakdown of collective life. A better social mix, for example, through the return of middle-class housing and small enterprises to city centers could be expected to improve the morale, services, and living standards of these areas.

A number of structural features in public housing have been found to have a direct relationship with aspects of mental health. In New York, Newman (1972) showed that the number of dwellings per entrance was the most important factor affecting the rate of crime in an apartment block, that is, the more dwellings, the more crime. Though crime levels are not a direct proxy for mental ill-health, fear of crime and the psychological and social consequences of having been exposed to it should represent two important elements in any overall measure of such morbidity. Coleman (1985) also found that design features that are bad from the human point of view tend to cluster together in the same scheme, and so reinforce each other. Newman's concept of "defensible space" has been of great heuristic value in considering these questions: Personal control over one's home environment and its immediate surroundings was shown to be important to the morale of both individuals and communities, as well as favorably influencing their behavior.

PSYCHOSOCIAL STRESS IN URBAN AREAS

In investigating the mental health aspects of the environment, an important general model is that of stress, though demonstrating its effects in any specific terms has proved to be difficult (Freeman, 1988). Other than the study of Cohen, Evans, Stokols, and Kranz (1986) in California, there have been few attempts to examine either the interplay between multiple environmental stressors or the influence they may have on health. In fact, the direct effects of such stressors on either behavior or bodily physiology may be less harmful than the consequences of an individual's coping responses (Evans, 1982). It appears that the combination of multiple stressors results in a much greater combined adverse effect than the mere summation of the effects of the separate stressors (Rutter, 1979).

Though city living seems to be associated with decline of social support from neighbors and of participation in the local community life, this pattern is not homogeneous across urban populations (Mueller, 1981). It might be especially characteristic of areas such as the inner city or public housing developments, where there tends to be a high turnover of residents and changing ethnic composition. Within such areas, the effects of reduced supportive ties would be greater in those not in contact with people outside the immediate locality, for example, housewives (particularly with young children at home or not working) and the elderly. A greater prevalence of depression has been found both in urban working-class women, and in the elderly (Gurland et al., 1976).

In high-rises particularly, people complain of feeling remote and cut off from any community life, with no real neighborly contacts, yet at the same time lacking privacy because of the absence of sound insulation and so on. Such disadvantaged groups as the elderly and physically handicapped often find these situations hazardous and stressful because of their dependence on elevators and garbage chutes that often fail to work, because of their isolation, and because they are often harassed by groups of adolescents who hang around public areas and are remote from any adult observation or control. The pollution of public areas by litter, vandalism, graffiti, urine, or feces is also a source of much distress to residents, not only because it is offensive, but also because it demonstrates the breakdown of the moral order of society—a situation out of control (Coleman, 1985).

With economic recession, a vicious circle of environmental decline often begins: Functioning families try to find accommodation elsewhere, and tend to be replaced by families with multiple social problems. In this process, the chief sufferers are those who start by being already disadvantaged; they now find themselves trapped in an escalation of vandalism, crime, and the despoiling of their surrounding environment.

THE MENTAL HEALTH OF CHILDREN
AND ADOLESCENTS IN CITIES

The connection between high rates of social deviance and psychiatric disorder, which tends to be found in certain areas of cities, is most marked in the case of children. Rutter (1981) pointed out that for them, inner-city life is associated with a wide range of problems—not only crime and delinquency, but depression, emotional disturbance, educational difficulties, and family breakdown. However, the critical factors do not appear to be overall population density, migration, or urbanization. In fact, the inner-city excess of childhood psychiatric disorder could be accounted for by the combined adverse effects of certain schools and certain families; no broader ecological influence needs to be invoked (Rutter & Quinton, 1977).

Yet even in a deprived neighborhood, many children show no evidence of antisocial behavior or delinquency (West & Farrington, 1977). There is considerable individual variation, probably of genetic origin, in response to environmental stress, though of course, such stressors should still be removed whenever possible. However, it may be useful to focus help on the most vulnerable, when these can be identified. Children exposed to a single risk factor were found to be no more likely to have psychiatric disorders than children with no such factors, but when two or more factors were present, the risk of disorder increased greatly (Rutter & Quinton, 1977).

Children and adolescents have suffered particularly from the consequences of contemporary environmental changes in many cities—destruction of established neighborhoods, high-rise housing, urban motor ways, loss of public transport, et cetera. Sherlock (1990) pointed out that they "can no longer play spontaneously in their street or cycle to school. They may now live in more hygienic houses, but their peer community has been destroyed" (p. 26). Because streets have been taken over by traffic, the usual response is to provide fenced-off play areas, but in fact, these tend either to be largely unused or become centers for vandalism, delinquency, and drugs.

Jacobs (1961) first pointed out that established neighborhoods are self-policing, in that children outside their homes are constantly seen by passing neighbors or relatives, as well as observed by "the eyes in the street"—people who watch the passing scene from their homes. Contact with many adults then provides a variety of role models for the process of socialization into the society's mores. However, in redeveloped areas, particularly with high-rise buildings, this informal supervision can no longer take place, whereas the lack of distinction between public and private space means that it becomes largely impossible for children to learn the limits of privacy. Young people also tend to remain separate from adults in these environments, for example, in the gang territory of empty spaces (Coleman, 1985).

For adolescents, many urban environments are unfriendly and fail to provide opportunities for the kind of social interactions and physical activity they need. In these circumstances, vandalism, drug-taking, and the defacement of every accessible surface with graffiti are likely to be on a massive scale. Such incivilities are especially frightening to older people, leading to a deterioration in the community's morale and so to poorer mental health.

REFERENCES

Abey-Wickrama, I., A'Brook, M. F., Gattoni, F. E. G., & Herridge, C. F. (1969). Mental hospital admissions and aircraft noise. *Lancet, 2,* 1275–1277.

Anderson, C. M. B. (1971). *The measurement of attitude to noise and noises* (Acoustics Report No. AC 52). Teddington, Middlesex, United Kingdom: National Physical Laboratory.

Bagley, C., Jacobson, S., & Palmer, C. (1973). Social structure and the ecological distribution of mental illness, suicide and delinquency. *Psychological Medicine, 3,* 177–187.

Baldessare, M. (1979). *Residential crowding in urban America.* San Francisco: University of California Press.

Barker, S. M., & Tarnopolsky, A. (1978). Assessing bias in surveys of symptoms attributed to noise. *Journal of Sound and Vibration, 59,* 349–354.

Bennett, E. (1945). Some tests for the discrimination of neurotic from normal subjects. *British Journal of Medical Psychology, 20,* 271–277.

Broadbent, D. E. (1953). Noise, paced performance, and vigilance tasks. *British Journal of Psychology, 44,* 295–303.

Broadbent, D. E. (1972). Individual differences in annoyance by noise. *Sound, 6,* 56–61.

Broadbent, D. E. (1983). Recent advances in understanding performance in noise. In G. Rossi (Ed.), *Proceedings of 4th International Congress: (Vol. 2). Noise as a public health problem* (pp. 719–738). Milan: Centro Ricerche e studi amplifon.

Burchell, B. (1994). The effects of labour market position, job insecurity, and unemployment on psychological health. In D. Gallie, C. Marsh, C. Vogler (Eds.), *Social change and the experience of unemployment* (pp. 188–212). Oxford: Oxford University Press.

Burke, T. (1990, June). *Supportive environments for health.* World Health Organization Workshop on Briefing Books, Copenhagen.

Cameron, P., Robertson, D., & Zaks, J. (1972). Sound pollution, noise pollution and health: Community parameters. *Journal of Applied Psychology, 56,* 67–74.

Cappon, D. (1975). Designs for improvements in the quality of life in downtown cores. *International Journal of Mental Health, 4,* 31–47.

Choldin, H. M. (1978). Urban density and pathology. *Annual Review of Sociology, 4,* 91–113.

Chowns, R. H. (1970). Mental hospital admissions and aircraft noise. *Lancet, 1,* 467–468.

Cohen, A. (1976). The influence of a company hearing conservation program on extra-auditory problems in workmen. *Journal of Public Safety, 8,* 146–161.

Cohen, S., Evans, G. W., Stokols, D., & Kranz, D. (1986). *Behavior, health and environmental stress.* New York: Plenum.

Cohen, S., & Spacapan, S. (1978). The after effects of stress: An attentional interpretation. *Environmental Psychology and Non-verbal Behaviour, 3,* 43–57.

Cohen, S., & Weinstein, N. (1981). Non-auditory effects of noise on behaviour and health. *Journal of Social Issues, 37,* 36–70.

Coleman, A. (1985). *Utopia on trial.* London: Hilary Shipman.

Crook, M. A., & Langdon, F. J. (1974). The effects of aircraft noise on schools around London airport. *Journal of Sound and Vibration, 34,* 221–232.

Davis, H. (Ed.). (1958). *Project Anehin USN School of Aviation Medicine* (Project NM 130199, Subtask 1, Report No. 7). Pensacola, FL.

Dunleavy, P. (1981). *The politics of mass housing in Britain, 1945–75.* Oxford: Clarendon Press.

Evans, G. W. (1982). General introduction. In G. W. Evans (Ed.), *Environmental stress* (pp. 1–11). Cambridge: Cambridge University Press.

Evans, G. W., Palsane, M. N., Lepore, S. J., & Martin, J. (1989). Residential density and psychological health: The mediating effects of social support. *Journal of Personality and Social Psychology, 57,* 994–999.

Evans, G. W., & Tafalla, R. (1987). Measurement of environmental annoyance. In H. S. Koelaga (Ed.), *Developments in toxicology and environmental science* (pp. 11–25). Amsterdam: Elsevier.

Faria, J. S. (1989). *Notes on the promotion of mental health within the health promotion concept.* Dresden: WHO Working Group.

Ferrie, J. E., Shipley, M. J., Marmot, M. G., Stansfeld, S., & Davey Smith, G. (1995). Health effects of anticipation of job change and non-employment: Longitudinal data from the Whitehall II Study. *British Medical Journal, 311,* 1264–1269.

Fields, J. M. (1994). The effect of numbers of noise events on people's reactions to noise. An analysis of existing survey data. *Journal of the Acoustic Society of America, 75,* 447–467.

Finke, H. O., Guski, R., Martin, R., Rohrmann, B., Schumer, R., & Schumer-Kohrs, A. (1974). *Effects of aircraft noise on man.* Proceedings of the Symposium on Noise in Transportation, section III, paper 1. Institude of Sound and Vibration Research: Southampton.

Freeman, H. L. (Ed.). (1984). Mental health and the environment. London: Churchill Livingstone.

Freeman, H. L. (1985). Housing. In H. L. Freeman (Ed.), *Mental health and the environment* (pp. 197–225). London: Churchill Livingstone.

Freeman, H. L. (1988). Psychiatric aspects of environmental stress. *International Journal of Mental Health, 17,* 13–23.

Freeman, H. L. (1993). Mental health and high-rise housing. In R. Burridge & D. Otmandy (Eds.), *Aspects on unhealthy housing.* London: E. & F. SPON.

Freeman, H. L. (1994). The relationship between schizophrenia and city residence. *British Journal of Psychiatry, 164* (Suppl. 23), 40–51.

Frerichs, R. R., Beeman, B. L., & Coulson, A. H. (1980). Los Angeles airport noise and mortality—Faulty analysis and public policy. *American Journal of Public Health, 70,* 357–362.

Fried, M. (1963). Grieving for a lost home. In L. J. Duhl (Ed.), *The urban condition* (pp. 151–171). New York: Basic Books.

Fryer, D., & Payne, R. (1986). Being unemployed: A review of the literature on the psychological experience of unemployment. In C. L. Cooper & I. Robertson (Eds.), *International review of industrial and organizational psychology* (pp. 235–278). Chichester, United Kingdom: Wiley.

Gans, H. (1968). *People and plans.* New York: Basic Books.

Gattoni, F., & Tarnopolsky, A. (1973). Aircraft noise and psychiatric morbidity. *Psychological Medicine, 3,* 516–520.

Globus, G., Friedmann, J., Cohen, H., Pearson, K. S., & Fidell, S. (1973). The effects of aircraft noise on sleep electrophysiology as recorded in the home. In W. D. Ward (Ed.), *Proceedings of the International Congress on Noise as a Public Health Problem* (pp. 587–592). Washington, DC: U.S. Environmental Protection Agency.

Goldberg, D. P. (1972). *The detection of psychiatric illness by questionnaire.* London: Oxford University Press.

Goldberg, D. P., Cooper, B., Eastwood, M. R., et al. (1970). A standardised psychiatric interview suitable for use in community surveys. *British Journal of Preventive and Social Medicine, 24,* 18–23.

Gore, S. (1978). The effect of social support in moderating the health consequences of unemployment. *Journal of Health and Social Behavior, 19,* 157–165.

Gove, W. R., Hughes, M., & Galle, O. R. (1979). Overcrowding in the home—An empirical investigation of its possible pathological consequences. *American Sociological Review, 44,* 59–80.

Granati, A., Angelepi, F., & Lenzi, R. (1959). L'influenza dei rumori sul sistema nervoso. *Folia Medica, 42,* 1313–1325.

Grandjean, E., Graf, P., Cauber, A., Meier, H. P., & Muller, R. (1973). A survey of aircraft noise in Switzerland. *Proceedings of the International Congress on Noise as a Public Health Problem* (USEPA Publication No. 500:1973–008, pp. 645–659). Washington, DC.

Griffiths, I. D., & Langdon, F. J. (1968). Subjective response to road traffic noise. *Journal of Sound and Vibration, 8,* 16–32.

Gunn, W. J. (1987). The importance of the measurement of annoyance in prediction of effects of aircraft noise on the health and well-being of noise exposed communities. In H. S. Koelaga (Ed.), *Developments in toxicology and environmental science* (pp. 237–255). Amsterdam: Elsevier.

Gurland, B., Copeland, J., Kuriansky, J., Kelleher, M., Sharpe, L. & Dean, L. L. (1976). *The mind and mood of aging.* London: Croom Helm.

Hall, F. L., Taylor, S. M., & Birnie, S. E. (1985). Activity interference and noise annoyance. *Journal of Sound and Vibration, 103,* 237–252.

Hall, P. (1966). Some clinical aspects of moving house as an apparent precipitant of psychiatric symptoms. *Journal of Psychosomatic Research, 10,* 59–70.

Halpern, D. (1995). *Mental health and the built environment.* London: Taylor & Francis.

Hamilton, V. L., Hoffman, W. S., Broman, C. L., & Rauma, D. (1993). Unemployment, distress and coping: A panel study of autoworkers. *Journal of Personality and Social Psychology, 65,* 234–247.

Hansen, J., & Hiller, W. (1984). The architecture of a community. *Architecture and Behavior, 2,* 20–29.

Hepworth, S. J. (1980). Moderating factors of the psychological impact of unemployment. *Journal of Occupational Psychology, 53,* 139–145.

Iversen, L., & Sabroe, S. (1988). Psychological well-being among unemployed and employed people after a company close down: A longitudinal study. *Journal of Social Issues, 44*(4), 141–152.

Iwata, O. (1984). The relationship of noise sensitivity to health and personality. *Japanese Psychological Research, 26,* 75–81.

Jacobs, J. (1961). *The death and life of great American cities.* New York: Random House.

Jansen, G. (1961). Adverse effects of noise on iron and steel workers. *Stahl und Eisen, 81,* 217–220.

Jelinkova, A. (1988). Coping with noise in noise sensitive subjects. In B. Berglund (Ed.), *Noise 88: Noise as a public health problem: Vol. 3. Performance, behaviour, animal, combined agents and community responses* (pp. 27–30). Stockholm: Swedish Council for Building Research.

Jenkins, L. M., Tarnopolosky, A., & Hand, D. J. (1981). Psychiatric admissions and aircraft noise from London Airport: Four-year, three hospitals' study. *Psychological Medicine, 11,* 765–782.

Jenkins, L. M., Tarnopolsky, A., Hand, D. J., & Barker, S. M. (1979). Comparison of three studies of aircraft noise and psychiatric hospital admissions conducted in the same area. *Psychological Medicine, 9,* 681–693.

Job, R. F. S. (1988). Community response to noise: A review of factors influencing the relationship between noise exposure and reaction. *Journal of the Acoustic Society of America, 83,* 991–1001.

Jones, D. M., Chapman, A. J., & Auburn, T. C. (1981). Noise in the environment: A social perspective. *Journal of Environmental Psychology, 1,* 43–59.

Kasl, S. V. (1979). Changes in mental health status associated with job loss and retirement. In J. E. Barrett, R. M. Rose, & G. L. Klerman (Eds.), *Stress and mental disorder.* New York: Raven Press.

Kellett, J. M. (1984). Crowding and territoriality: A psychiatric view. In H. Freeman (Ed.), *Mental health and the environment* (pp. 71–96). Edinburgh: Churchill Livingstone.

Knipschild, P., & Oudshoorn, N. (1977). VII Medical effects of aircraft noise: Drug survey. *International Archives of Occupational and Environmental Health, 40,* 97–100.

Kokokusha, D. (1973). *Report of investigation of living environment around Osaka International Airport.* Osaka, Japan: Aircraft Nuisance Prevention Association.

Kryter, K. D. (1990). Aircraft noise and social factors in psychiatric hospital admission rates: A re-examination of some data. *Psychological Medicine, 20*, 395–411.

Langdon, F. J. (1976). Noise nuisance caused by road traffic in residential areas: Part 1. *Journal of Sound and Vibration, 47*, 243–263.

Langdon, F. J., Buller, I. B., & Scholes, W. E. (1981). Noise from neighbours and the sound insulation of party walls in houses. *Journal of Sound and Vibration, 79*, 205–228.

Leighton, A. H., & Murphy, J. M. (1994). Contributions to psychiatric epidemiology in Ödegård's multifactorial inheritance. In L. F. Saugstad, H. L. Freeman, & M. K. Palomäki (Eds.), *Psychiatry and mental health—The legacy of Örnulv Ödegård* (pp. 29–42). Oslo: LFSF.

Lewis, G., David, A., Andreasson, S., & Allebeck, P. (1992). Schizophrenia and city life. *Lancet, 340*, 137–140.

Loeb, M. (1986). *Noise and human efficiency*. Chichester: Wiley.

Magaziner, J. (1989). Living density and psychopathology. *Psychological Medicine, 18*, 419–431.

McCulloch, J. W., Philip, A. E., & Carstairs, G. M. (1967). The ecology of suicidal behaviour. *British Journal of Psychiatry, 113*, 313–319.

Meecham, W. C., & Smith, H. G. (1977). Effects of jet aircraft noise on mental hospital admissions. *British Journal of Audiology, 11*, 81–85.

Melamed, S., Najenson, T., Luz, T., Jucha, E., & Green, M. (1988). Noise annoyance, industrial noise exposure and psychological stress symptoms among male and female workers. In B. Berglund (Ed.), *Noise 88: Noise as a public health problem. (Vol. 2). Hearing, communication, sleep and non-auditory physiological effects* (pp. 315–320). Stockholm: Swedish Council for Building Research.

Mitchell, R. E. (1976). Cultural and health influences on building, housing and community standards. *Human Ecology, 4*, 297–330.

Mueller, D. P. (1981). The current status of urban—rural differences in psychiatric disorder. *Journal of Nervous and Mental Disease, 169*, 18–27.

Newman, O. (1972). *Defensible space*. New York: Macmillan.

Newman, O. (1980). *Community interest*. New York: Anchor.

Öhrström, E. (1982). *On the effects of noise with special reference to subjective evaluation and regularity*. Göteborg, Sweden: Department of Environmental Hygiene.

Öhrström, E. (1989). Sleep disturbance, psychosocial and medical symptoms—a pilot survey among persons exposed to high levels of road traffic noise. *Journal of Sound and Vibration, 133*, 117–128.

Öhrström, E. (1993). Long-term effects in terms of psychosocial wellbeing, annoyance and sleep disturbance in areas exposed to high levels of road traffic noise. In M. Vallet (Ed.), *Proceedings 6th International Congress on Noise as a Public Health Problem* (pp. 209–212). Nice: Institut National De Recherche Sur Les Transports Et Leur Securite.

Öhrström, E., Björkman, M., & Rylander, R. (1988). Noise annoyance with regard to neurophysiological sensitivity, subjective noise sensitivity, and personality variables. *Psychological Medicine, 18*, 605–611.

Öhrström, E., Rylander, R., & Björkman, N. (1988). Effects of night time road traffic noise—An overview of laboratory and field studies on noise dose and subjective noise sensitivity. *Journal of Sound and Vibration, 127*, 441–448.

Paulus, P. B., McCain, G., & Cox, V. C. (1978). Death rates, psychiatric commitments, blood pressure and environment. *Journal of Applied Social Psychology, 5*, 91.

Payne, R. L., & Hartley, J. (1984). *Financial situation, health, personal attributes as predictors of psychological experience amongst unemployed men* (Memo No. 599). University of Sheffield, MRC/ESRC Social and Applied Psychology Unit.

Platt, S. (1984). Unemployment and suicidal behaviour: A review of the literature. *Social Science and Medicine, 19*, 93–115.

Pulles, T., Biesiot, W., & Stewart, R. (1988). *Adverse effects of environmental noise on health: An interdisciplinary approach. Noise 88: Noise as a public health problem*. Stockholm: Swedish Council for Building Research.

Reich, R. B. (1990). Review. *Times Literary Supplement*, 925–926.

Rutter, M. L. (1979). Primary prevention of psychopathology. In M. M. Kent & J. E. Rolf (Eds.), *Primary prevention of psychopathology* (pp. 610–625). Hanover, NH: University Press of New England.

Rutter, M. L. (1981). The city and the child. *American Journal of Orthopsychiatry, 51,* 610–625.

Rutter, M. L., & Quinton, D. (1977). Psychiatric disorder. In H. McGurk (Ed.), *Ecological factors in human development.* Amsterdam: North-Holland.

Rutter, M., Yule, B., Quinton, D., Rowlands, O., Yule, W., & Berger, M. (1975). Attainment and adjustment in two geographical areas II: Some factors accounting for area differences. *British Journal of Psychiatry, 126,* 520–533.

Sainsbury, P. (1955). *Suicide in London.* London: Chapman Hall.

Schultz, T. J. (1978). Synthesis of social surveys on noise annoyance. *Journal of Acoustic Society of America, 64,* 377–405.

Sherlock, H. (1990). *Cities are good for us.* London: Transport 2000.

Smith, A. P., & Broadbent, D. E. (1981). Noise and levels of processing. *Acta Psychologica, 47,* 129.

Stansfeld, S. A. (1992). Noise, noise sensitivity and psychiatric disorder: Epidemiological and psychophysiological studies. *Psychological Medicine Monographs* (Suppl. 22). Cambridge: Cambridge University Press.

Stansfeld, S. A., Clark, C. R., Jenkins, L. M., Turpin, G., & Tarnopolsky, A. (1985). Sensitivity to noise in a community sample. I. The measurement of psychiatric disorder and personality. *Psychological Medicine, 15,* 243–254.

Stansfeld, S. A., Sharp, D. S., Gallacher, J., & Babisch, W. (1993). Road traffic noise, noise sensitivity and psychological disorder. *Psychological Medicine, 23,* 977–985.

Stokols, D. (1972). A socio-psychological model of human crowding phenomena. *Journal of the American Institute of Planners, 38,* 72–84.

Tarnopolsky, A., Barker, S. M., Wiggins, R. D., & McLean, E. K. (1978). The effect of aircraft noise on the mental health of a community sample: A pilot study. *Psychological Medicine, 8,* 219–233.

Tarnopolsky, A., & Morton-Williams, J. (1980). *Aircraft noise and prevalence of psychiatric disorders, research report.* London: Social and Community Planning Research.

Tarnopolsky, A., Watkins, G., & Hand, D. J. (1980). Aircraft noise and mental health: I. Prevalence of individual symptoms. *Psychological Medicine, 10,* 683–698.

Taylor, S. M. (1984). A path model of aircraft noise annoyance. *Journal of Sound and Vibration, 96,* 243–260.

Taylor, S. (1938). Suburban neurosis. *Lancet, I,* 759–761.

Thomas, J. R., & Jones, D. M. (1982). Individual differences in noise annoyance and the uncomfortable loudness level. *Journal of Sound and Vibration, 82,* 289–304.

Vallet, M., & Francois, J. (1982). Evaluation physiologique et psychosociologique de l'effect du bruit d'avion sur le sommeil. *Travail Humain, 45,* 155–168.

Van Dijk, F. J. H. (1987). Non-auditory effects of noise in industry. II. A review of the literature. *International Archives of Occupational and Environmental Health, 58,* 325–332.

Warr, P. B. (1984). Job loss, unemployment loss and psychological well-being. In V. Allen & E. van de Vliert (Eds.), *Role transitions* (pp. 263–285). New York: Plenum Press.

Warr, P., & Jackson, P. (1987). Adapting to the unemployed role: A longitudinal investigation. *Social Science and Medicine, 25*(11), 1219–1224.

Watkins, G., Tarnopolsky, A., & Jenkins, L. M. (1981). Aircraft noise and mental health: II. Use of medicines and health care services. *Psychological Medicine, 11,* 155–168.

Webb, S. D. (1985). Urban rural differences. In H. L. Freeman (Ed.), *Mental health and the environment* (pp. 226–249). London: Churchill Livingstone.

Wedmore, K., & Freeman, H. L. (1985). Social pathology and urban overgrowth. In H. L. Freeman (Ed.), *Mental health and the environment* (pp. 293–326). London: Churchill Livingstone.

Weinstein, N. D. (1978). Individual differences in reactions to noise: A longitudinal study in a college dormitory. *Journal of Applied Psychology, 63*, 458–466.

Weinstein, N. D. (1978). Individual differences in critical tendencies and noise annoyance. *Journal of Sound and Vibration, 68*, 241–248.

West, D. J., & Farrington, D. P. (1977). *The delinquent way of life.* London: Heinemann Educational.

Willmott, P. (1974, August 27). Population and community in London. *New Society*, 357–358.

Willner, P., & Neiva, J. (1987). Brief exposure to uncontrollable but not to controllable noise biases the retrieval of information from memory. *British Journal of Clinical Psychology, 25*, 93–100.

Wilson, W. J. (1987). *The truly disadvantaged.* Chicago: University of Chicago Press.

Wing, J. K., Cooper, J. E., & Sartorius, N. (1974). *The measurement and classification of psychiatric symptoms.* London: Cambridge University Press.

Chapter 11

Nature and Mental Health: Biophilia and Biophobia

Randall White
Emory University

Judith Heerwagen
Pacific Northwest National Laboratory

Posttraumatic stress disorder (PTSD) following natural and human-caused disasters demonstrates the sometimes devastating psychological effects of unusual environmental events. The more subtle psychological responses to the natural world have seldom attracted clinical attention. Given our species' long history as subsistence hunters, gatherers, and farmers, the natural environment must have helped shape our cognitive and emotional apparatus. A growing body of research substantiates that we demonstrate consistency in our psychological responses to animals and landscapes, and that these responses do not depend solely on the cultural or symbolic significance of the objects.

Wilson (1984) published an influential book entitled *Biophilia*, which he defined as "an innate tendency to focus on life and lifelike processes" (p. 1). He proposed that such a tendency enhanced the fitness of our ancestors and that we have received the legacy: a brain and mind attuned to extracting, processing and evaluating information from the natural world (Wilson, 1993). These processes operate on a largely unconscious level leaving the mind free to concentrate on complex problems that require decision making (Orians, 1980). Bowlby (1982) brought the evolutionary perspective to psychiatry, but his work focused on human social functioning. Wilson went beyond Bowlby's theory to propose interaction with nature as part of our emotional and behavioral repertoire. This idea is more fully treated by a diverse group of scholars in the book *The Biophilia Hypothesis*

(Kellert & Wilson, 1993). Whereas biophilia denotes attraction, aversion to nature or *biophobia* has also been defined.

FEAR OF NATURE AND PHOBIC DISORDERS

Specific phobias are common, and emerged as the most prevalent non-substance-use mental disorders in the Epidemiologic Catchment Area Study (Regier et al., 1988). Torgersen (1979), in a study of male and female same-sex twins, performed a factor analysis of their fears. He found that fears of animals and of nature formed two of five coherent types, although the nature category included man-made as well as natural environments (tunnels, the ocean). Using Torgersen's categories, a study of phobias among Canadian women demonstrated that animals and nature were the most frequent phobic objects (even when including social phobias; Costello, 1982). In a sample of elderly urban British people, 36% of diagnosed phobias involved animals or specific environments (open and enclosed spaces, heights and thunderstorms; Lindsay, 1991). These data explain why *DSM–IV* lists animal-type and natural-environment-type as two of the five types of specific phobia.

Despite the many deaths each day in traffic accidents, few people develop automobile phobia. Why do we develop excessive fear and avoidance responses to relatively low-risk environmental stimuli such as animals and thunderstorms, and not to common and more dangerous ones? Psychologists realized the limitations of the learning–conditioning model in understanding how we acquire fears, and applied the evolutionary–adaptive model to this question. As a result, Seligman (1971) offered the influential concept of preparedness that postulates that repeated experience over many generations with certain dangerous situations has resulted in selection for innate avoidance responses, adaptive for early hominids. These situations have become prepotent stimuli that find the human mind prepared for them. Marks (1981) explained prepotency as "selective attention of the species to particular stimuli rather than to others when these are encountered without previous experience" and preparedness as "the selective facility to associate only certain stimuli with certain other responses" (p. 194). These concepts add a dimension of understanding lacking from Pavlovian learning theory, which cannot adequately explain why certain objects are more likely to become foci of phobic behavior. We have a long and eventful history with animals and consequently fear them more than automobiles.

Many of the animals that evoke fear, such as spiders, are difficult to see in advance because of their size, cryptic coloration, or because they hide in vegetation or under rocks. Under these circumstances reactions such as negative emotional states and rapid motor responses (e.g., freezing or jumping back) are highly adaptive. Other animals evoke varied responses depending on the situation. If seen up close and with threatening facial features, predators evoke fear (Ohman, 1986). When viewed from a distance or when the head is in profile, predators elicit interest. Both wariness and fascination with hazards in the environment are adaptive: Watching them from a safe vantage point permits one to gain important information about the habits, behaviors, and movements of predators (Heerwagen & Orians, 1993).

In an essay from *Biophilia*, "The Serpent," Wilson (1984) discussed his adventures with snakes when he was a boy, and presented the archetypal animal, more evil and dangerous than any real snake. Fascination with snakes, manifest in religion, myths, visual art and in individuals such as the young Wilson, illustrates the prepotency of snakes for *Homo sapiens*. Wilson emphasized that snakes would have caused significant morbidity among people in hunter–gatherer societies in tropical and subtropical regions. Snakes, like large predators, evoke both fear and fascination, and humans have ascribed paradoxical properties to them: the power both to harm and to heal. People who are compelled to handle snakes, such as herpetologists and members of certain evangelical sects, may in part act from a counterphobic impulse, an active attempt to master the feared object by conquering its mystery.

Research on Specific Phobias—the Evolutionary Perspective

Research using conditioning models with certain fear-relevant stimuli, reviewed by Ulrich (1993) supports the role preparedness plays in human response. Fear-relevant stimuli are overrepresented as phobic objects because they presented hazards to pretechnological people, whereas fear-irrelevant stimuli did not (Ohman, 1986). The snake is a prominent fear-relevant stimulus, and Ohman, who has conducted much of this work, went further than Wilson in speculating about the biological origins of fear of reptiles. His studies employed differential conditioning: Each of two groups of subjects observed pictures of either two fear-relevant (a spider and a snake) or two fear-irrelevant (a flower and a mushroom) stimuli, with one of the stimuli accompanied by an unconditioned aversive costimulus, electric shock. A physiologic response was monitored, either skin conductance or heart rate, over the three phases of the experiment: habituation, acquisition, and extinction. The actual conditioning occurred during the acquisition phase. During the other phases only the stimulus was presented. The preparedness hypothesis predicts that the magnitude of the physiologic response during acquisition and extinction, reflecting the magnitude of the affective response, would be greater for fear-relevant than for fear-irrelevant stimuli.

Studies have found that during the acquisition phase, accelerated heart rate but not increased skin conductance significantly distinguished subjects conditioned to fear-relevant stimuli (E. Cook, Lang, & Hodes, 1986). During the extinction phase, however, increased skin conductance and not accelerated heart rate persisted longer in subjects conditioned to fear-relevant stimuli than in other subjects (E. Cook et al., 1986; Ohman, 1986).

Simply put, more acceleration of heart rate occurs once electric shock begins and hand sweating lasts longer after shock ceases when the subjects see a picture of a snake, than when they see a picture of a mushroom. E. Cook et al. (1986) also found that specifically tactile aversive stimuli permitted conditioning to fear-relevant animal stimuli, since substitution of an aversive sound for electric shock resulted in quicker extinction of the conditioned response. This suggests that we expect that these creatures will bite, and that our fear, or what Ohman (1986) called our innate predatory defense system, responds more robustly when the experiment satisfies this expectation. One can interpret these results as supporting the preparedness hypothesis, although other conditions must be met to substantiate the model fully. Interpretations other than the evolutionary–adaptive might explain the phenomena (Delprato, 1980; McNally 1987).

Learning and Biophobia

A competing hypothesis is that of a learned response: Stories, images, and reports from victims teach us to fear snakes and spiders. An experiment to rule out learned responses compared conditioning with animal stimuli to conditioning with technological stimuli: snakes (phylogenetically fear-relevant) versus guns (ontogenetically fear-relevant; E. Cook et al., 1986). Guns have considerable lethal potential, although some people may perceive them as protective rather than threatening (McNally, 1987). Conditioned skin conductance responses to the animal stimuli demonstrated greater resistance to extinction than did responses to the technological stimuli, which indicates preparedness for fear of phylogenetically relevant objects, for example, snakes.

Learning from others may nonetheless play an important role in acquiring fear. Specific animal phobias tend to begin in childhood (Burke, Burke, Regier, & Rae, 1990; Kendler, Neale, Kessler, Heath, & Eaves, 1992), an age when predators would have taken a significant toll on early hominids (Ohman, 1986). Although humans may readily develop aversive responses to certain animals, this aversion may not require direct exposure to the stimuli: Vicarious experience probably serves as a more adaptive learning stimulus (Ulrich, 1993). Why should a child wait until meeting a real tarantula and getting bitten to learn to avoid spiders? Conditioning trials in which subjects received verbal warnings of electric shock associated with fear-relevant stimuli, or observed others react fearfully to such stimuli, produced more persistent physiologic responses than did similar trials with fear-irrelevant stimuli (Ohman, 1986).

An interesting series of experiments demonstrated that rhesus monkeys have a prepared fear response to reptiles that naive, laboratory-reared monkeys can learn from wild monkeys. The naive monkeys, after habituation to either a toy snake, a toy crocodile, a toy rabbit, or plastic flowers, observed a videotape of another monkey responding fearfully to the ersatz stimulus. Upon re-exposure, the observing monkeys responded with evident fright to the toy reptiles but without fright to the toy rabbit or flowers (M. Cook & Mineka, 1989).

The mutually reinforcing aspects of culture (i.e., learned responses) and atavistic responses could provide a model for understanding the extreme reactions to such rare events as maulings of humans by mountain lions in the United States; calls for exterminating the species contrast with the general indifference to daily reports of fatal auto accidents.

Electrophysiologic studies on preparedness of human responses to predators such as large felines and canines remain to be done, but an intriguing experiment (Webb & Davey, 1992) elucidated an aspect of the fear with which we regard these animals. Subjects rated their fear to a series of animals before and after viewing one of three videos: one depicted "extreme violence," one "revulsive scenes from a hospital operation," and one a "neutral landscape scene." Fear of predators increased after viewing the violent video, whereas fear of smaller animals and insects increased after viewing the revulsive video, which suggests that fear of predators stems from anticipation of maiming or violent death.

This prepotency/preparedness model of avoidance implies that people react before they think, for even without knowing whether a snake is poisonous or not (and most are not), people will have a more persistent physiologic response to an image of a snake than to an image of a flower. The debate over the primacy of affect versus that of cognition is a primary feature of the literature of psychiatry and psychology. In an evolutionary-adaptive analysis, affect emerges as phylogenetically primary because emotional responses (mediated by limbic structures) long preceded thought, language and the development of the cerebral cortex (Zajonc, 1980). Izard (1978) has made a convincing argument that in humans this holds true ontogenetically as well. Ohman (1986), building on these ideas, hypothesized that the predatory defense system "is rapidly and automatically recruited, with little room for inhibitory influences from higher cognitive control loci" (p. 128): We flee before we reflect.

In testing this hypothesis and ensuring the use of what he called automatic stimulus-analysis mechanisms, Ohman developed a conditioning model that permitted subliminal presentation of fear-relevant and fear-irrelevant stimuli. During the extinction phase (following usual methods of acquisition of a conditioned response), subjects viewed the visual stimuli very briefly (for 30 ms) immediately followed by another image presented for sufficient time (100 ms) to permit conscious perception. In this procedure, called *backward masking*, the subject cannot recall having seen the first (or "target") stimulus, but only the second (or "masking") stimulus. The conditioned skin conductance response to fear-relevant stimuli persisted during the backward masked extinction trials, whereas the conditioned response to fear-irrelevant stimuli did not. These results tend to support the idea of an automatic and prepared stimulus analysis (Ohman & Soares, 1993). Among phobic subjects, the masked presentation of a feared animal without an aversive costimulus elicited increased skin conductance, whereas an identically presented control stimulus alone failed to do so.

Ohman and Soares (1993) speculated that these prepared responses may involve subcortical structures, perhaps direct connections between the thalamus and amygdala, which play a role in conditioned autonomic responses in rats. This may explain why a phobic person experiences the fear response as uncontrollable despite being aware that it is excessive. A case study of arachnophobia illustrates this point:

> P. H. is a 58-year-old woman who has feared spiders her entire life. Her earliest vivid memory of spiders is from age 13 when she was surprised by "a huge spider" in the kitchen and had persistent anxiety and insomnia for several days. On another occasion, at approximately age 25, she found a group of small spiders while cleaning her house and felt "paralyzed with overwhelming fear." She once saw a tarantula in the southwest desert and has since ruled out a return trip to that region. She enjoys outdoor activities but participates in them less than she might like out of her need to avoid spiders. She even avoids toy spiders and would refuse to keep one in her house. She also reports having many nightmares involving spiders. Although she realizes that most spiders are harmless, her fear seems beyond her control and she would not consider *in vivo* desensitization because she worries that she might have "a heart attack."

Clinically significant phobic behavior causes distress partly because it seems irrational even to the patient, but both clinician and patient should remember that biophobia evolved as a protective mechanism. Although a salient focus of clinical attention, specific phobias do not perfectly represent the adaptive kind of fearfulness of most interest in considering biophobia. This latter fear may likely be more easily modified by learning, and is not an incapacitating dread. Why some people develop specific phobias remains unknown, although recent studies suggest a genetic diathesis interacting with specific environmental factors (Kendler et al., 1992; Kendler, Neale, Kessler, Heath, & Eaves, 1993).

The Role of Disgust in Biophobia

Emotions other than fright probably play a role in biophobia. Davey (1994a) examined self-reported fear of animals indigenous to Britain in nonclinical subjects and discovered that 53% and 28% of this population are anxious about snakes and spiders, respectively, and at least 20% are anxious about wasps, rats, cockroaches, and bats. The aversion to such animals may arise from their ability to provoke disgust (Matchett & Davey, 1991). This poorly understood emotion may have originated as a response to contaminated food, and disgusting contaminants are almost always of animal origin (prototypically feces; Rozin & Fallon, 1987). Disgust may ultimately serve to prevent ingestion of pathogens, although cultural elaborations of this basic response abound (Rozin & Fallon, 1987).

In a series of experiments, Davey and associates tested the hypothesis that disgust mediates the fear of animals considered vermin or associated with "dirt, disease, or contagion." They used self-ratings to measure the "disgust sensitivity" of nonclinical subjects to hypothetical food contamination, and correlated these with self-ratings of fear of animals. The authors discerned three coherent categories of feared animals: predators (e.g., lions, wolves), invertebrates (e.g., slugs, spiders), and a group they called "fear-relevant" (e.g., snakes, rats). Disgust correlated with fear of the animals in the latter two categories (except wasps and bees; Davey, 1994a; Ware, Jain, Burgess, & Davey, 1994).

Matchett and Davey (1991) proposed that disgust toward most nonpredatory animals serves the adaptive function of reducing contact with vectors of disease, and although some disgusting animals in actuality do not transmit disease, they resemble others that do. Davey (1994b) argued that culture plays a dominant role in determining animal fears. Wasps and bees present a special case among nonpredatory animals: risk of a painful sting and, less frequently, of a fatal systemic reaction. Fear of them may result from "simple processes of associative learning" (Davey, 1994a, p. 553). Snakes fall into both predatory and disgust-evoking categories (Ware et al., 1994). Despite the fact that snakebite resembles a grave bee sting, Webb and Davey (1992) attributed the prepotency of snakes to their resemblance to feces, a peculiar post-Freudian Freudianism. A more cogent explanation may be that some prepotent animal stimuli, even nonpredators like wasps, evoke a prepared anxiety (predatory–defense) response; some, disgust; and some, a combination of both.

In two studies of nonpatient adult subjects, self-rated fear of animals (invertebrates, reptiles, and mammals) explicitly designated as harmless by the investigators correlated significantly with unpleasant characteristics of the animals. Sliminess, strange sounds and odors, and perceived unpredictability and speediness of movement all contributed to higher fear ratings (Bennett-Levy & Marteau, 1984; Merckelbach, Van den Hout, & Van der Molen, 1987). Certain of these attributes, such as sliminess, may provoke disgust (Matchett & Davey, 1991), whereas others, such as quick, erratic movement, may provoke anxiety, which perhaps explains the complex response to snakes. Some creatures of mythology resemble chimera (a fire-breathing she-monster often represented as a composite of lion, goat, and snake), assembled from the most prepotent attributes of several feared or unpleasant animals.

Treatment of Specific Phobias

The most effective treatment for phobias requires that the person confront the feared object. Clinicians have developed different methods of bringing this about, either actually (*in vivo* desensitization) or imaginally (covert desensitization), gradually (systematic desensitization) or abruptly and intensely (flooding). Probably *in vivo* systematic desensitization is most effective and well tolerated. Medication seems to have little effect in long-term diminution of specific phobias and asssociated avoidance behavior (Andrews, Crino, Hunt, Lampe, & Page, 1994).

The automatic stimulus response mechanism, if preconscious and subcortical, would not likely respond solely to cognitive and verbal techniques of intervention. Ohman (1996) believes that the efficacy of exposure supports his model of phobias, and postulated that exposure permits habituation, the "ubiquitous mechanism of response inhibition through repeated exposures," to diminish the anxiety toward the feared object (p. 284). He even suggested that masked exposure, which would avoid conscious anxiety in the patient, may prove therapeutic.

BIOPHILIA AND MENTAL HEALTH

The positive responses to natural stimuli have received much less attention in psychiatry and psychology than the negative. This may be due in part to the difficulty of conducting positive conditioning studies (Ulrich, 1993). The emotional and physiological responses to fear are more obvious than the responses to delight. It is likely that these responses are difficult to measure and observe because of an unevenness in the evolutionary payoffs of biophobic and biophilic responses. The consequences of not attending to potential dangers could mean death or serious injury; those of failure to respond to stimuli that may enhance fitness are less dire.

The uneven payoffs of biophobic and biophilic responses do not mean that biophilia is less important to human well-being. On the contrary, positive responses to nature may have a good deal to do with living well, as opposed to merely surviving. Living well means having continual access to nourishing food, a safe and healthy environment, and supportive social relationships. Such conditions allow successful reproduction, and biophilia, the innate human tendency to focus on and respond to the natural world, must have evolved in enhancing the fitness of our ancestors.

Katcher and Wilkins (1993) carried Wilson's idea of biophilia further and argued that particular kinds of natural events capture our attention and promote positive emotions. They describe these events as having "Heraclitean motion that is always changing but always remaining the same" (p. 176). These phenomena, associated with safety and comfort, include gently moving water, soft patterns of light and shade under a tree canopy, a camp fire, or waterfowl swimming. Events signaling hazard, on the other hand, are characterized by erratic and forceful motion—forest fires, animals fleeing from a predator, lightning, or bursts of wind from a thunderstorm.

Humphrey (1980) similarly hypothesized that aesthetic responses arose from biophilic impulses. He reasoned that our sense of beauty evolved from a fascination with classifying and collecting natural objects and events, skills that were critical for survival (e.g., being able to distinguish between toxic and nourishing foods), and that the characteristics of nature lend themselves particularly well to this process. According to Humphrey's hypothesis our fondness for finding patterns as well as incongruities stems from necessity. The places and objects we regard as beautiful exhibit "rhyming," which he defined as sameness coupled with differences that occur in a patterned way. Similar ideas have been expressed by Platt (1961).

The notion that our sense of aesthetics derives from the functional evaluation of nature is also at the heart of the habitat selection hypothesis advanced by Orians (1980; see also Heerwagen & Orians, 1993; Orians & Heerwagen, 1992). Orians and Heerwagen argued that humans, like other species, innately prefer habitats that provide adequate food and water as well as protection from physical hazards, predators, and hostile members of their own species. Although we now live in a habitat immensely altered by human ingenuity, there is no reason to believe that our basic needs differ from those of our ancestors.

Underlying this theory is the notion that preferences serve as an intuitive guide for behavior. Suitable human habitats must provide resources over long periods of time and in different seasons, which makes quick evaluation of a place difficult. For this reason, humans (as well as many other species) must rely on the features of habitats that predict future conditions. Of particular importance are the presence of food, water, and shelter and the absence of obvious hazards. A desirable environment must also provide opportunities to perceive and assess dangers far enough in advance that appropriate action can be taken. Heerwagen and Orians (1993) further argued that people seek out particular settings conducive to supporting important human activities such as foraging, exploring, sleeping, child care, mating, socializing, planning, and resting. Habitats and settings that fulfill these needs should elicit positive emotional responses, and those that do not should elicit negative responses.

Orians and Heerwagen hypothesized that preferences are likely to vary according to age, gender, and life experience. For instance, the desire for refuge and enclosure might be stronger in young children and in people who are ill or otherwise vulnerable to social or physical hazards. Women in pretechnological societies, especially if primary caretakers for children, were vulnerable to strange men or to large predators. To test aspects of this hypothesis, they compared the landscape paintings of Irish and French male and female artists from the 18th century. They predicted that women would be more sensitive to refuge features of the environment because of their greater vulnerability, and that their paintings would contain more refuge symbolism than the paintings of men. The analysis of 107 paintings (52 by women and 55 by men) showed that women painted significantly more refuge settings, such as gardens and enclosed spaces near residences, whereas men painted more expansive settings with views of the horizon (Heerwagen & Orians, 1993). It is certainly possible that the results are related to different experiences of men and women of the time, given women's more home-centered lives. Nevertheless, women painters probably were exposed to expansive open spaces and panoramic views. The fact that they did not choose to paint such scenes does not indicate lack of opportunity, but rather suggests an intense interest in safe spaces.

Paintings of heaven and hell reflect the very notions that habitat selection theory predicts. Images of hell are often desolate and dark, with dead or dying trees, sick people, lack of refuge, and the presence of menacing creatures. Heaven and paradise, in contrast, have lush vegetation, fruiting trees, sunshine, water, places to rest, distant views of an endless green space, quietly grazing animals, and well fed people with plump babies and rosy-cheeked children. Such images are frequently used by advertisers to sell products such as cigarettes, cars, and liquor that have virtually nothing to do with the happy habitat featured in the advertisement.

What might be the consequences for human emotional functioning of being in "the right place"? Kellert (1993) argued that "the adaptational value of the aesthetic experience of nature could further be associated with derivative feelings of tranquillity, peace of mind, and a related sense of psychological well-being and self-confidence" (p. 50). If there is an evolved relaxation response (Benson, 1975; Everly & Benson, 1989), its origins must lie in the life experiences of our ancestors. Did the sight of lush green grass and large trees next to a gently running stream evoke feelings of relief, comfort, and tranquillity after a day of hunting? Did the camp fire create a sense of security and pleasure? Did views of the horizon and the setting sun evoke contemplation and quiet reflection? Recent studies increasingly show that exposure to pleasant nature stimuli promotes positive emotional states and restoration from stress (Ulrich, 1993; Ulrich et al., 1991). Despite the increasing evidence that nature has potentially profound implications for human well-being, clinicians have paid surprisingly little attention to the natural environment. Nor has there been much interest in searching for the origins of relaxation and restoration responses, the stimuli that evoke such responses, and their significance for human welfare and survival. Given the enormous social and economic costs of emotional distress and mental illness, it is worth looking at ways in which nature can be used in healing.

Existing studies suggest three possibilities for introducing nature into mental health treatments and programs: (a) the intentional use of nature stimuli in relaxation therapy; (b) the active experience of nature in outdoor settings, such as wilderness challenge programs; and (c) the design of therapeutic settings that include both indoor and outdoor vegetation, water, small animals, nature paintings, and natural daylight.

Nature Stimuli in Relaxation Therapy

Relaxation therapy often calls on patients to visualize pleasing natural places, such as meadows, streams, gardens, and gently flowing water (Overholser, 1991). Most of this work proceeded from an intuitive sense of the stress-reducing qualities of nature and did not draw on any theoretical work in biology and psychology. However, habitat selection theory suggests that relaxed enjoyment of the environment originated in the sense of pleasure associated with a place that is safe, comfortable, and rich in resources. Empirical research supports this perspective. Scenery associated with quiet fascination, positive moods, physiological relaxation, and cognitive tranquillity include distant views to the horizon, water, flowers, and park-like settings with clustered trees and shrubbery (Coss, Clearwater, Barbour, & Towers, 1989; Kaplan & Kaplan, 1989; Ulrich, 1983).

A recent study by Golletz (1995) indicates how biophilia can guide identification of clinical problems that would benefit from nature-centered therapy and selection of appropriate stimuli in treatment. He proposed that relaxation therapy may be especially helpful in the treatment of anxiety and anger in which patients find it difficult to eliminate negative, intrusive thoughts. He argued that nature stimuli work well in promoting relaxation by inducing a positive and passive emotional state thereby allowing patients to block out intrusive, negative ideation. In a series of laboratory experiments he first induced anxiety and irritability in subjects by asking them to solve difficult anagrams and to describe a situation that had produced stress and anger. Subjects were then randomly assigned to one of four treatment conditions: a standard verbal relaxation protocol; nature sounds; nature slides; and a control condition of quiet rest with neither stimuli nor a verbal relaxation protocol. Although the experimental stress induction produced only mild indicators of stress and anxiety, subjects who scored the highest on trait anxiety or anger (using the State-Trait Anxiety Inventory and the State-Trait Anger Scale) also showed the most positive response to the nature stimuli. They experienced more positive moods than those receiving the standard verbal protocol and acheived lower heart rates than subjects in the control group. Here is an example of the use of these principles:

> A 51-year-old White male was referred for relaxation therapy and biofeedback training as adjunct to pharmacotherapy for panic disorder and posttraumatic stress disorder. His symptoms occurred subsequent to combat experience in Vietnam and he complained of increasingly low stress tolerance and extreme irritability causing workplace conflicts. He initially learned a standard focused-breathing relaxation procedure but had difficulty implementing this between sessions. The therapist then gave him an audiotape with ocean sounds on one side and a guided verbal relaxation procedure on the other and instructed him to practice relaxation once a day. He reported a strong preference for the ocean sounds. He used them exclusively three to six times per week at home and, occasionally, at work when angry at his supervisor. Biofeedback training progressed during therapy sessions and the patient gained greater control over emotional reactions and reported less overall anxiety.

In this case, nature stimuli improved compliance with a prescribed treatment. For certain patients it may be a useful alternative to other relaxation techniques. Studies by Ulrich further suggest that nature stimuli can elicit emotional and behavioral relaxation. In the experimental model developed by Ulrich (1993; see also Ulrich et al., 1991), participants were subjected to stress, usually by viewing films of industrial accidents. They then attended one of two stress recovery groups in which they sat passively and viewed slides or videos of either nonspectacular nature scenes (the nature group) or urban scenes lacking in vegetation (the control group). A number of physiological responses were monitored. Subjects in both the nature and control groups showed decreases in physiological indicators of stress; however, the subjects who viewed the nature scenes typically showed more rapid stress reduction as well as a greater degree of physiological recovery. Subjects who viewed the nature scenes also experienced more positive emotion than the control group. Ulrich (1993) argued that "acquiring a capacity for restorative responding to certain natural settings had major advantages for early humans including, for instance, fostering the recharge of physical energy, rapid attenuation of stress responses following an encounter with a threat, and perhaps rapid reduction of aggression following antagonistic contacts with other humans" (p. 98).

The Experience of Nature

Nature challenge programs, most notably Outward Bound, have undertaken the goal of promoting self-confidence, self-efficacy, and self-esteem, often in troubled adolescents. Although there is considerable anecdotal evidence of positive results, there is limited empirical support due to numerous methodological problems, including lack of appropriate or use of inappropriate controls, lack of random assignment, and use of in-house evaluations and subjective measures (Levitt, 1994).

Another problem is the notable lack of theory to guide research protocols, with only rudimentary predictions of outcomes, the psychological and social mechanisms contributing to the outcomes, or the characteristics of people for whom the programs would be most beneficial. Despite the theoretical problems, therapists continue to show a strong belief in the therapeutic value of wilderness experiences. In recent years, wilderness programs have been used in a wide range of situations including rape recovery (Powch, 1994), cancer recovery (Johnson & Kelly, 1990), diabetes treatment programs (Herskowitz, 1990), alcohol and drug abuse treatment (Kennedy & Minami, 1993), and bereavement programs (Birnbaum, 1991; Moyer 1988).

Most claims about the therapeutic effects of wilderness programs center on the notion that nature settings and challenges are in some fundamental way different from life in man-made environments. A number of wilderness therapy advocates have begun to identify the elements contributing to its hypothesized benefits. According to Kiewa (1994), one benefit is the concrete and immediate feedback from nature. The consequences of actions are evenhanded in fundamentally different ways from those of human interactions in other settings. Herman (1992) contended that the challenges of nature require "realistic coping" such that making demands, waiting passively to be rescued, and complaining are not effective responses in situations that require both team effort and individual skill such as crossing difficult terrain, setting up camp, and preparing meals. Although a number of programs place high value on the group experience, the literature does not address how group interactions in nature settings are different from interactions in other settings. Numerous authors point to the sense of peacefulness, spirituality, and timelessness evoked by the aesthetic and sensory experiences of natural settings (Dorfman, 1979; Kaplan & Kaplan, 1989; Rossman & Ulehla, 1977; Shafer & Mietz, 1969).

An important distinction in program outcomes relates to active versus passive experiences of nature. For a number of programs, most notably

Outward Bound, the real value comes from meeting challenges such as rock climbing, long-distance canoeing, hiking through difficult terrain, and surviving on resources from the environment. The ability to meet these challenges successfully, to master new situations, and to solve problems in group settings, as well as alone, form the basis for enhanced confidence, self-esteem, and self-efficacy. In other programs, the real basis for positive outcomes appears to be the psychological restoration that comes not from conquering, but from living with nature. These programs are frequently designed for adults, especially women, in recovery from highly stressful events such as rape, cancer, and bereavement.

Recently there have been attempts to identify more rigorously the behavioral and psychological outcomes associated with wilderness challenge programs. Kaplan and Kaplan (1989) summarized their own studies that have shown that gains in "self-concept" are especially strong and enduring. They found that youth who had taken part in a nature challenge program showed more realism with respect to their own strengths and weaknesses, a greater sense of self-sufficiency, a greater concern for others, and a more positive overall view of themselves than did a control group. They also found that the nature group experienced more feelings of peacefulness, an absence of time pressure, and an ability to attend to and find pleasure in common sounds and sights of nature.

Herskowitz (1990), in a program with diabetic youth, compared a group of patients who took part in an Outward Bound sea course with a group of similar patients who did not. Because of the small sample size ($n = 8$), this is best viewed as an expanded case study. Comparing responses to standardized instruments before the program and at 7 to 11 months afterward, he found that several of the Outward Bound patients showed dramatic improvement in problem scores on the Achenbach Youth Self-Report Profile and somewhat less improvement in locus of control and in self-esteem. Patients who took part in the Outward Bound program also showed improvement in their ability to cope with their illness. Qualitative data gathered from patient comments showed that participants had a better understanding of the causes of fluctuating blood sugar levels and an improved sense of being able to manage the disease.

In a study of chemically dependent youth, Kennedy and Minami (1993) looked at behavior for 1 year prior to and 1 year after a 22-day wilderness program. The wilderness activities were designed to teach experientially how to cope with stress and how to interact effectively with others to solve problems. The program included regular group and individual therapy sessions and discussions about chemical dependency and recovery. Results indicated that 38% of the youth regularly attended Alcoholics Anonymous and 47% had maintained complete abstinence after 1 year. The participants also reported fewer legal and school problems and improved family relationships and physical health. The study, however, did not have a control group and no comparative data were available to indicate how these outcomes compared with other treatments.

Clinical Environments

The physical setting in mental health clinics and hospitals could also benefit from the inclusion of nature stimuli. Views of nature are highly effective in eliciting positive emotional states and physiological relaxation. A pleasant outdoor landscape, water, indoor vegetation, nature posters and paintings, fresh flowers, daylight, fish tanks, and bird feeders—all can be readily incorporated into the physical environment with minimal expense. Results from other studies suggest that nature contact benefits patients as well as caregivers.

Although most studies of the positive effects of nature have been done in laboratory settings, work by Kaplan and Kaplan (1989) in an office environment and by Ulrich (1984) in a hospital deal with views from windows. In the Kaplans' study, workers who had a view of vegetation experienced less stress and more job satisfaction than similar workers who did not have a window view of the outdoors. In Ulrich's hospital study, patients with a window view of a small grove of trees had a more positive postsurgical experience than did patients with a view of a brick wall without vegetation. Patients with the view of trees needed fewer strong analgesics, stayed in the hospital fewer days, and had fewer minor postoperative complications than patients in the control group.

Although Ulrich's study focused on patients, the impact of views is likely to be experienced by caregivers as well. For instance, in a discussion following a presentation by Heerwagen, a nurse in the audience described the struggle among staff at her hospital over being located on the side of the building with an expansive view of the Olympic mountains and the water. The other side of the building looked out on a parking lot. We know little about how regularly such sentiments are experienced in health care settings, nor do we know much about the impact of a pleasant window view on those who work in a building all day.

We also know little about the effects of nature on interpersonal relationships. For instance, would settings rich in nature stimuli promote more positive feelings among physicians, therapists and patients, and reduce the amount of time needed to develop trust? Would such settings help patients feel less anxious and, perhaps, more readily able to disclose painful or shameful memories? Might they decrease incidents of violence on inpatient wards? At the present time, there is virtually no research on these important topics.

In the past, psychiatric hospitals were located in bucolic settings, perhaps for some perceived benefit to both the afflicted and society. More recently the physical setting has not been regarded as a mental health concern, and is at best treated as an afterthought rather than as an important aspect of therapy. Failure to look at the physical environment ignores a potentially powerful, inexpensive, and noninvasive adjunct to treatment that may benefit both patients and health care providers.

ACKNOWLEDGMENT

The authors wish to thank Dan Golletz, PhD for his contribution to the manuscript.

REFERENCES

Andrews, G., Crino, R., Hunt, C., Lampe, L., & Page, A. (1994). *The treatment of anxiety disorders: Clinicians's guide and patient manuals.* Cambridge: Cambridge University Press.

Bennett-Levy, J., & Marteau, T. (1984). Fear of animals: What is prepared? *British Journal of Psychology, 75,* 37–42.

Benson, H. (1975). *The relaxation response.* New York: William Morrow.

Birnbaum, A. (1991, September/October). Haven hugs & bugs. *American Journal of Hospice and Palliative Care,* 23–29.

Bowlby, J. (1982). *Attachment* (2nd ed.). New York: Basic Books.

Burke, K. C., Burke, J. D., Regier, D. A., & Rae, D. S. (1990). Age at onset of selected mental disorders in five community populations. *Archives of General Psychiatry, 47,* 511–518.

Cook, E. W., Lang, P. J., & Hodes, R. L. (1986). Preparedness and phobia: Effects of stimulus content on human visceral conditioning. *Journal of Abnormal Psychology, 95,* 195–207.

Cook, M., & Mineka, S. (1989). Observational conditioning of fear to fear-relevant versus fear-irrelevant stimuli in rhesus monkeys. *Journal of Abnormal Psychology, 98,* 448–459.

Coss, R. G., Clearwater, Y. A., Barbour, C. G., & Towers, S. R. (1989). *Functional decor in the international space station: Body orientation cues and picture perception.* Mountain View, CA: NASA-Ames Research Center.

Costello, C. G. (1982). Fears and phobias in women: A community study. *Journal of Abnormal Psychology, 91,* 280–286.

Davey, G. C. L. (1994a). Self-reported fears to common indigenous animals in an adult UK population: The role of disgust sensitivity. *British Journal of Psychology, 85,* 541–554.

Davey, G. C. L. (1994b). The "disgusting" spider: The role of disease and illness in the perpetuation of fear of spiders. *Journal of Agricultural and Environmental Ethics, 2,* 17–25.

Delprato, D. J. (1980). Hereditary determinants of fears and phobias: A critical review. *Behavior Therapy, 11,* 79–103.

Dorfman, P. W. (1979). Measurement and meaning of recreation satisfaction: A case study of camping. *Environment and Behavior, 11,* 483–510.

Everly, G. S., & Benson, H. (1989). Disorders of arousal and the relaxation response: Speculations on the nature and treatment of stress-related diseases. *International Journal of Psychosomatics, 56,* 15–21.

Golletz, D. (1995). *Uses of nature stimuli in relaxation therapy for anxiety and anger.* Unpublished doctoral dissertation. University of Washington, Seattle.

Herman, J. L. (1992). *Trauma and recovery.* New York: HarperCollins.

Heerwagen, J. H., & Orians, G. H. (1993). Humans, habitats, and aesthetics. In S. R. Kellert & E. O. Wilson (Eds.), *The biophilia hypothesis* (pp. 138–172). Washington, DC: Island Press.

Herskowitz, R. D. (1990). Outward Bound, diabetes and motivation: Experiential education in a wilderness setting. *Diabetic Medicine, 7,* 633–638.

Humphrey, N. K. (1980). Natural aesthetics. In B. Mikellides (Ed.), *Architecture for people* (pp. 59–73). London: Studio Vista.

Izard, C. E. (1978). Emotions as motivations: An evolutionary–developmental perspective. In R. Dienstbier (Ed.), *Nebraska Symposium on Motivation* (Vol. 27, pp. 163–200). Lincoln: University of Nebraska Press.

Johnson, J. B., & Kelly, A. W. (1990). A multifaceted rehabilitation program for women with cancer. *Oncology Nursing Forum, 17,* 691–695.

Kaplan, R., & Kaplan, S. (1989). *The experience of nature: A psychological perspective.* Cambridge and New York: Cambridge University Press.

Katcher, A., & Wilkins, G. (1993). Dialogue with animals: Its nature and culture. In S. R. Kellert & E. O. Wilson (Eds.), *The biophilia hypothesis* (pp. 173–197). Washington, DC: Island Press.

Kellert, S. R. (1993). The biological basis for human values of nature. In S. R. Kellert & E. O. Wilson (Eds.), *The biophilia hypothesis* (pp. 42–69). Washington, DC: Island Press.

Kellert, S. R., & Wilson, E. O. (Eds.). (1993). *The biophilia hypothesis.* Washington, DC: Island Press.

Kendler, K. S., Neale, M. C., Kessler, R. C., Heath, A. C., & Eaves, L. J. (1992). The genetic epidemiology of phobias in women: The interrelationship of agoraphobia, social phobia, situational phobia and simple phobia. *Archives of General Psychiatry, 49,* 273–281.

Kendler, K. S., Neale, M. C., Kessler, R. C., Heath, A. C., & Eaves, L. J. (1993). Major depression and phobias: The genetic and environmental sources of comorbidity. *Psychological Medicine, 23,* 361–371.

Kennedy, B. P., & Minami, M. (1993). The Beech Hill Hospital/Outward Bound adolescent chemical dependency treatment program. *Journal of Substance Abuse Treatment, 10,* 395–406.

Kiewa, J. (1994). Self-control: The key to adventure? Towards a model of adventure experience. *Women & Therapy, 15,* 29–41.

Levitt, L. (1994). What is the therapeutic value of camping for emotionally disturbed girls? *Women & Therapy, 15,* 129–137.

Lindsay, J. (1991). Phobic disorders in the elderly. *British Journal of Psychiatry, 159,* 531–541.

Marks, I. M. (1981). *Cure and care of neuroses.* Washington, DC: American Psychiatric Press.

Matchett, G., & Davey, G. C. L. (1991). A test of a disease-avoidance model of animal phobias. *Behaviour Research and Therapy, 29,* 91–94.

McNally, R. J. (1987). Preparedness and phobias: A review. *Psychological Bulletin, 101,* 283–303.

Merckelbach, H., Van den Hout, M. A., & Van der Molen, G. M. (1987). Fear of animals: Correlations between fear ratings and perceived characteristics. *Psychological Reports, 60,* 1203–1209.

Moyer, J. A. (1988, March/April). Bannock bereavement retreat: A camping experience for surviving children. *American Journal of Hospice Care,* pp. 26–30.

Ohman, A. (1986). Face the beast and fear the face: Animal and social fears as prototypes for evolutionary analyses of emotion. *Psychophysiology, 23,* 123–145.

Ohman, A. (1996). Preferential preattentive processing of threat in anxiety: Preparedness and attentional biases. In R. M. Rapee (Ed.), *Current controversies in the anxiety disorders* (pp. 253–290). New York: Guilford Press.

Ohman, A., & Soares, J. J. F. (1993). On the automatic nature of phobic fear conditioned electrodermal responses to masked fear-relevant stimuli. *Journal of Abnormal Psychology, 102,* 121–132.

Orians, G. H. (1980). Habitat selection: General theory and applications to human behavior. In J. S. Lockard (Ed.), *The evolution of human social behavior* (pp. 49–66). New York: Elsevier.

Orians, G. H., & Heerwagen, J. H. (1992). Evolved responses to landscapes. In J. Barkow, L. Cosmides, & J. Tooby (Eds.), *The adapted mind: Evolutionary psychology and the generation of culture* (pp. 601–624). Oxford and New York: Oxford University Press.

Overholser, J. C. (1991). The use of guided imagery in psychotherapy: Modules for use with passive relaxation training. *Journal of Contemporary Psychology, 21,* 159–172.

Platt, J. R. (1961). Beauty: Pattern and change. In D. W. Fisker & S. R. Maddi (Eds.), *Functions of varied experience* (pp. 402–430). Homewood, IL: Dorsey.

Powch, I. G. (1994). Wilderness therapy: What makes it empowering for women? *Women & Therapy, 15,* 11–27.

Regier, D. A., Boyd, J. H., Burke, J. D., Rae, D. S., Myers, J. K., Kramer, M., Robins, L. N., George, L. K., Karno, M., & Locke, B. Z. (1988). One-month prevalence of mental disorders in the US, based on five epidemiologic catchment area sites. *Archives of General Psychiatry, 45,* 977–986.

Rossman, R. R., & Ulehla, Z. J. (1977). Psychological reward values associated with wilderness use: A functional-reinforcement approach. *Environment and Behavior, 9,* 41–66.

Rozin, P., & Fallon, A. E. (1987). A perspective on disgust. *Psychological Review, 94,* 23–41.

Seligman, M. E. P. (1971). Phobias and preparedness. *Behavior Therapy, 2,* 307–320.

Shafer, E. L., & Mietz, J. (1969). Aesthetic and emotional experiences rate high with Northeast wilderness hikers. *Environment and Behavior, 1,* 187–197.

Torgersen, S. (1979). The nature and origin of common phobic fears. *British Journal of Psychiatry, 134,* 343–351.

Ulrich, R. S. (1983). Aesthetic and affective response to natural environment. In I. Altman & J. F. Wohlwill (Eds.), *Human behavior and the natural environment: Vol. 6. Behavior and the natural environment* (pp. 85–125). New York: Plenum.

Ulrich, R. S. (1984). View through the window may influence recovery from surgery. *Science, 224,* 420–421.

Ulrich, R. S. (1993). Biophilia, biophobia and natural landscapes. In S. R. Kellert & E. O. Wilson (Eds.), *The biophilia hypothesis* (pp. 73–137). Washington, DC: Island Press.

Ulrich, R. S., Simons, R. F., Losito, B. D., Fiorito, E., Miles, M. A., & Zelson, M. (1991). Stress recovery during exposure to natural and urban environments. *Journal of Environmental Psychology, 11,* 201–230.

Ware, J., Jain, K., Burgess, I., & Davey, G. C. L. (1994). Disease-avoidance model: Factor analysis of common animal fears. *Behaviour Research and Therapy, 32,* 57–63.

Webb, K., & Davey, G. C. L. (1992). Disgust sensitivity and fear of animals: Effect of exposure to violent or revulsive material. *Anxiety, Stress and Coping, 5,* 329–335.

Wilson, E. O. (1984). *Biophilia.* Cambridge, MA: Harvard University Press.

Wilson, E. O. (1993). Biophilia and the conservation ethic. In S. R. Kellert & E. O. Wilson (Eds.), *The biophilia hypothesis* (pp. 31–41). Washington, DC: Island Press.

Zajonc, R. B. (1980). Feeling and thinking: Preferences need no inferences. *American Psychologist, 35,* 151–175.

Chapter 12

Animal-Assisted Therapy in the Treatment of Disruptive Behavior Disorders in Children

Aaron Katcher
University of Pennsylvania
Devereux Foundation, Villanova, Pennsylvania

Gregory G. Wilkins
William Penn School District, Darby, Pennsylvania

At a time when the largest European cities could fit into a modern shopping mall, poets recommended retreat to the countryside as a cure for the psychological ills induced by urban living. Hesiod's *Works and Days*, written around 700 BC, offers the placid, ordered life of the farm as a cure for the stress of a life in the city (Evelyn-White, 1950). Since Hesiod's day, retreat to the country has been the perennially suggested remedy for the malaise of city life (Williams, 1973). The Arcadian myth, viable even today, holds that at some time in the past, life in the country had an almost Elysian beauty and that farmers and herdsmen enjoyed a life of health and tranquillity unknown today (Harrison, 1992; Rousseau, 1947). The myths contain some shrewd clinical observations: Until this century, death rates were always higher in the cities than in the country (Davis, 1965). They fueled the Quaker reform of English mental institutions with their prescription of rural residence, solitary activity, and farm work. Even in the present century, mental hospitals, prisons, and reform schools were frequently built in association with working farms that were abandoned only in the 1970s. The reasons were numerous and complex: Passage of peonage laws made employment of inmates difficult, the number of farming jobs declined, the need for hospital beds decreased, and the powerful effects of new medications obscured subtler environmental influences (Morrison, 1992). Unfortunately, the use of farm work and animal contact as treatment was abandoned before it could be evaluated.

Just when mental hospitals and other institutions were abandoning their farms and summer camps, a new environmental sentiment developed. It found political, scientific, and popular expression in the environmental movement, the interest in animal rights, a belief that healing could emanate from people who were seen as closer to nature and, most recently in the concept of *biophilia* (Kellert & Wilson, 1993; Wilson, 1984). *Biophilia* asserts that humans have inborne responses to animals and natural settings in which they have evolved. These ideas also directed attention to human dependence on the few remaining links between urban populations and the natural world—companion animals and scenic greenery.

COMPANION ANIMALS AND SCENIC GREENERY

Watching Animals and Scenic Greenery

Researchers find similar effects from contemplating an aquarium, or an animal in the room, and from viewing images of natural spaces like parks, streams, mountains, or gardens. In both cases the influence of the stimulus is assessed over a brief period. Several studies (Ulrich, 1979, 1983a, 1983b) describe a large and consistent body of data on the stress-reducing effects of viewing natural settings and still pictures of natural settings. The same kinds of stress reduction and physiological change are evident in reduced blood pressure and heart rate (observed) when people contemplate moving animals, specifically tropical fish swimming in a tank (Bataille-Benguigui, 1992; DeSchriver & Riddick, 1990; Katcher, Friedmann, Beck, & Lynch, 1983).

In a clinical experiment, contemplating an aquarium was as effective as hypnosis in relaxing patients prior to elective oral surgery (Katcher, Segal, & Beck, 1984). Similar effects have been observed when a dog is introduced in the room with an experimental subject. One study reported decreased test anxiety when the experimenter's dog was present (Sebkova, 1978). Friedmann, Katcher, Lynch, and Thomas (1983) reported that children had lower blood pressures, both when resting and reading aloud if a dog were present. Such results have been replicated with adults (Baun, Bergstrom-Langston, & Thomas, 1984; Grossberg & Alf, 1985).

Interacting With Pets

In a study of the physiological and behavioral responses during interactions with pets, subjects were recruited from a veterinary clinic and were asked to pet their animals while their heart rate and blood pressure were measured (Katcher, 1981). A study in a coronary care unit showed that gentle touch reduced the frequency of dangerous arrhythmia (Lynch, Thomas,

Mills, Malinow, & Katcher, 1974). When subjects touched their pets, they invariable talked to them as well and gave their interactions the form of a human relationship (Katcher, 1981). Blood pressure recorded from people during this kind of exchange is consistently lower than blood pressure recorded during speech directed at the experimenter or when reading aloud (Katcher, 1981).

Long-Term Relationships With Pets

Because the immediate effects of interactions with companion animals are large and easy to measure, and because people describe pets as close companions, equivalent to family members, it is reasonable to inquire whether long-term relationships with pets have similar benefits for psychological state and health as do human relationships. Social support, family composition, and friendship have powerful effects on health and well-being (House, Landis, & Umberson, 1988). There is some direct evidence that the companionship of animals makes a difference in health (Anderson, Reid, & Jennings, 1992; Friedmann et al., 1983; Siegel, 1990). However, most of the scientific literature suggests that, if pets have any generalized effect on health and emotional well-being, this effect is small and restricted to subgroups of the population (Ory & Goldberg, 1983; Stallones, Marx, Garrity, & Johnson, 1990).

Therapeutic Use of Pets

There is ample evidence that the introduction of an animal into a therapeutic milieu has significant immediate effects on the behavior of patients, therapists, and the interaction between them, but these effects are usually limited to the time when the animal is present, and there is little evidence of enduring and general effects (Beck & Katcher, 1984). The introduction of animals resulted in more focused attention (to the animal), increased social responding, first to the animal and then to the therapist, positive emotion, and favorable social attributions from patient to therapist and from the caregiver to the patient. The increased social interaction has been associated with increased verbal response by the patient and even with autistic children (Redefer & Goodman, 1989) or severely withdrawn patients with Alzheimer's disease (Corson & Corson, 1977). The results have been comparable with a wide variety of organic and functional mental disorders (Beck, Seradarian, & Hunter, 1986; Levinson, 1969; McCulloch, 1981) across a broad spectrum of ages.

This chapter illustrates ways in which contact with animals can be integrated into treatment programs by describing a series of clinical studies with children and adolescents in residential treatment for severe attention deficit/hyperactive disorder (ADHD) and conduct disorders (CD; American Psychiatric Association, 1994).

ATTENTION DEFICIT / HYPERACTIVITY DISORDER

ADHD is a biological condition characterized by developmentally inappropriate degrees of inattention, impulsivity, and hyperactivity (Barkley, 1990). It is a relatively stable disorder that emerges in early childhood and persists with tenacity into adolescence and adulthood (Halloway & Ratey, 1994; Weiss & Hechtman, 1986). Inattention, impulsivity, and hyperactivity are typically transsituational in nature and accordingly are manifest across academic, occupational, home, and community contexts. People with ADHD often tend to be more spontaneous than others. Their thinking is at times unrestrained and creative, but more frequently quite disorganized and tangential. Their speech patterns are often compromised by inarticulations, speech dysfluencies, and other psycholinguistic impairments. They act unpredictably and often lack sufficient intermediate reflection between impulse and action for adequate goal-directed or context-regulated behavior.

The disinhibited behavior of ADHD children and adolescents adversely affects almost every aspect of their daily lives: lining up for lunch in school, waiting for turns in games, listening to directions, compliance with structure and regulations, and so on (Barkley, 1989). They lack any appreciation of probable consequences and their behavior can be quite dangerous (e.g., darting across a congested highway without looking in either direction). They are unable to complete school work, and are socially disruptive, intruding on others, and respond minimally to traditional psychological interventions.

The problems of ADHD patients are seldom limited to the core ADHD symptoms. These youngsters frequently suffer from a cluster of psychosocial problems including internalizing disorders, aggression, defiant behavior, academic underachievement, diminished self-esteem, depression, and peer rejection. Treatment of ADHD is multimodal and focuses particularly on their oppositional, defiant, or noncompliant behavior which, in combination with ADHD, is a significant predictor of maladjustment during adolescence and young adulthood.

Theories of ADHD

ADHD has been the object of rigorous scientific investigation during the last decades. A number of theoretical formulations have been proposed with respect to its characteristics, etiology, developmental trajectory, and treatment. Despite the consensus on the essential dimensions, there has been considerable substantial controversy concerning the central and causative deficits. Over the years, shifting emphasis has been focused on distractibility (Strauss & Lehtinen, 1947); hyperarousal, decreased activity in the brain's behavioral inhibition system (Quay, 1989); deficient regulation of behavior by rules and consequences (Barkley, 1990); diminished sensitivity to partial schedules of consequences (Barkley, 1989; Douglas, 1985, 1990); and most important, deficient levels of neurotransmitters that facilitate arousal, motivation, and attention, dysfunctions in the orbital-frontal cortex and its rich associated limbic pathways (Heilman, Voeller, & Nadeau, 1990; Lou, Henriksen, Bruhn, Borner, & Nielsen, 1989).

A recently proposed unified theory of ADHD (Barkley, 1997) has impressive empirical support and permits an optimal assimilation of the present study's research model. Relying heavily on the seminal essays of Bronowski (1967, 1977), Barkley postulated that the cardinal impairment is one of impaired response inhibition. This impairment is linked and negatively affects the four executive neuropsychological functions of working memory, self-regulation of affect-motivation-arousal, internalization of speech, and reconstitution or behavioral analysis and synthesis. He suggested that the failure to delay responses is the central feature of ADHD and is integrally related to the numerous problems experienced by people with this disorder.

A STUDY OF ANIMAL-ASSISTED THERAPY

Animal-assisted interventions were designed to ameliorate the CD and ADHD conditions and to attenuate somewhat their negative long-term prognosis. Interventions were based on a number of assumptions:

1. Animals capture and hold children's attention. The behavior of small animals is predictably unpredictable. Although the child becomes familiar with the animal's behavior, he or she must still pay close attention because the nuances and structural details of the creature's reactions cannot be readily anticipated from experience. This sustained attention is associated with the prolongation of the idea or image of the animal in the child's mind. At the same time, the child is uncertain how best to respond to the animal.

2. The animal creates a captivating uncertainty for the child that tends to inhibit rapid responding and affords increased opportunities for speech. This in turn stimulates the child's curiosity, initiating dialogue requisite for therapy and learning.

3. The presence of the animal directs the child's attention outward, which gives the child the opportunity to perceive the behavior of therapists and other children more accurately, and curtails the child's use of preformed negative attributions. This favors the development of positive attributions toward the animal, the staff associated with the animal, and other children involved.

4. The play of CD children is frequently aggressive and insufficiently modulated (Wilkins & Sholevar, 1995). Animals provide an opportunity for affectionate and nurturing play.

5. Mastery of fear of the animals and learning to care for them gives these children a sense of competence. Their growing capacity to experience interaction with animals, staff, and other children increases their self-esteem and potentiates learning in other contexts.

METHODS AND RESULTS

A controlled crossover experimental design was used with initially 52 children at the Devereux Foundation. They were randomly assigned to one of two voluntary experiences that complemented, but did not replace, their regular school and treatment curriculum. The control group participated in an Outward Bound (OB) type course for 5 hours per week, which consisted of such supervised activities as rock climbing, canoeing, swimming, and water safety. The experimental treatment consisted of a 5-hour nature and companiable zoo (CZ) program during every school week. After 6 months, the outdoor group was transferred to the zoo program, and the students in the original experimental group were returned to their regular school program. They were, however, permitted to visit their animals in their free time. The clinical rationale for the partial crossover design was based on the conviction that it was unethical to separate children from their pets for research purposes.

The center of the nature program was a small prefabricated building (14 ft by 32 ft) that housed a collection of small animals that included rabbits, gerbils, hamsters, mice, chinchillas, iguanas, and other lizards, turtles, doves, chicks, and a Vietnamese pot-bellied pig. One of the nature educators also owned dogs that were present most of the time. The children were given only two general rules: be gentle with the animals, which included talking softly while in the zoo; and respect the animals and each other and avoid speech that devalued the animals or other children. The rules of speaking softly and gently, and focusing attention on the animals' rather than on personal needs facilitated behavior that demands motor inhibition and impulse control.

The term *respect* was chosen to define the animals anthropomorphically. This enabled the children to think reflexively with the animal as an intermediary (i.e., thinking about their own feelings by conjecturing and reasoning about the animals' feelings and relationships). The first task was to learn the general requirements for the care of animals and the proper way of holding them. The second task was to learn the biology and care of the one animal the child chose to adopt as his pet. After this adoption, the child could master more than 20 other areas of knowledge and skill. In one term, the average child progressed through eight such areas completely, and partially completed three or four more. Once the child adopted his or her pet, there were no other incentives for learning and mastering other skills. Areas of mastery included how to weigh and measure the pet, charting growth, computing food and bedding requirements, learning to breed the animals and to care for the mother and young, and learning to demonstrate a pet to children in other special education classes within the Devereux Foundation or at facilities for adults in geriatric or rehabilitation hospitals.

The program also included hikes through the woods of the Devereux campus, fishing and camping trips, visits to local state parks, to pet stores, to farms, and to a veterinarian's office. On these trips children learned about the water cycles; the gross aspects of wetlands, pasture and woodlot; identification of indigenous birds, trees, reptiles, and small mammals. The zoo maintained spaces for wildlife such as insects, amphibians, and reptiles brought in by the children. These guests were housed in the zoo for a few days for identification and study, and then returned to their natural habitats. In addition to their regularly scheduled time, the children could visit the zoo to care for, or play with, the animals on their free time. The program was voluntary and provided as a supplement to the regular therapeutic and educational programs.

The details of the crossover study have been reported elsewhere (Katcher & Wilkins, 1993). In comparison to the outdoor group experience, therapy structured around animal contact and nature resulted in significantly fewer aggressive episodes. It also accelerated learning and decreased pathological behavior in the regular school program. On the basis of the frequency of restraints and aggressive episodes in the regular school program 35 restraints were expected in the CZ program within the first 6 months. None were observed. The program was also rewarding and attendance was significantly better than in the OB program. The Achenbach (1991) Teacher Report Form (TRF), a standardized and empirically derived behavior rating scale, was used to assess the frequency and severity of the children's behavioral problems. This rating scale was completed at four intervals by the teachers in the students' regular school program. A significant reduction in total behavioral pathology was evident in the zoo group compared to the outdoor group.

Once the clinical trial was completed, all children participated in the zoo. The efficacy of the program was examined by contrasting children who were successful or unsuccessful in the zoo program as rated by their instructors. Their scores (Total Problem and Externalizing Scores) on the Achenbach TRF were then compared. Children who were successful in the zoo program had significantly lower scores of psychopathology in their regular school program.

The authors concluded that animal-assisted therapy and nature education has large, persistent, and broadly distributed therapeutic effects on highly aggressive and disturbed children and adolescents, particularly those with ADHD and CD. These effects carried over to the regular school where the treated children were less symptomatic.

These effects were, however, strongly influenced by context. Immediate changes were seen in the zoo programs, which carried over to the school setting within a 6-month period, a short interval when attempting to realize positive behavioral changes in conduct-disordered children. However, the authors never observed improvement in the less structured milieu of the residences, and the positive effects on behavior were always greatest within the zoo program.

Some important conclusions can be drawn from the dependence of performance on context. Initially, the CZ program should be evaluated by measuring change in the presence of the animal, or in the natural setting. As improvement occurs, the significant caregivers should observe the child in contact with the animals to assess positive change. Behavior should be measured in more than one context outside the CZ program. If behavior had been examined solely in the residences, a conclusion would have been reached that the program had no therapeutic effect. The therapy must also include techniques to transfer favorable changes from the program to other significant contexts.

Case History

Steve was 10 years old when enrolled at the Brandywine Programs of Devereux's Beneto Center with a diagnosis of ADHD with comorbid oppositional and defiant characteristics. Steve's mother traced his hyperactivity to the first months after birth. Within 6 months he was placed in foster care because of maternal abuse and neglect, and before he was 2 years old, he had been in five foster families. In each of them he was a severe management problem and was moved to the next family. At age 2 he was adopted. His new parents noted that he had a very short attention span and required close supervision for his own safety. At age 4 he was put on medication; the greatest success was achieved with the conjoint use of Desipramine and Methylphenidate. From ages 7 to 9 his behavior became increasingly violent, uncontrollable, aggressive, and impulsive.

On admission Steve was tested and found to have a verbal IQ of 107, a performance IQ of 126, and a full-scale IQ of 117. In treatment he rapidly achieved a campus reputation for temper tantrums lasting as long as 10 hours, aggression toward staff and peers requiring frequent physical restraints—more than any other child in treatment at that time—and several episodes of vandalism. In school, except for his favorite classes of art and cooking, he spent much of his time in the discipline room.

On his initial visits to the zoo, staff noted both his extreme hyperactivity and his consuming interest in the animals. He needed constant redirection and was initially unsuccessful in handling the animals because of his erratic behavior. He never became aggressive toward staff or animals and gradually was able to modulate his physical activity. He was rewarded by the increasing comfort the animals displayed with him, and by increasing praise from staff for his growing knowledge of animals and his ability to work in the zoo.

In the first year, he mastered more skills than any other child in the program, and achieved the level of assistant zoo keeper. He spent large blocks of time in the zoo because teachers sent him there when he was unable to control his behavior in class. Although peer relationships remained a problem as a result of his invasive desire to join and control anyone's activity, he became able to lead activities because of his creative abilities. He constructed elaborate habitats and mazes for animals that the other children used. He was the first to suggest a pet cemetery, and built monuments for the animals. Despite all these abilities, he still required frequent instructions to complete tasks and put away equipment.

In the presence of animals he was able to interact appropriately and fluidly with adults and other children, conducting tours of the zoo and teaching about animals when he was taken on visits to residences for the aged or other schools. Although he was able to demonstrate control in the presence of animals, his behavior in other contexts did not start to improve significantly until the middle of his third year of treatment. He was in high school at that time and enrolled in the 4H program where he continued his involvement with animals. From then on he improved rapidly and was discharged to a special education day school.

DISCUSSION

There is substantial cultural evidence that children are able to keep images of animals in their minds for long periods of time. The nursery, books, and children's programs are usually full of animals. The ambiguous world of grown-ups becomes more comprehensible when different types of behavior and emotion are linked to different types of animals, which is the technique of the fable. To paraphrase Levi-Strauss, animals are long to think. Children's dreams (Van de Castle, 1983) are dominated by animal features that decrease with age.

A tendency toward anthropomorphism (Lockwood, 1983) permits the children with ADHD to ask questions about animals whose behavior and needs they do not understand. They can ask because they reason anthropomorphically and think of the animal as a social other. Interestingly, they can see the animal as other, even when their social interactions with peers are quite primitive. This permits the therapist to ask what they think the animal wants and needs, to what they themselves and other children want and need. With proper intervention from the therapist, anthropomorphic reasoning makes them more aware of the human social milieu. When the animal becomes a child's friend or playmate, a wider display of emotion and behavior becomes possible. Aggressive children can become tender and nurturing in their play and responsible in their behavior toward the animals. This wider range of behavior, from arranging a mock marriage between two pets to burying a pup that died, permits a therapeutic discussion of issues that would not surface otherwise.

REFERENCES

Achenbach, T. M. (1991). *Manual for the teacher's report form and 1991 profile*. Burlington: University of Vermont, Department of Psychiatry.

American Psychiatric Association. (1994). *Diagnostic and statistical manual of mental disorders* (4th ed.). Washington, DC: Author.

Anderson, W., Reid, P., & Jennings, L. G. (1992). Pet ownership and risk factors for coronary artery disease. *Medical Journal of Australia, 157*, 298–301.

Barkley, R. A. (1989). *The problem of stimulus control and rule-governed behavior with attention deficit disorder with hyperactivity*. Paper presented at the Highpoint Conference, Toronto, Canada.

Barkley, R. A. (1990). *Attention deficit hyperactivity disorder: A handbook for diagnosis and treatment*. New York: Guilford.

Barkley, R. A. (1997). Behavioral inhibition, sustained attention, and executive functions: Constructing a unifying theory of ADHD. *Psychological Bulletin, 121*, 65–94.

Bataille-Benguigui, M. (1992). Man–fish relationship in the therapy of conflict. *Proceedings of the International Conference on Science and the Human-Animal Relationship*. Holland.

Baun, M., Bergstrom, N., Langston, N., & Thomas, I. (1984). Physiological effects of petting dogs: Influences of attachment. In R. Anderson, B. Hart, & A. Hart (Eds.), *The pet connection: Influences on our health and quality of life*. St. Paul: Grove Publishing.

Beck, A. M., & Katcher, A. H. (1984). A new look at pet-facilitated therapy. *Journal of American Veterinarian Medical Association, 184*, 414–421.

Beck, A. M., Seradarian, L., & Hunter, G. F. (1986). Use of animals in the rehabilitation of psychiatric inpatients. *Psychological Reports, 58*, 63–66.

Bronowski, J. (1967). *Human and animal languages: To honor Roman Jakobson* (Vol. 1). The Hague, Netherlands: Mouton.

Bronowski, J. (1977). *Human and animal languages. A sense of the future* (pp. 104–131). Cambridge, MA: MIT Press.

Corson, S. A., & Corson, E. (1977). The socializing role of pet animals in nursing homes: An experiment in non-verbal communication therapy. In L. Lewvi (Ed.), *Society, stress, and disease* (pp. 1–47). London: Oxford University Press.

Davis, K. (1965). The urbanization of the human population. In D. Flanagan (Ed.), *Cities* (pp. 3–24). New York: Knopf.

DeSchriver, M., & Riddick, C. (1990). Effects of watching aquariums on elders' stress. *Anthrozoos, 4*(1), 44–48.

Douglas, V. I. (1985). The response of ADD children to reinforcement: Theoretical and clinical implication. In L. M. Bloomindale (Ed.), *Attention deficit disorder: Identification, course, and treatment rationale.* New York: Spectrum Publications, Inc.

Douglas, V. I. (1990). Can Skinnerian psychology account for the deficits in attention deficit disorder? A reply to Barkley. In L. M. Bloomindale & J. Swanson (Eds.), *Attention deficit disorder* (Vol. 4). New York: Pergamon.

Evelyn-White, H. G. (1950). *Hesiod and the Homeric hymns.* Cambridge: Harvard University Press.

Friedmann, E., Katcher, A., & Thomas, S. (1983). Social interaction and blood pressure: Influence of animal companions. *Journal of Nervous and Mental Disease, 171,* 461–465.

Grossberg, J., & Alf, E. (1985). Interaction with pet dogs: Effects on human cardiovascular response. *Journal of the Delta Society, 2,* 20–27.

Halloway, E. M., & Ratey, J. J. (1994). *Answers to distraction.* New York: Pantheon.

Harrison, R. (1992). *Forest's shadow of civilization.* Chicago: University of Chicago Press.

Heilman, K. M., Voeller, K. K. S., & Nadeau, S. E. (1990). A possible pathophysiological substrate of attention deficit hyperactivity disorder. *Journal of Child Neurology, 6,* 74–79.

House, J., Landis, K., & Umberson, D. (1988). Social relationships and health. *Science, 241,* 540–545.

Katcher, A. (1981). Interactions between people and their pets: Form and function. In B. Fogle (Ed.), *Interrelations between people and pets.* Springfield: Charles C. Thomas.

Katcher, A., Friedmann, E., Beck, A., & Lynch, J. (1983). Looking, talking and blood pressure: The physiological consequences of interaction with the living environment. In A. Katcher & A. Beck (Eds.), *New perspectives on our lives with companion animals.* Philadelphia: University of Pennsylvania Press.

Katcher, A., Segal, H., & Beck, A. (1984). Comparison of contemplation and hypnosis for the reduction of anxiety and discomfort during dental surgery. *The American Journal of Clinical Hypnosis, 27,* 14.

Katcher, A., & Wilkins, G. G. (1993). Dialogue with animals—Its nature and culture. In S. R. Kellert & E. O. Wilson (Eds.), *The biophilia hypothesis: A theoretical and empirical inquiry* (pp. 173–203). New York: Island Press.

Kellert, S., & Wilson, E. O. (1993). *The biophilia hypothesis.* Washington, DC: Island Press.

Levinson, B. (1969). *Pet oriented child psychotherapy.* Springfield: Charles C. Thomas.

Lockwood, R. (1983). The influence of animals on social perception. In A. Katcher & A. Beck (Eds.), *New perspectives on our lives with companion animals* (pp. 64–71). Philadelphia: University of Pennsylvania Press.

Lou, H. C., Henriksen, L., Bruhn, P., Borner, H., & Nielsen, J. B. (1989). Striatal dysfunction in attention deficit and hyperkinetic disorder. *Archives of Neurology, 46,* 48–52.

Lynch, J., Thomas, S. A., Mills, M. E., Malinow, L., & Katcher, A. (1974). Human contact and heart arrhythmia: The effect of human contact on cardiac arrhythmia in coronary care patients. *Journal of Nervous Mental Disease, 158,* 88.

McCulloch, M. (1981). The pet as prosthesis: Defining criteria for the adjunctive use of companion animals in the treatment of medically ill, depressed outpatients. In B. Fogle (Ed.), *Interrelations between people and pets.* Springfield: Charles C. Thomas.

Morrison, E. (1992). *The city on the hill.* Harrisburg, PA: Harrisburg State Hospital.

Ory, M. G., & Goldberg, E. L. (1983). Pet possession and life satisfaction in elderly women. In A. Katcher & A. Beck (Eds.), *New perspectives on our lives with companion animals* (pp. 342–351). Philadelphia: University of Pennsylvania Press.

Quay, H. C. (1989). The behavioral reward and inhibition systems in childhood behavior disorder. In L. M. Bloomindale (Ed.), *Attention deficit disorder III: New research in treatment, psychopharmacology, and attention* (pp. 176–186). New York: Pergamon.

Redefer, L., & Goodman, J. (1989). Brief report: Pet-facilitated therapy with autistic children. *Journal of Autism and Developmental Disabilities, 19*(3), 461–467.

Rousseau, J. J. (1947). *The origins of inequality in the social contract and discourses* (G. D. H. Cole, Trans.). New York: Dutton and Co.

Sebkova, J. (1978). *Anxiety levels as affected by the presence of a dog.* Unpublished senior thesis, University of Lancaster, Lancaster, England.

Siegel, J. (1990). Stressful life events and use of physician services among the elderly: The moderating role of pet ownership. *Journal of Personality and Social Psychology, 58*(6), 1081–1086.

Stallones, L., Marx, M., Garrity, T. F., & Johnson, T. P. (1990). Pet ownership and attachment in relation to the health of U.S. adults, 21 to 64 years of age. *Anthrozoos, 4*(2), 100–112.

Strauss, A. A., & Lehtinen, L. E. (1947). *Psychopathology and education of the brain-injured child.* New York: Grune and Stratton.

Ulrich, R. (1979). Visual landscapes and psychological well-being. *Landscape Research, 4*(1), 17.

Ulrich, R. (1983a). Aesthetic and affective response to natural environment. In I. Atman & J. Wohlwill (Eds.), *Behavior and the natural environment.* New York: Plenum.

Ulrich, R. (1983b). View through a window may influence recovery from surgery. *Science, 224,* 420.

Van de Castle, R. L. (1983). Animal figures in fantasy and dreams. In A. Katcher & A. Beck (Eds.), *New perspectives on our lives with companion animals* (pp. 167–293). Philadelphia: University of Pennsylvania Press.

Weiss, G., & Hechtman, L. (1986). *Hyperactive children grown up.* New York: Guilford.

Wilkins, G., & Sholevar, G. P. (1995). Manual-based psychotherapy. In G. P. Sholevar (Ed.), *Conduct disorders in children and adolescents* (pp. 173–192). Washington, DC: American Psychiatric Press.

Williams, R. (1973). *The country and the city.* New York: Oxford University Press.

Wilson, E. O. (1984). *Biophilia.* Cambridge: Harvard University Press.

Chapter 13

Psychiatry and Ecopsychology

Randall White
Emory University

Clinical problems typically involve difficulties in the social and not the natural environment and psychiatrists have not concerned themselves with their patients' relationship to the natural world. One critic of psychiatric nosology has pointed out that the *Diagnostic and Statistical Manual of Mental Disorders*, (3rd ed. [*DSM–III*]; American Psychiatric Association, 1982) mentions the natural environment in regard only to zoophilia (Roszak, 1992). *DSM–IV* (American Psychiatric Association, 1994) admits that specific phobias and posttraumatic stress disorder also may occur in relation to nature.

Psychiatry and behavioral sciences, however, are beginning to pay some attention to the environment. Concern over environmental problems has led to investigations beyond traditional boundaries in attempts to understand human ecology and to diminish our deleterious impact on the biosphere. For instance, environmental ethics or ecophilosophy developed as a branch of ethics, and environmental studies programs have become common in universities as an outgrowth of ecology, a subdiscipline of biology. In the social sciences, including psychology, geography, history, and sociology, two approaches have developed that focus on the cultural, behavioral, and subjective components of our interactions with the natural world:

1. Empirical research on how humans relate to nature, aiming to uncover the aspects of emotion, cognition, and behavior that permit, impede, or compel us toward such relations.

2. Metapsychological investigations of humans' relationship with the natural world and speculations on changes required in human thought and behavior to avoid increasing environmental degradation.

Empirical research typically employs methods of psychology but often borrows a theoretical framework from evolutionary biology. Hominids evolved in close relationship to the natural world, probably on the savannas of Africa (a terrain of scattered trees and grassland), and the behavior humans exhibit now should in part be a legacy of adaptations evolved in response to that environment (Orians, 1980). Wilson (1984) proposed the term *biophilia* to denote the "urge to affiliate with other forms of life" that, he hypothesized, all human beings possess, along with *biophobia*, the tendency to avoid potentially dangerous elements of nature (p. 85). No organism can survive without a behavioral repertoire to find food, water, and protection from harsh weather and natural enemies. *Homo sapiens*, according to the biophilia hypothesis, developed such adaptations to the wilderness of the Pleistocene and they remain with us.

This idea resembles an assertion by Roszak (1992) that humans possess an ecological unconscious that represents "the living record of . . . evolution." Those with a scientific bias will prefer Wilson's testable formulation, but its sociobiological implications, and the new age context of Roszak's formulation, do create problems: The nature or nurture debate fosters mutually suspicious intellectual camps with overlapping concerns but limited dialogue. This chapter examines these two approaches to understanding human relationships to nature. They each bring a useful perspective. The ecopsychology movement fostered by Roszak aspires among other things to change clinical psychotherapy practice.

RESPONSES TO NATURE

Research has demonstrated that inhabitants of industrialized societies prefer specific landscapes. Kaplan and Kaplan (1989) studied responses to nature among diverse populations and published a synopsis of their empirical work, *The Experience of Nature*. In a series of investigations, subjects rated photographs of various landscapes on a preference scale. Their answers showed high ratings for scenes of parklike landscapes or open forest; and low ratings for highly urban scenes, and for very open (such as treeless fields) and very closed (such as dense forest) natural scenes.

In general, subjects preferred natural scenes to those showing human influence, but preferences differed by age and cultural group. Urban African Americans preferred parklike landscapes with a built element such as a concrete pathway or picnic shelter. One intriguing finding is that children ages 8 to 11 distinctly preferred pictures of savanna over those of deciduous and coniferous forests, and rated desert and rain forest scenes lowest. One can speculate that children have the least cultural bias and that their preferences reflect basic human preferences.

Appleton (1975), a geographer, advanced a coherent approach to understanding landscape aesthetics that he called *habitat theory*, which has provided a base for investigation. Heerwagen and Orians (1993) examined the history of European landscape aesthetics from this perspective by looking at paintings and gardens and, as discussed in chapter 11, have empirically verified aspects of habitat theory. They suggested four unconscious considerations by which people make aesthetic judgments about landscapes. We respond positively to places where we would have a good chance of survival because of resources, shelter, absence of hazards, and ease of movement. Our basic needs rather than a notion of abstract, ideal beauty shape our preferences. This view may seem to reduce our relationship to the land to a pragmatic, narrow level: The exalted landscapes painted by Bierstadt and written about by John Muir become potential habitats, nothing more. Yet our relationship to the landscape, especially in America, has always contained a conflict between exploitive pragmatism and romantic idealism. The power of habitat theory lies in its ability to explain both responses to landscape, the mundane and the exultant, for they both arise from our basic biological requirements.

"A KIND OF MADNESS"

If people possess innate preferences for certain landscapes along with the "innate tendency to focus on life and lifelike processes" (p. 1), as Wilson (1984) suggested, why do we damage our habitat? Shepard, Roszak, and others have borrowed ideas from dynamic psychiatry to explain the increasing alienation from the natural world of people in agricultural and industrial societies. In this view alienation from and destructiveness toward the environment arise during psychological development and represent "an irrationality beyond mistakenness, a kind of madness" (Shepard, 1982, p. 4). An attempt to understand a global crisis of our age becomes both an examination of individual thought, motive, and behavior, and an application of psychology to societal problems.

Environmental degradation is unarguably the consequence of human behavior. Psychiatry and psychology have not provided solutions to other kinds of destructiveness, so one might wonder why psychologists and psychiatrists should care about this social problem. Most clinicians seldom delve beyond cursory considerations of social psychology, because the people they see in their offices seem removed from, or powerless before the larger forces shaping their world. Nonetheless, individuals do feel the effects of environmental degradation just as they do the effects of war. Some clinicians have begun to explore the implications of alienation from nature in therapy.

Ecopsychology is a term associated with a metapsychological or humanistic approach to understanding the problem of human environmental destructiveness (Roszak, 1992). An important aspect of this movement is the critique of consumerism, the culture of spending and buying that propels industrial societies forward. Almost all activities in industrialized societies harm natural systems: building houses, driving cars, growing food. Durning (1992) in his book *How Much is Enough?* argued that the accumulation and disposal of possessions are major contributors to environmental degradation. Consumption in industrial societies has increased exponentially to maintain the standard of living as the population increases. Environmentalists have promoted sustainable development, that is, long-term growth at a rate that is environmentally benign. Ecopsychologists have called unsustainable economic activity a kind of insanity, thus equating the pursuit of sustainability with the pursuit of sanity. If psychopathology requires treatment, in this case the patient is the entire society.

Shepard's (1982) book, *Nature and Madness,* begins with the question "(w)hy do men persist in destroying their environment?" (p. 1). He explicitly avoided clinical jargon but employed psychoanalytic ideas to examine the effects on human development of the transition from hunter–gatherer to agricultural to industrial society. He maintained that a lack of deep experience with the natural world during childhood and adolescence has distorted our development, alienated us from nature, and thereby permitted environmental degradation to progress.

Shepard used madness as a metaphor for human folly, but Sontag (1978) observed that "(i)llnesses have always been used as metaphors to enliven charges that a society was corrupt or unjust," which, she argued, invariably stigmatizes the people with the illnesses (p. 71). Although Shepard probably had no intention of contributing to the stigmatization of the mentally ill, he perpetuated certain misconceptions about mental illness: literary notions of psychosis as paradoxical thinking and behavior, the result of "arrested development," and a reaction to the discredited double-bind. Yet his speculations on the consequences of ignoring the influence of nature on human development merit serious attention, and his writings have influenced the subsequent development of ecopsychology.

Roszak went beyond using madness as metaphor in attempting to uncover the roots of neurosis in our alienation from nature. Since the publication of *The Voice of the Earth* Roszak (1992) has become a leader of the ecopsychology movement. He derived his idea of madness from Laing (1969), who defined mental illness as a protest against society, thereby reversing the attribution of sanity: "the species that destroys its own habitat in pursuit of false values, in willful ignorance of what it does, is 'mad' if the word means anything" (Roszak, 1992, p. 68). This diagnosis surpasses Shepard's "a kind of madness" and challenges psychiatry and psychology to redefine their nosology and practice. In an epilogue containing the "principles of ecopsychology" Roszak stated, "repression of the ecological unconscious is the deepest root of collusive madness in industrialized society," the treatment for which entails recovering "the child's innately animistic quality of experience in functionally 'sane' adults" (p. 320). He argued for a nature-based therapy based on the human-potential movement and the animistic spirituality of nonindustrialized societies.

Because psychiatrists have defined sanity in terms of the dominant world view and are themselves alienated from nature, Roszak holds little hope that psychiatry will embrace his ideas. He mentioned a crucial point: "The issue we raise here is at once both ethical and psychological, a debate that pits many increasingly distressed environmental scientists against a far greater number of invincibly optimistic entrepreneurs" (Roszak, 1992, p. 70). Michels (1991), in discussing the differences between psychiatric and ethical interpretations of behavior, noted that behavioral scientists view behavior as an observable phenomenon flowing from antecedent causes, biological and psychosocial, whereas ethicists view behavior as the result of a choice among alternatives with causation playing a small role. Roszak does not fully acknowledge this distinction and defines psychiatry as a political undertaking. He hopes that some therapists will begin to inform their work with ecopsychological concepts, and take on an activist role. Certainly activism has a place in the life of a therapist, but the debate between environmental scientists and entrepreneurs is political, not psychological, and does not belong in the consulting room unless the client brings it in.

Roszak (1992) rightly observed that environmentalists have too often resorted to censure and negativity, which make their message unpalatable. The degradation of biodiversity and impoverishment of less developed nations, although discouraging to some, has little effect on the "optimistic entrepreneurs." He pointed out that "environmentalists overlook the unreason, the perversity, and the sick desire that lie at the core of the psyche" (p. 38). Yet he concluded that the unreason results from shared neurosis. An ethical plea has little effect on an irrational mind; ergo, society requires psychiatric intervention. But unethical behavior and mental disorders are not equivalent, and the destructive activities of an entire society cannot be treated as the product of mental illness.

A major deficit of Roszak's analysis lies in the fact that individuals with mental disorders suffer, and although they occasionally do not have insight enough to seek treatment, they can almost always convey their pain. The typical American would not describe much pain resulting from ownership of a house, a car, and a television. Poor people may feel deprived for not having such possessions. In contrast, certain people experience anguish in perceiving the decline of the natural world, in knowing that other organisms may die off in large numbers at our hands, but these people are probably already trying to reduce their personal impact on the planet. Understanding why only some of us have this sensitivity seems a cardinal problem for ecopsychological investigation.

In an interview Roszak pointed out that, although we all make daily decisions that affect the natural world, such decisions are not calculated to harm the environment but follow from our semivoluntary participation in the consumer oriented industrial society. We are ensnared in the madness by virtue of living in such a society. The massive efforts of advertising have succeeded in creating a desire for objects, such as fast and sleek automobiles, that did not exist two or three generations ago. Ecopsychology hypothesizes that people buy things in order to alleviate depression, or out of a desire to be admired; "legitimate, understandable human aspirations" as Roszak put it (Gablik, 1995). This is an intriguing hypothesis worth investigating, but in carrying the idea further some authors seem to equate the act of buying with addiction (Glendining, 1995). Recent research suggests that in some people buying has pathologic, even ego-dystonic, features (Lejoyeux, Andes, Tassain, & Solomon, 1996). Most people, however, do not seek treatment for consumeristic behavior.

Michels (1991) wrote, "the knowledge that psychiatry has developed may be of relevance and value to a wide variety of enterprises, but psychiatry and psychiatrists have no privileged competence in assessing the value of those enterprises" (p. 72). Treating the mentally ill, a stigmatized and sometimes disenfranchised group, is the "privileged competence" of psychiatry. Still, behavioral scientists can contribute to understanding the psychology of consumerism and the influence of the natural world on human mental functioning and development. But in the end, determining how our society will use its resources sustainably entails scientific and ethical analysis and political action, not psychiatric analysis and treatment.

CONFRONTING HUMAN NATURE

Hypotheses about what drives destructive attitudes and indifference to humans' impact on the world have come from the evolutionary-adaptive approach to understanding human nature (Ornstein & Ehrlich, 1989). The "unreason, the perversity, the sick desire" that Roszak (1992, p. 38) recognized may be part of human nature, along with a capacity for benevolence and appreciation of beauty. Ecopsychology shrinks from this complexity and casts unattractive human traits as manifestation of a disorder. Konner (1982), an anthropologist and physician, traced this optimistic but naive interpretation of the human condition to the trope of society as organism. Attempts to eliminate dysfunction in the organism he calls the "tinker theory"; by "tinkering" with human institutions we will eventually cure our collective ailments. In Shepard's and Roszak's version, providing ecopsychotherapy and changing our child rearing practices will reunite us with nature and help us avert environmental catastrophe. Konner allowed that tinkering may sometimes help but he dismissed the "article of faith" that such approaches can erase all human misery. As psychiatrist Anthony Storr (1991) argued, "We cannot abolish man's potential for cruelty and destructiveness, but we may be partially able to control the circumstances which lead to their overt expression" (p. 142).

Denying the violent and destructive impulses in human nature results in simplistic approaches to complex problems, and denial of our impact on nature stems in part from denial of our modest status as inhabitants of the planet with many other organisms. We share 99% of our genome with the bonobo (erroneously called the pygmy chimpanzee; Gribbin & Gribbin, 1993), but acknowledging this fact need neither dehumanize us nor abrogate the significance of culture, for in cultural adaptation lies our uniqueness among animals and our greatest hope for survival. Under our cloak of culture we find an intelligent primate, not a sick angel.

Sontag (1978) recognized the operation of denial in the metaphor of disease: "(O)ur views about cancer, and the metaphors we have imposed on it, are so much a vehicle for the large insufficiencies of this culture, . . . for our anxieties about feeling, for our reckless improvident responses to our real problems of growth, for our inability to construct an advanced industrial society which properly regulates consumption, and for our justified fears of the increasingly violent course of history" (pp. 84–85).

One could easily substitute "mental illness" for "cancer" in her sentence. This denial has served humanity well in the past, but is tragically maladaptive for long-term survival. Perhaps for some individuals this denial will diminish through a self-exploratory process with a therapist, but this remedy will never be available to everyone.

The humanities and sciences both grapple with ways to expand awareness of the contribution the more-than-human world makes to our happiness and survival. A positive message to temper the negative messages of political environmentalism may emerge, but many people face the consequences of environmental damage in their lives right now. Living near a toxic waste site causes clinically significant stress (Foulks & McLellen, 1992), and studies of victims of technological disasters such as Three Mile Island corroborate the psychophysiological significance of such events (Davidson & Baum, 1986). Ecopsychology proposes an emotional response to loss of revered plants, animals, or places (Windle, 1995), a corollary of biophilia and an hypothesis worth investigating. Clinicians should not interpret such concerns about the environment as displaced anxiety, but should foster open exchange with patients concerning these issues. Likewise, a collaboration between behavioral scientists and humanistic thinkers will promote the development of a coherent ecopsychology.

REFERENCES

American Psychiatric Association. (1982). *Diagnostic and statistical manual of mental disorders* (3rd ed.). Washington, DC: Author.

American Psychiatric Association. (1994). *Diagnostic and statistical manual of mental disorders* (4th ed.). Washington, DC: Author.

Appleton, J. (1975). *The experience of nature.* Chichester, England: Wiley.

Davidson, L. M., & Baum, A. (1996). Chronic stress and posttraumatic stress disorder. *Journal of Consulting and Clinical Psychology, 54,* 303–308.

Durning, A. (1992). *How much is enough?* New York: W. W. Norton & Co.

Foulks, E., & McLellen, T. (1992). Psychologic sequelae of chronic toxic waste exposure. *Southern Medical Journal, 85,* 122–126.

Gablik, S. (1995, March/April). A few things beautifully made. *Common Boundary, 13,* 41–46.

Glendining, C. (1995). Technology, trauma and the wild. In T. Roszak, M. E. Gomes, & A. D. Kanner (Eds.), *Ecopsychology: Restoring the earth, healing the mind* (pp. 41–54). San Francisco: Sierra Club Books.

Gribbin, M., & Gribbin, J. (1993). *Being human: Putting people in an evolutionary perspective.* London: J. M. Dent.

Heerwagen, J. H., & Orians, G. H. (1993). Humans, habitats and aesthetics. In S. R. Kellert & E. O. Wilson (Eds.), *The biophilia hypothesis* (pp. 138–172). Washington, DC: Island Press.

Kaplan, R., & Kaplan, S. (1989). *The experience of nature: A psychological perspective.* Cambridge, England, and New York: Cambridge University Press.

Konner, M. (1982). *The tangled wing: Biological constraints on the human spirit.* New York: Holt, Rinehart & Winston.

Laing, R. D. (1969). *The divided self.* New York: Random House.

Lejoyeux, M., Andes, J., Tassain, V., & Solomon, J. (1996). Phenomenology and psychopathology of uncontrolled buying. *American Journal of Psychiatry, 153,* 1524–1529.

Michels, R. (1991). Psychiatry: Where medicine, psychology and ethics meet. In D. S. Browning & I. S. Evison (Eds.), *Does psychiatry need a public philosophy?* (pp. 61–73). Chicago: Nelson-Hall, Inc.

Orians, G. H. (1980). Habitat selection: General theory and applications to human behavior. In J. S. Lockard (Ed.), *The evolution of human social behavior* (pp. 49–66). New York: Elsevier.

Ornstein, R., & Ehrlich, P. (1989). *New world, new mind.* New York: Doubleday.

Roszak, T. S. (1992). *The voice of the earth.* New York: Simon & Schuster.

Shepard, P. (1982). *Nature and madness.* San Francisco: Sierra Club.

Sontag, S. (1978). *Illness as metaphor.* New York: Random House.

Storr, A. (1991). *Human destructiveness.* New York: Grove Weidenfeld.

Wilson, E. O. (1984). *Biophilia.* Cambridge, MA: Harvard University Press.

Windle, P. (1995). The ecology of grief. In T. Roszak, M. E. Gomes, & A. D. Kanner (Eds.), *Ecopsychology: Restoring the earth, healing the mind* (pp. 136–145). San Francisco: Sierra Club Books.

Appendix
Environmental Information
Resources for the Clinician

An abundance of information is available to professionals and the public about pollutants, disaster relief, and other topics related to health and the environment, especially through the Internet. This appendix lists a selection of telephone hotlines, Internet addresses, and World Wide Web sites. Most are federal agencies, or sponsored by them.

Telephone information numbers, hotlines

The National Pesticide Telecommunications Network (NPTN):
Telephone: 1-800-858-7378 (General public), 1-800-858-7377 (Medical and government personnel), Fax: 1-503-737-0761

Information about

- Chemical, health, and environmental information on the 600+ active ingredients incorporated into over 50,000 different products that have been registered for use in the United States since 1947.
- Information on recognition and management of pesticide poisonings.
- Toxicology and symptomatic reviews.
- Referrals to local laboratories for environmental testing of air, water, or soil for pesticide residues.
- Product label information.
- Investigation of pesticide incidents.

- Cleanup and disposal procedures.
- General information on the regulation of pesticides in the United States.

The Indoor Air Quality Information Clearing House: 1-800-438-4318

Answers questions, provides literature for professionals and private individuals, can perform literature searches. Operated under contract with EPA.

National Radon Hotline: 1-800-SOS-RADON (Fax 202-293-0032)

People calling the Hotline receive a packet of information about radon and a coupon for a low-cost radon test kit. Callers are also referred to a public information specialist at the Radon Helpline, **1-800-55-RADON** if they have specific questions. In addition, the public may fax requests for documents or information.

EMF InfoLine: 1-800-EMF-2383 (Fax 703-821-8236)

The EMF InfoLine was established to help the general public by providing accurate, up-to-date, and balanced information in response to questions on electric and magnetic fields (EMF). Hotline staff respond to EMF inquiries relating to both Extremely Low Frequency (ELF) fields produced in the generation, distribution, and use of electricity and radiofrequency (RF) fields from sources such as broadcast and communication technologies and radars.

The Safe Drinking Water Hotline: 1-800-426-4791

The Hotline is intended to assist Public Water Systems, State and local officials, and members of the public with information on EPA regulations and programs authorized by the Safe Drinking Water Act Amendments of 1986. This includes drinking water regulations, other related drinking water topics, wellhead protection and ground water protection program information.

The Environmental Justice Hotline:. 1-800-962-6215

The Environmental Justice Hotline was established by EPA's Office of Environmental Justice (OEJ) to receive calls from concerned citizens about justice issues in their communities. The purpose of the Hotline is to make information easily accessible to the public and to the media, and to assist in the resolution of environmental justice issues. The Hotline is answered by staff of OEJ. A procedure has been established to ensure follow-up. A brochure describing the Hotline (in both English and Spanish) is available.

Internet, World Wide Web sites

Each listing includes a World Wide Web (WWW) address and, in most cases, a brief description of the service. The WWW offers a convenient way to retrieve information from and pose questions to these organizations. The sites are updated regularly and can usually be searched for specific topics.

Agency for Toxic Substances and Disease Registry (ATSDR)

http://atsdr1.atsdr.cdc.gov:8080/atsdrhome.html

Among datasets and other resources offered are

The HazDat Database

ATSDR's Hazardous Substance Release/Health Effects Database, is the scientific and administrative database developed to provide access to information on the release of hazardous substances from Superfund sites or from emergency events and on the effects of hazardous substances on the health of human populations.

ATSDR Science Corner

Toxicology—the Health Effects of Hazardous Substances

- ToxFAQs—short, easy-to-read summaries about hazardous substances that have been excerpted from the ATSDR Toxicological Profiles.
- Public Health Statements—Text search enables the World Wide Web user to search for specific words or combination of words occurring in ATSDR's Public Health Statements. Taken from the Toxicological Profiles, the Public Health Statements offer easy-to-read summaries of many hazardous substances to which people might be exposed.
- ATSDR/EPA Top 20 hazardous substances
- Minimal Risk Levels (MRLs) for hazardous substances

Health Assessments and Consultations

- Environmental data needed for Public Health Assessments (guidance manual)

Health Education and Communication

- Hazardous Substances & Public Health (Newsletter)
- Primer on Health Risk Communication Principles and Practices
- Case Studies in Environmental Medicine (CME/CEU credit)

Special Initiatives and Projects

- ATSDR Great Lakes Human Health Effects Research Program

- ATSDR Mississippi Delta Project
- ATSDR Minority Health Program

Best Environmental Resources Directory

http://www.ulb.ac.be/ceese/cds.html
An extensive, alphabetically arranged list of the best web directories for more than 400 environmental subjects.

Center for Health and the Global Environment, Harvard Medical School.

http://www.med.harvard.edu/chge/

Centers for Disease Control (CDC)

http://www.cdc.gov/cdc.html

EcoNet

http://www.econet.apc.org/econet/
EcoNet serves organizations and individuals working for environmental preservation and sustainability. The site contains a directory of organizations with resources on EcoNet's World Wide Web and Gopher services, and elsewhere on the Internet. EcoNet's web pages can be searched by keyword or concept.

Envirolink

www.envirolink.org
A library of websites arranged by subject, an environmental news service and other environmental resources are offered at this nonprofit, nicely designed site.

Environmental Organization Web Directory

http://www.webdirectory.com

Environmental Protection Agency (EPA)

http://www.epa.gov
This site offers access to a wide range of databases and information systems including the Toxic Release Inventory (TRI).

National Association of Physicians for the Environment (NAPE)

http://intr.net/napenet

National Institute of Environmental Health Sciences (NIEHS)

http://www.niehs.nih.gov

- Environmental Health Clearinghouse is found here. It is open from 9:00 am to 8:00 pm, Eastern time, and can be reached by calling toll free, 800-643-4794, or from outside the United States, call 919-361-0570. You can also send e-mail to: envirohealth@niehs.nih.gov.
- The EHC is staffed by junior and senior scientists trained in environmental health issues and can answer many calls over the phone. Factsheets on specific health issues or specific chemicals can be mailed or faxed. In addition, for questions that are best answered by other clearinghouses, hotlines, or support groups, referrals to the best place to get the answers you need are provided.

National Library of Medicine (NLM)

http://www.nlm.nih.gov

NLM offers a range of on-line services, including free Medline searches at the sites below. The toxicological databases require a billable user code and password. Information on how to obtain a code and password can be found here. Of particular note for clinicians is the peer-reviewed summary of the chemicals indexed in the Hazardous Substances Data Bank (HSDB). Emergency medical treatment described for the over 5,000 substances included in the Data Bank.

- **Internet Grateful Med** (http://igm.nlm.nih.gov): free full access to Medline and some other medical databases.
- **PubMed** (http://www.ncbi.nlm.nih.gov/PubMed): free access to Medline, searches especially designed for the clinicians who want "a few good articles."

Rachel's Environment & Health Weekly

http://www.nirs.org/rehw/rehwbbs.htm

An electronic newsletter.

Author Index

Subject Index